797,885 Books
are available to read at

www.ForgottenBooks.com

Forgotten Books' App
Available for mobile, tablet & eReader

ISBN 978-1-331-37112-0
PIBN 10180632

This book is a reproduction of an important historical work. Forgotten Books uses state-of-the-art technology to digitally reconstruct the work, preserving the original format whilst repairing imperfections present in the aged copy. In rare cases, an imperfection in the original, such as a blemish or missing page, may be replicated in our edition. We do, however, repair the vast majority of imperfections successfully; any imperfections that remain are intentionally left to preserve the state of such historical works.

Forgotten Books is a registered trademark of FB &c Ltd.
Copyright © 2015 FB &c Ltd.
FB &c Ltd, Dalton House, 60 Windsor Avenue, London, SW19 2RR.
Company number 08720141. Registered in England and Wales.

For support please visit www.forgottenbooks.com

1 MONTH OF FREE READING

at

www.ForgottenBooks.com

By purchasing this book you are eligible for one month membership to ForgottenBooks.com, giving you unlimited access to our entire collection of over 700,000 titles via our web site and mobile apps.

To claim your free month visit:

www.forgottenbooks.com/free180632

* Offer is valid for 45 days from date of purchase. Terms and conditions apply.

Similar Books Are Available from
www.forgottenbooks.com

Beautiful Joe
An Autobiography, by Marshall Saunders

Theodore Roosevelt, an Autobiography
by Theodore Roosevelt

Napoleon
A Biographical Study, by Max Lenz

Up from Slavery
An Autobiography, by Booker T. Washington

Gotama Buddha
A Biography, Based on the Canonical Books of the Theravādin, by Kenneth J. Saunders

Plato's Biography of Socrates
by A. E. Taylor

Cicero
A Biography, by Torsten Petersson

Madam Guyon
An Autobiography, by Jeanne Marie Bouvier De La Motte Guyon

The Writings of Thomas Jefferson
by Thomas Jefferson

Thomas Skinner, M.D.
A Biographical Sketch, by John H. Clarke

Saint Thomas Aquinas of the Order of Preachers (1225-1274)
A Biographical Study of the Angelic Doctor, by Placid Conway

Recollections of the Rev. John Johnson and His Home
An Autobiography, by Susannah Johnson

Biographical Sketches in Cornwall, Vol. 1 of 3
by R. Polwhele

Autobiography of John Francis Hylan, Mayor of New York
by John Francis Hylan

The Autobiography of Benjamin Franklin
The Unmutilated and Correct Version, by Benjamin Franklin

James Mill
A Biography, by Alexander Bain

George Washington
An Historical Biography, by Horace E. Scudder

Florence Nightingale
A Biography, by Irene Cooper Willis

Marse Henry
An Autobiography, by Henry Watterson

Autobiography and Poems
by Charlotte E. Linden

THE SPY UNMASKED;

OR,

MEMOIRS

OF

ENOCH CROSBY, ALIAS HARVEY BIRCH,

THE HERO OF MR. COOPER'S TALE OF THE

NEUTRAL GROUND;

BEING AN AUTHENTIC ACCOUNT OF THE SECRET SERVICES WHICH HE RENDERED HIS COUNTRY DURING THE REVOLUTIONARY WAR,

(Taken from his own lips, in short hand),

COMPRISING MANY INTERESTING FACTS AND ANECDOTES, NEVER BEFORE PUBLISHED.

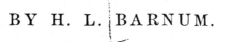

BY H. L. BARNUM.

EMBELLISHED WITH ENGRAVINGS.

PRINTED IN NEW YORK CITY, 1828, BY J. & J. HARPER,
AND RE-PRINTED BY
THE FISHKILL WEEKLY TIMES,
WITH ADDITIONAL APPENDIX AND ILLUSTRATIONS,
1886.

CONTENTS.

	Page.
DEDICATION	5
INTRODUCTION	9
CHAP. I.—Early Impressions	13
II.—Leaving Home	17
III.—The First Campaign	21
IV.—The Tories	28
V.—Secret Service	31
VI.—The Spy and the Haystack	38
VII.—The Escape	44
VIII.—The Mountain Cave	49
IX.—Chaderton's Hill	56
X.—The Secret Pass	63
XI.—Lights and Shadows	71
XII.—Quaker Hill	75
XIII.—The Spy Unmasked	79
XIV—The Spy and the Traitor	85
CONCLUSION	91
APPENDIX	93
ADDITIONAL APPENDIX:	
The Old Senate House, Kingston, N. Y.	119
A Revolutionary Heroine	120
The Old Brinckerhoff Mansion, Swartwoutville, N. Y.	121
Washington's Headquarters, Newburgh, N. Y.	122
The Crosby Memoirs	129
The Fishkill Centennial	129
The Old Trinity Church, Fishkill, N. Y.	143
The Old Reformed Dutch Church, Fishkill, N. Y.	145
The Wharton House, Fishkill, N. Y.	147
Anecdote on Continental Money	148
Fishkill in Olden Time	149
Revolutionary Reminiscences	150
Our Nation's Progress	152
ILLUSTRATIONS:	
Enoch Crosby	2
Old Reformed Dutch Church	47
Wharton House	61
Old Trinity Church	93 & 143
Old Senate House	119
Old Colonel Brinckerhoff Mansion	121
Washington's Headquarters	123
Bartholdi's Statue of Liberty Enlightening the World	152

DEDICATION.

TO JAMES F. COOPER, Esq.,
AUTHOR OF "THE SPY," "RED ROVER," &c.

SIR,

As it was your fascinating pen that first immortalized the subject of the following Memoir, while it elevated the literary reputation of our free and happy country, the Compiler has ventured to prefix your name to this unauthorized dedication.

Rest assured, Sir, that in taking this liberty, the undersigned had no other incentive but a profound respect for your talents as an author, and a warm esteem for your virtues as a man.

Under the hope that the motive will justify the act, he begs leave to subscribe himself

Your most obedient, and very humble servant,

H. L. BARNUM.

INTRODUCTION.

Since the first publication of Mr. Cooper's interesting novel of "The Spy, A Tale of The Neutral Ground," much curiosity has been excited in the reading community, respecting the or*iginal* of that excellent portraiture, Harvey Birch. It seemed to be generally admitted, that the Spy was not a fictitious personage, but a real character, drawn from life; and the author himself intimates as much in his preface, where he admits that "a good portion of the tale is true."

But we are happy to assure the reader, that the fact does not rest upon the slender basis of fanciful conjecture. A gentleman of good standing and respectability, who has filled honourable official stations in the county of Westchester, and who has long enjoyed the friendship and confidence of Mr. Cooper, informed the writer of this article, on the authority of Mr. Cooper himself, that the *outline* of the character of Harvey Birch, was actually sketched from that of Enoch Crosby; but filled up, partly from imagination, and partly from similar features in the lives of two or three others, who were also engaged in *secret services*, during the revolutionary war. But Mr. Cooper has frequently assured our informant' that, though he had borrowed incidents from the lives of others, to complete the portrait, yet Enoch Crosby was certainly the or*iginal* which he had in his "mind's eye."

That there were several such *secret agents* in the service of the leaders of the revolution, is a fact that is now well known; a fact to which the author alludes in the first chapter of "The Spy," where he says, "*Many* an individual has gone down to the tomb stigmatized as a foe to the rights of his countrymen, while, in *secret*, he has been the useful agent of the leaders of the revolution." Each of these individuals might have contributed a tint, a shade, a line, or perhaps a feature, to the character of Harvey Birch; but we think no one can peruse the following pages without being convinced that Enoch Crosby was the original model from which that character was formed.

It is highly probable, however, that Mr. Cooper never saw Crosby; and, of course, could not have received the incidents of his life from his own lips, as did the compiler of the following Memoir. But the honourable John Jay, it will be recollected, was chairman of the "Committee of Safety," under whose sanction Crosby's secret services were performed; and we understand, it was at Mr. Jay's residence that the novel of "The Spy" was first conceived and brought into existence. This venerable patriot, (better than any one else, not even excepting the *secret agents* themselves,) could furnish Mr. Cooper with every requisite material for the character of Harvey Birch; although he was under the erroneous impression, that Enoch Crosby had long since paid the debt of nature.

On learning the foregoing facts, from the gentleman alluded to above, the writer of this narrative, being then about twenty miles from the residence of Mr. Crosby, was induced to pay him a visit, for the purpose of hearing some of the incidents of his life related by himself; but without the least intention of ever committing them to paper.

Although perfect strangers to each other, the old gentleman gave his visitor a cordial reception, and readily complied with his request, by relating several particulars of his own eventful life. Some of these were of so interesting a nature, as induced his auditor to suggest the propriety of laying them before the public. The aged veteran modestly waived such a proposition, considering the events of his life as of too little consequence to claim attention from the patrons of literature. He had never seen "The Spy," as novels were not included in his present course of reading; he was consequently ignorant of being himself the very hero of the tale. When advised of this fact, and solicited to peruse the work, he consented; and the visitor took his leave.

A short time subsequent to this interview, Mr. Crosby was called to the city of New York, to give his testimony in an important law suit, respecting the transfer of some valuable real estate. While attending Court, in the City Hall, he was recognized by an old gentleman, who, not having heard of him for a number of years, supposed (like Jay and Cooper,) that Crosby had been, long since, numbered with the dead. After such mutual greetings as are usual on similar occasions, Crosby's old acquaintance turned to the Court, and introduced his friend as "the original Harvey Birch of Mr. Cooper's '*Spy*.'"

This anecdote being published in some of the daily papers, Mr. Sandford, proprietor of the LaFayette Theatre, politely invited Mr. Crosby to attend the representations of the drama of the "*Spy*;" which was performed expressly for that occasion. Mr. Crosby complied; and, the circumstance being announced in the papers, a numerous audience attended, who received the old soldier with several rounds of applause, which he modestly acknowledged. He appeared to be much interested in the performance, and readily admitted, that some of the incidents resembled transactions in which he himself had been an actor in "olden time," on "the Neutral Ground."

How Mr. Crosby was pleased with his reception in the city, will be seen from the following letter, which he sent to the Editors of the "*Journal of Commerce*," in which paper it appeared on the twenty-first day of December last, 1827.

"*For the Journal of Commerce.*
MESSRS. EDITORS.

It would be an unsatisfactory restraint of my feelings, should I not express my gratitude to the citizens of New York, for their kind attention to me during my late visit to that city, and particularly to the managers of the theatre, who politely invited me to witness the play called the '*Spy.*'

I was much gratified with the performance; for, while it called to mind those trying scenes of the revolutionary war, it also created happy emotions in reflecting upon the glorious result of our labours during that perilous time, which brought with it Independence and Prosperity; and having been spared to enjoy those blessings for half a century, and see them still continued, I can lay down my weary and worn-out limbs in peace and happiness, to see my feeble labours rewarded, and my greatest wishes answered, in gaining our independence, and the blessings attending it; and my most earnest and fervent prayer is, and shall be, that they may be perpetuated to the latest posterity.

Yours, very respectfully,
ENOCH CROSBY.
December 15, 1827."

The writer of these pages now felt convinced that the public curiosity demanded an authentic narrative of Enoch Crosby's *secret services*, during the revolutionary war. Under this impression, he paid him a second visit; and, after much persuasion, prevailed on him to relate the principal incidents of his life, in the order they occurred, while his visitor took them down, from his own lips, in *short-hand*. The *substance* of the following pages may, therefore, be depended upon, as *facts* related by Mr. Crosby himself. It is true, the *language* is, in the most instances, the Compiler's; but the *ideas*, with very few exceptions, are Crosby's own. The *language* was changed for the two following reasons:

First, The events and incidents of Crosby's life were related to the Compiler in the *first person*; which would have precluded many other facts, from various sources, which have a connection with, or bearing on, those furnished by himself. By changing the style to the third person, the Compiler was at liberty to interweave several important events which can certainly detract nothing from the merits of the work.

Secondly, The particulars of Crosby's adventures, as narrated in the following pages, were elicited in a catechetical colloquy; the style of which is seldom sufficiently accurate, or elevated for the page of history. But the facts themselves did all actually occur, with very trifling variation.

The following work has been divided into chapters, for the convenience of the reader, in making references, &c.; each of which has been headed with a motto, in order that his path, as he proceeds through the narrative, might be diversified with a few flowers of acknowledged sweetness. They may be "read or sung, at the discretion of" those who honor the book with a perusal; or they may be passed over unnoticed; for a motto, like a parenthesis. "can always be omitted without injuring the sense."

THE SPY UNMASKED

OR,

MEMOIRS OF ENOCH CROSBY.

CHAPTER I.

EARLY IMPRESSIONS.

Be this brief precept carefully imprest,
By every parent, on the infant breast;
"Thy best affections let thy God command,
But next to Heaven, adore thy native land."

Enoch Crosby, the subject of the following memoir, is a native of Harwich, in the county of Barnstable, state of Massachusetts.* He was born on the fourth day of January, 1750; a year rendered somewhat remarkable by the first indication of a wish, on the part of the British parliament, to infringe the rights and privileges of the American colonies.†

It would not be an unpardonable hyperbole to say, that the adventures of Enoch Crosby commenced at the early age of *three years*; as, at that period, he left the place of his nativity, and, after a journey of more than two hundred miles, became a resident in the state of New York. His father had purchased a farm in the township of Southeast,‡ then in the county of Dutchess, but since set off as part of the county of Putnam, to which place he removed his family in 1753.

In this delightful retreat, Enoch passed the happy period of childhood, blest with parents whose tenderness and affection were only equalled by the rectitude of their lives; and indulged with every reasonable gratification that moderate affluence could procure.

The natural scenery which surrounded his paternal mansion, was picturesque, wild, and romantic; and, no doubt, contributed to tinge his infantile mind with that cast of romance and adventure which so eminently influenced the actions of his riper years. His earliest recreations were among cragged rocks and dizzy steeps; frightful precipices, roaring cataracts, and placid lakes. A high and romantic eminence called Joe's Hill, which rises near the centre of the town, and extends several miles into the state of Connecticut,

---

* "Harvey Birch," says Cooper, in his interesting novel of the Spy, "was supposed to be a native of one of the Eastern colonies."—Spy, Vol. 1. p. 81.

† It is well known, that the "mother country" had, for a long period, reaped a rich harvest from the trade of her colonial subjects in North America. In order to secure a perpetuity of these commercial advantages, by compelling her colonists to "let their workshops remain in Europe," sundry prohibitory acts were passed by parliament, in the year alluded to, which produced considerable excitement on this side the Atlantic.

‡ This town derives its name from its situation, being the southeast corner of Putnam county. In extent it is about six miles square; bounded by Connecticut on the East, and the county of Westchester (the neutral ground) on the South. The face of the country is rather mountainous and hilly, with numerous little valleys running Southwest and Northeast. It is well watered by the Croton and Mill rivers, and their tributary streams. There are, in the town, five natural ponds, the largest of which is two miles in length and one in breadth.

was the theatre of many of his juvenile exploits; as were, also, the flowery banks of the meandering Croton, and the borders of several beautiful ponds, which lie like mirrors in the bottom of valleys, reflecting from their lucid surface the mountains and the sky. Endowed by nature with more than ordinary physical advantages, he generally bore away the palm from his play-fellows, in every athletic exercise; especially such as required a combination of personal courage, strength, and activity.

Thus, for several years, glided the smooth current of his existence, sparkling in the sunbeams of hope, and unruffled by any intruding cares, save such as are incidental to the April morning of life. As his mental faculties gradually developed themselves, they were doubtless assisted by such precarious literary instruction as could be conveniently obtained in a thinly populated district, at a period when the state of education was not very promising in any part of the country.

Under such circumstances, it is not to be presumed that a lad of fourteen years could have a very clear idea of the political relations existing between different countries; yet there is little doubt, that the political discussions to which, at that age, he was frequently a silent listener, had considerable influence in preparing his mind for the part he was destined to perform in the great drama of the revolution.

These discussions originated in certain acts of the British parliament, which were passed in the year 1764; one of which commenced in the following alarming terms: "Whereas it is just and necessary, that a revenue be raised in America, for defraying the expenses of defending, protecting, and securing the same,* we, the commons, &c., give and grant unto your majesty, the sum of,' &c. Here followed a specification of duties on certain articles of foreign produce, such as sugar, indigo, coffee, silks, calicoes, molasses, and syrups.

This being the first act of the kind (avowedly for the purpose of raising a revenue from the colonies,) that had ever disgraced the parliamentary statute book, it naturally produced much excitement and animadversion on this side the Atlantic. The merits of the question were freely and warmly canvassed by persons of all conditions and ages, and in every

---

* Tudor, in his life of Otis, gives us the following interesting anecdote: "When President Adams was minister at the court of St. James, he often saw his countryman, Benjamin West, the late president of the royal academy. Mr. West always retained a strong and unyielding affection for his native land. Mr. West one day asked Mr. Adams, if he should like to take a walk with him, and see the cause of the American revolution. The minister, having known something of this matter, smiled at the proposal, but told him that he should be glad to see the cause of that revolution, and to take a walk with his friend West any where. The next morning he called according to agreement, and took Mr. Adams into Hyde Park, to a spot near the Serpentine river, where he gave him the following narrative. The king came to the throne a young man, surrounded by flattering courtiers; one of whose frequent topics it was, to declaim against the meanness of his palace, which was wholly unworthy a monarch of such a country as England. They said that there was not a sovereign in Europe who was lodged so poorly; that his sorry, dingy, old, brick palace of St. James, looked like a stable, and that he ought to build a palace suitable to his kingdom. The king was fond of architecture, and would therefore more readily listen to suggestions, which were in fact all true. This spot that you see here, was selected for the site, between this and this point, which were marked out. The king applied to his ministers on the subject; they inquired what sum would be wanted by his majesty, who said that he would begin with a million; they stated the expenses of the war, and the poverty of the treasury, but that his majesty's wishes should be taken into full consideration. Some time after the king was informed, that the wants of the treasury were too urgent to admit of a supply from their present means, but that a revenue might be raised in America to supply all the king's wishes. This suggestion was followed up, and the king was in this way first led to consider, and then to consent to the scheme for taxing the colonies."

situation where two or three happened to be congregated; by females as well as males, and even by children in their seasons of recreation. The village lasses felt indignant at the interference of parliament in matters connected with the regulation of their wardrobes; while the children justly apprehended some economical restrictions in their usual allowance of gingerbread and sweetmeats.

Master Enoch, of course, was not an indifferent auditor of these perpetual discussions; but regularly reiterated, to an audience of school fellows, such of his father's arguments and observations, as his juvenile mind partially comprehended. Each of his comrades could, from a similar source, furnish his own quota or remark; and thus a determined spirit of opposition to ministerial encroachments on colonial rights, was permanently, and almost instinctively, established in the bosoms of the rising generation, even before they were capable of understanding the nature or extent of the subject.

Ere these newly awakened feelings, in the minds of Americans, were allowed time to subside, the celebrated stamp act was received from England. The astonishment, alarm, and indignation, which now agitated every patriotic breast, would not be restrained, but burst forth in expressions and acts that could not be misunderstood by the friends and abettors of the obnoxious measure. A string of patriotic resolutions on the subject, offered by the celebrated Patrick Henry, and adopted by the legislature of Virginia, were printed, and circulated through all the provinces. Wherever they were read, they were hailed with enthusiasm; even school-boys were encouraged to recite them in their respective classes, and exhorted to imbibe the spirit by which they had been dictated.†

A new mode of expressing the popular resentment against this odious act, began with the whigs in Boston, and was soon adopted by those of the neighboring colonies. This was by hanging or burning, in effigy, such of the principal loyalists as had openly avowed themselves friendly to the revenue system. The temper which prompted these tumultuous proceedings rapidly spread through the colonies, until popular commotions prevailed to a degree that gave serious alarm to those cool and reflecting citizens who regarded the morals as well as the liberties of their country. Scarcely a day passed without furnishing the peaceful inhabitants of Southeast with some new account of riots,‡ mobs, and summary chastisements, inflicted on the friends of the stamp act, in Boston, Newport, New York, Baltimore, and other populous towns. This was certainly a dangerous spirit to let loose in society; and though, in the present instance, its excesses were, perhaps, in some measure, sanctified by its motives, still the necessity of its existence was deeply deplored by the best friends of their country.

The mind of youth is easily dazzled by such vivid coruscations of patriotic fervour; and there is little doubt that they had a due share of influence

---

† When these resolutions were first read in the house of burgesses, in Virginia, the boldness and novelty of them affected one of the members to such a degree that he cried out "Treason! treason!"

‡ In all America there had been but seven presses issuing newspapers, previous to the year 1750. In 1765 they had increased to twenty-six on the continent, and five in the West India Islands.

in the formation of Enoch Crosby's character.

About this period, patriotic associations were formed, the members of which were denominated the "*Sons of Liberty*," and they agreed "to march with the utmost expedition, (at their own proper cost and expense), with their whole force, to the relief of those who should be in danger from the stamp act, or its *promoters* and *abettors*, on account of any thing done in opposition to its obtaining." This agreement was subscribed to by such numbers in New York and the Eastern states, that nothing short of a repeal of the offensive act could have prevented the immediate commencement of a civil war. It was accordingly repealed on the 18th of March, 1766.

The subject of this memoir very distinctly remembers the unusual rejoicings which took place in his vicinity, in consequence of this highly interesting event. Similar demonstrations of joy were exhibited throughout the colonies. The names of Camden and Pitt were cheered to the skies. Every indignant resolution was immediately rescinded; the churches resounded with thanksgivings; illuminations and bonfires were every where exhibited; and a joyful holiday was held throughout the country. This was another circumstance that made a lasting impression on the youthful mind of Enoch, and assisted in the formation of a character which has since been so admirably delineated by the pen of a master.

But while the whole country was thus dissolved in joy, there were not wanting a few enlightened patriots, who maintained "that the immoderate transports of the colonists were disproportioned to the advantage they had gained;" for at the same time that the stamp act was repealed, the *absolute unlimited supremacy of parliament* was, in words, asserted.

"Wherefore do we rejoice?" asked the good clergyman, to whose pious exhortations, both in public and private, the Crosby family ever listened with pleased and devout attention. "Is it because the parliament of Great Britian has been graciously pleased to exchange our handcuffs for fetters? Is it because she claims the power and right to bind the colonies in all cases whatsoever? Are we prepared for this? Shall the petty island of Great Britian, scarce a speck on the map of the world, control the free citizens of the great continent of America? God forbid!"

"I believe, sir," replied the elder Crosby, "that we are hallooing before we are fairly out of the woods. Our politicians seem to overlook the degrading condition which is tacked to this boasted repeal, that we must make *compensation* to those who have suffered, in person or property, through their own wilful adherence to the cause of our oppressors. If we submit to this, we deserve to be slaves."

"It appears to me," observed the village schoolmaster, who happened to be present, and who was strongly suspected of leaning to the ministerial side of the question; "it appears to me, that if we look at this subject by the pure light of sober reason, and not by the illusive flashes of excited passion, we shall see the propriety of waiving all debate and controversy; and, for the sake of internal peace, of making the trifling compensation required. It cannot amount to much."

"It is not the amount of the sum that I object to," returned the other. "It is the principal that I am contending for. If we yield in one point, there is no telling how far their encroachments may extend."

"Is not their compliance with our petitions for repealing the stamp act an evidence of their respect for the rights of the colonies?"

"No sir," replied the clergyman. "In this measure, the ministry have not been so much actuated by principles of equity, as impelled by necessity."

"Necessity!" reiterated the pedagogue. "To me it appears an act of favour and lenity "

"The doctrine of submission, passive obedience, and non resistance, may do very well in the discipline of your school," answered Crosby; "but I hope my son will never imbibe from you, or any other man, such sentiments as applied in politics."

Here the conversation terminated; and Enoch, who was present, did not feel any great increase of respect towards his preceptor in consequence; nor was it long afterwards, that his father placed him under the tuition of an elderly gentleman, of superior literary acquirements, whose political sentiments were in accordance with his own. As this personage will again appear on the stage, in the progress of our little drama, we beg the reader to bear in mind that he is not only a "staunch whig," but, in every other respect, a worthy man.

CHAPTER II.
LEAVING HOME.

"Here, as, with wearied steps, I bent my way,
 I mark'd each dear and well-remembered spot,
Where youth had buoyed my mind with visions gay,
Nor thought I then how hard would be my lot."

At the period of which we are writing, it was the earnest wish of all parties, that harmony might be re-established between Great Britian and her American colonies. The severities of the British government "had not yet taught the colonists to express themselves in any other modes of language, but what indicated their firm attachment to the mother country: nor had they erased the habitual ideas, even of tenderness, conveyed in their usual modes of expression. When they formed a design to visit England, it had always been thus announced, 'I am going home.' *Home*, the seat of happiness, the retreat of all the felicities of the human mind, is too intimately associated with the best feelings of the heart, to renounce without pain, whether applied to the natural or the political parent."*

But although a strong desire for the re-establishment of harmony was manifested by persons of every description, there still existed a great diversity of opinion as to the best means of producing so desirable a result. "There were several classes in America, who were at first exceedingly opposed to measures that militated with the designs of administration. Some, impressed by long

---
* Mrs. Warren.

connection, were intimidated by her power, and attached by affection to Britain; others, the true disciples of passive obedience, had real scruples of conscience with regard to any resistance to 'the powers that be;' these, whether actuated by affection or fear, by principle or interest, formed a close combination with the colonial governors, custom-house officers, and all insubordinate departments who hung on the court for subsistence."*

The partizan distinction of *whig* and *tory* was adopted at an early stage of the controversy, and introduced in every political altercation to which it gave rise. It was no un common occurrence for members of the same family, not only to espouse opposite sides of the question, but to defend the stand they had taken with a zeal and pertinacity that ultimately sundered the tenderest ties of consanguinity. Thus, as the general ferment increased, the father was often arrayed "against the son, and the son against the father;" brothers became implacable enemies to each other; and even the fair sex were not unfrequently involved in this frightful whirlpool of political contention.

Fortunately for the subject of these memoirs, and happily for his country, his father's family, to adopt his own expression, were "staunch whigs;" so was a majority of their fellow-townsmen, particularly the good clergyman, the Rev. Mr. Gregory, before mentioned. Indeed, the clergy, of every denomination, throughout the country, with very few exceptions, warmly espoused the cause of the colonies; and embraced every opportunity, both in public and private, of exhorting their flocks manfully to resist every encroachment on their rights as freemen. Their influence was great, and its effects such as might have been expected.†

The attention of the elder Crosby, however, and that of his amiable family, were, for a time, diverted from political difficulties by domestic misfortunes. From a state of comfort and comparative affluence, he suddenly found himself reduced to poverty and distress.‡

This unexpected reverse of fortune rendered it necessary for the son, at the age of sixteen, to leave, for the first time, the shelter of his paternal roof, and seek his own fortune in an untried world.

The painful sensations incidental to the parting of an affectionate child

---

* Mrs. Warren's American Revolution.

† The clergyman of New England, in particular, were among the strongest advocates of "Whig principles;" there were a few instances only of a separation of a minister from his people, in consequence of a disagreement in political sentiment. It was recommended by the provincial congress of Massachusetts, that on other occasions than the Sabbath, ministers of parishes should adapt their discourses to the times, and explain the nature of civil and religious liberty, and the duties of magistrates and rulers. A zealous divine, who had been compelled to abandon the people of his charge in Boston, on one occasion used, in the pulpit, at P***, the following emphatic language: "O Lord, if our enemies *will* fight us, let them have fighting enough. If more soldiers are on their way hither, sink them, O Lord, to the bottom of the sea." *Thacher's Journal, p. 23.* "The clergy of New England were a numerous, learned, and respectable body, who had a great ascendancy over the minds of their hearers. They connected religion and patriotism, and, in their sermons and prayers, represented the cause of America as the cause of Heaven." *Ramsey.* "The clergy were among the first and most zealous patriots, both in speaking and writing in vindication of the rights of their country. No class of men had more deeply imbibed the spirit of their venerable ancestors, the first settlers of New England, than they. None more generally engaged in the cause of their injured country, nor had a greater and more general influence upon the people." *Morse's Rev.*

‡ Mr. Cooper frequently intimates that the parents of Harvey Birch had been suddenly "reduced from competence to poverty." *See Spy. Vol. i. p. 33, and* 154.

from indulgent parents, and the home of his childhood, are seldom forgotten by the parties concerned; but in the present instance, their impression was left with a vividness of colouring which the lapse of more than sixty years has not been able to obliterate. In reverting to this incident, at the age of seventy-eight, the subject of this memoir expressed himself, in substance, as follows:

"At the age of sixteen the scene changed, and I was compelled to leave the home of my childhood, to seek the protection of strangers, and depend upon my own exertions for support. With the scanty outfit of a change of clothes and a few shillings in my pocket, I bade a long adieu to the friends I best loved, and the scenes of my happiest days. After receiving the blessing of my parents, with much good advice, and a small Bible, which they assured me would prove my greatest consolation in every trial and affliction that might befall me, I shouldered my pack, clasped their hands in silence—for I dared not trust my voice to say 'farewell!'—and hastened away, leaving my poor mother in an agony of tears.

"I proceeded a short distance, with a burden at my heart much heavier than the one on my back. I then paused, and cast back a 'longing lingering look,' on the spot that I could once call my home—but now no longer a home for me. I then resumed my march, and after proceeding a little further, again turned; when, for the last time, I saw my weeping mother through the widow, gazing, with streaming eyes, after her exiled son. I hurried away—I could not look again. The hills which surrounded the beloved mansion soon hid it from my view, and I felt myself alone in the world, cut off from all that I held dear; while the future appeared like a dark impenetrable cloud, scarcely illumined by a ray of hope."

Painful as these sensations must have been to a youth in his circumstances, they were soon dissipated by the novelty ever attendant on a change of scene and associations. He became an apprentice to a worthy man who resided in the eastern part of Phillipstown, since called Kent, in the county of Putnam. Here he was taught the "art and mystery of a cordwainer," and faithfully fulfilled his term of service, which terminated on the fourth day of January, 1771, that day completing his twenty-first year.

Let it not be supposed, however, that during all this period he was an unconcerned spectator of the political movements around him. Far from it. The sentiments which he had imperceptibly imbibed in childhood, "grew with his growth, and strengthened with his strength," and now began to flow out into effective operation. Although military discipline had for several years been almost totally neglected, it now began to assume a more respectable attitude. New trainbands were organized, in one of which young Crosby soon became an active and efficient member; and he largely shared in the prevailing impression, that a most important crisis was fast approaching, for which it was the duty of every lover of his country to be duly and properly prepared. Nor was this impression weakened by an incident which occurred in the last year of his minority; an incident which forms a conspicuous chapter in the history of those times. We mean the massacre, in cold blood, of several citizens in the streets of Boston, by the British soldiery. This wanton act of barbarity was perpetrated in open day, on the fifth of March, 1770.

No previous outrage had produced such a general alarm as the one here alluded to. "Yet the accident that created a resentment which emboldened the timid, determined the wavering, and awakened an energy and decision that neither the artifices of the courtier, nor the terror of the sword, could easily overcome, arose from a trivial circumstance:

"A sentinel, posted at the door of the custom house, had seized and abused a boy, for casting some opprobrious reflections on an officer of rank; his cries collected a number of other lads, who took the childish revenge of pelting the soldier with snow balls. The main guard, stationed in the neighborhood of the custom house, was informed by some persons from thence, of the rising tumult. They immediately turned out under the command of a captain Preston, and beat to arms. The cry of fire was raised in all parts of the town; the mob collected. and the soldiery. from all quarters, ran through the streets, sword in hand, threatening and wounding the people, and with every appearance of hostility they rushed furiously to the centre of the town.

"The soldiers, thus ready for execution, and the populace grown outrageous, the whole town was justly terrified by the unusual alarm. This naturally drew out persons of higher condition and more peaceably disposed, to inquire the cause. Their consternation can scarcely be described, when they found orders were given to fire promiscuously among the unarmed multitude. Five or six persons fell at the first fire, and several more were dangerously wounded at their own doors."*

"How slightly soever historians may pass over this event, the blood of the martyrs, right or wrong, proved to be the 'seeds of *the congregation.*' Not the battle of Lexington or Bunker's Hill; not the surrender of Burgoyne or Cornwallis, were more important events in American history, than the battle of King street, on the 5th of March, 1770."†

The immediate result of this outrage is well known. Captain Preston and his party were taken into custody of a civil magistrate, tried for murder, and acquitted; and all the royal troops were subsequently removed from the town to the fort about three miles below. But the indignant feelings which it had created in every patriotic bosom were not to be appeased. The blood of their brethren cried from the ground for vengeance, and the appeal was felt in every section of the country. Like other young men of his age, Enoch Crosby ardently longed for an opportunity to mingle the blood of the assassin with that of their victims. But the hour had not yet come.‡

---

* See Appendix, No. 1.
* Mrs. Warren's American Revolution.
† John Adams' letters to Dr. Morse.
‡ The town of Boston instituted an annual oration in commemoration of this catastrophe, and among the first orators were such names a Hancock, Warren, and Lovell.

CHAPTER III.

THE FIRST CAMPAIGN.

"O, who, reclined in dastard ease,
Could hear his country's call in vain;
Or view her banner court the breeze,
Nor sigh to join the hostile train."
WOODWORTH.

As we are not writing a history of the rise and progress of the revolutionary war, but merely the memoirs of a private individual who took an active part in that momentous contest, it is only requisite to give a brief detail of such events as are connected, more or less remotely, with his own transactions.

The destruction of the tea in Boston,* the consequent port bill,† as it was called, the formation of a continental congress, and the arrival of General Gage with an army to reduce the "refractory colonists" to submission, are prominent features in the history of four years, from the period of our last chapter. But events of still greater importance were at hand, and anticipated with trembling anxiety.

Among the "signs of the times," was the newly awakened military ardour which prevailed throughout the colonies, more especially in the Eastern states. In almost every town, a certain quota of hardy youth were draughted from the militia trainbands, who voluntarily devoted a daily portion of their time to improve themselves in the military art, under officers of their own choice. These were styled "*minute men*," and stood ready to march at a moment's warning, to defend the rights of their countrymen.

At this period, the younger Crosby resided at Danbury, in the State of Connecticut; and though it was not his fortune to be draughted as a minute-man, he was still actuated by the same martial spirit which inspired the rest of his countrymen. The year 1775 had opened without the occurrence of any incident of much political importance; but while thousands of bosoms were throbbing with feelings of intense interest, every eye was directed to the capital of Massachusetts as the quarter from whence momentous intelligence might be hourly expected.

The public mind was in this state of feverish suspense, when, in the month of April, an express arrived at Danbury, with intelligence that "upwards of four-score of Americans had been inhumanly butchered on the plains of Lexington,* by a detachment of the British army, which had afterwards been put to flight by a few raw country militia. That houses had been rifled, plundered, and burnt; that neither sex, age, nor infirmity, had been respected by these ruthless marauders; and that women, with their new-born infants, had been compelled to fly naked, to escape the fury of flames in which their houses were enwrapped!" †

---

† The 1st day of June, 1774, the day when the Boston port-bill began to operate, was observed, in most of the colonies, with uncommon solemnity, as a *day of fasting* and prayer.

* When General Washington heard of the battle of Lexington, April 19, 1775, and of the slaughter of the Americans on that occasion, he said, "I grieve for the death of my countrymen; but rejoice that the British are still so determined to keep God on our side; for the smiles of Heaven can never be expected on a nation that disregards the eternal rules of order and right, which Heaven itself has ordained."—*Weems's Life of Washington.*

† The celebrated Rev. John Horne (Tooke,) two years after the event, was tried, in England, and found guilty of publishing an advertisement, in which it was asserted, "that the king's troops had committed *murder* at Lexington, in America;" he was consequently, sentenced to imprisonment for a year, to pay a fine of ℔200, and to find security for his good behaviour for three years!—*Fordyce's Chronology.*

The sensation produced by this intelligence not only at Danbury, but in every other place, can be better conceived than described. The shock was electric, and the whole country flew to arms.‡

Within twenty-four hours after the routed "regulars" had regained the protection of their shipping, the town of Boston was invested by several thousands of our exasperated countrymen; while the colonies of Connecticut, Rhode Island, and New Hampshire, seemed all to be in motion. Indeed, "such was the resentment of the people, and the ardour of enterprise, that it was with difficulty they were restrained from rushing into Boston, and rashly involving their friends, in common with their enemies, in all the calamities of a town taken by storm."§

The outrage at Lexington occurred on Wednesday, the 19th of April; but the news did not reach the city of New York until late on Saturday evening, nor was it generally known until Sunday morning. A meeting of the citizens immediately took place; who, without much ceremony, seized upwards of five hundred stands of muskets and bayonets belonging to his Britannic majesty.

On the following day, the keys of the custom-house were secured by the whigs; who soon made themselves masters of all the public stores in the king's ware-houses in the city and at Turtle Bay.

At this time there were about three hundred regular British troops in the city, commanded by a Major; and very serious apprehensions were entertained, that the confused and disorderly manner in which the foregoing transactions were conducted, would produce a rupture between the soldiers and the populace. A regular general meeting of the citizens was therefore called, and a committee of fifty appointed, who were invested with full powers to act as the exigency and circumstances of the times might require. At this meeting a set of spirited resolutions were passed, and signed by the citizens at large, in which they pledged themselves, their lives, their fortunes, and their sacred honour, to support their committee in all its operations, and also every measure of the general congress, then in session at Philadelphia.

One of the first acts of the committee, was an order permitting the British troops to depart without interruption, taking with them their arms and accoutrements. In consequence of this order, the troops prepared to embark on the following day; when it was observed that they had several carts loaded with spare arms. Marinus Willett, and some others, immediately resolved to prevent this virtual infraction of their agreement; and meeting the troops in Broadway, stopped them, and without much difficulty took possession of the spare arms. With these Willett armed a new company of his own raising, with which he joined the first Canadian expedition.

‡ Israel Putnam (afterwards Major-general) was ploughing in his field when he heard the news. He instantly stopped his team, left the plough in the furrow, mounted a horse, and in eighteen hours was on the battle-ground, a distance of one hundred miles! He then returned to Connecticut, and raised an army; the provincial congress of Massachusetts having that day voted to raise thirty thousand men.

"They heard—and the plough in the furrow was stay'd.
Each art was relinquished for musket and blade;
The pipe of the swain in the valley was still.
While the bugle rang loud from each fortified hill."

§ Mrs. Warren's American Revolution.

The citizens of Danbury were not backward in this moment of general excitement. ‖ A rendezvous was opened, to which the youth of the county flocked from every quarter; and two regiments were immediately raised, one under the command of Colonel (afterward General) Wooster, and the other under the command of Colonel Waterbury. Within a few hours from the arrival of the express at Danbury, the name of Enoch Crosby was inscribed on the muster-roll of Captain Benedict, followed by those of one hundred and fifty young men, all residents of that town; forming the most efficient company in Waterbury's regiment.*

As soon as these regiments were duly organized, equipped, and reported to the provincial congress of Massachusetts, then in session at Watertown,† they impatiently waited for orders to move and act in defence of their Eastern brethren. Nor was their impatience abated by the successes of their enterprising neighbours at Ticonderoga and Crown Point, on the 10th of May following;‡ but on the news of the battle of Bunker Hill, § it was wrought up to a pitch of painful intensity. Every man longed to be in the field, and share in the dangers and glory that awaited the champions of liberty. This patriotic ardour was shortly to be gratified.

The continental congress was now in session at Philadelphia; and, at this period, the importance of possessing the Canadas, strongly impressed the minds of gentlemen of the first penetration, private citizens as well as the representatives of the several colonies, in that august legislative body. It was thought a favourable crisis to make the attempt "when the flower of the British troops, then in America, were shut up in Boston; and when the governors of the Southern provinces, interrupted in their negotiations with the Indians, had taken refuge on board the king's ships, either from real or imagined personal danger." ‖ It was, therefore, determined to employ Colonel Waterbury's regiment, together with two regiments of New York militia, in this important and hazardous service; the whole force consisting of about three thousand men, under the command of Generals Schuyler and Montgomery.

The reader may easily imagine

‖ This excitement was not confined to any class, age or sex. The females largely participate l in the patriotic ardour that prevailed, and exhibited instances of heroic virtue that were never surpassed by the celebrated women of Sparta. See Appendix, No. III.

* It is worthy of remark, that every one of these young men returned from the Northern campaign in safety; while, during their short absence, one hundred deaths occurred in the town where they belonged. Perhaps, by-going into danger, many of them preserved their lives.

† This legislative body had voted to raise thirty thousand men; thirteen thousand and six hundred of them to be of their own province, and that a letter and delegate be sent to the several colonies of New Hampshire, Connecticut, and Rhode Island. The Committee of safety also sent letters to the several towns in the colony soliciting assistance.

‡ This enterprise was managed by Colonels Easton, Arnold, and Allen; and so secretly, judiciously, and rapidly was the expedition conducted, that they entered the garrison before it was known that an enemy was near it. Arnold and Allen contended for the honour of entering the fort first; but it was finally agreed that they should both go in together. They advanced abreast, and entered the fortress at the dawning of day. A sentry snapped his piece at one of them, and then retreated through the covered way to the parade. The Americans followed, and immediately drew up. The commander, surprised in his bed, was called upon to surrender the fort. "By what authority?" exclaimed the astonished officer, rubbing his eyes, and scarcely knowing whether he was asleep or awake.

"I demand it in the name of the great Jehovah, and of the continental congress," was the reply of Colonel Allen.

The authority could not be disputed. The fort was surrendered without resistance, together with forty-eight prisoners, several brass and iron cannon, and a valuable quantity of warlike stores.

§ See Appendix, No. III.
‖ Mrs. Warren's American Revolution.

with what alacrity our hero and his fellow soldiers obeyed the orders of their superiors, to "strike their tents and march away." The language of each heart was,

"Strike up the drums; and let the tongue of war plead for our interest."

They were ordered to the city of New York, where they were joined by the New York militia, one corps of which was commanded by the gallant Willet; but encamped about two miles out of town, near the spot now occupied as Vauxhall garden.* After remaining in this position about three weeks, they removed to Harlaem, and encamped in the village. From thence they took boats, and proceeded up the Hudson to Albany, on their way to Lake Champlain.

General Schuyler being detained at Albany, for the purpose of negociating an Indian treaty, his coadjutor, the intrepid Montgomery, led on his gallant band of patriots to Ticonderoga, where they arrived on the twenty-first day of August.† As soon as a sufficient number of boats could be provided to convey the army down Lake Champlain, they embarked for *Isle aux Noix*, lying about eleven miles north of the lake, in the river Sorel, which connects the waters of Champlain with that of the St. Lawrence. On reaching Isle La Motte, they were rejoined by Gen. Schuyler, who had prepared an address to the inhabitants of Canada, inviting them to join the standard of liberty, and unite in the common cause of America.

From Isle aux Noix, the army proceeded to St. Johns, the first British post in Canada.‡ During their passage down the river, the soldiers were directed to hold themselves constantly in readiness for defence, as it was reasonably apprehended that they might be assailed by the Indians from the woods which skirted the stream.

On effecting a landing, at a short distance from fort St. Johns, the assailants, about one thousand in number, immediately formed in full view of the garrison, and prepared for hostile operations. Their movements, at this juncture, are thus described by Crosby himself:

"We were now in full view of the enemy, who kept up a constant cannonading, which only caused us to dodge now and then, merely serving to get us into a fighting mood. We were soon ordered to advance; but had only proceeded a few rods, when we were suddenly attacked by a body of Indians in ambush; who, after a

---

* In the year 1775, the city of New York (we mean the compact part of it) extended no farther north than Partition street, now called Fulton street, near St. Paul's church. Beyond this there were only a few scattering houses, with here and there a handsome country seat. It was considered a pleasant ramble "out of town" to go to "*the fields*," where the City Hall now stands.

† The fortress of Ticonderoga, so often mentioned in the history of the American wars, is now a heap of ruins, though many of the walls are so entire as to exhibit proofs of the excellency of their construction, and of the plan of the works. It was built by the French in 1756, on a point of land formel by the junction of Lake George creek with Lake Champlain, in N. lat. 43 degs. 50 min., and 31 min. E. long. from New York; elevation above Lake Champlain, 110 feet; above tide waters, 196 feet. The name is derived to us from the Indians, French field; and signified *noisy*. Che-on-der-oga: probably in allusion to the water. But the French called it Fort Carillon. It was a place of great strength, both by nature and art. On three sides, it is surrounded by water, and about half of the other side is occupied by a deep swamp, and the line of defence was completed by the French, with the erection of a breast-work, 9 feet high, on the only assailable ground. In 1768, Gene al Abercrombie, with the British army, assailed this fortress; was defeated July 9, with the loss of 1,911 men. But it was surrendered to General Amherst, in July of the following year. It was the first fortress carried by the arms of America in the war that established our Independence; it was taken by surprise, by Col. Allen, May 10, 1775, and retained till July, 1777, when it was evacuated, on the approach of Gen. Burgoyne with the British army.

‡ About 115 miles north of Ticonderoga.

short contest, were glad to show us a specimen of their speed in running.*

"Our sport, however, was soon interrupted by an order to *halt!*—when, after burying the dead, and providing for the wounded, a council of war was held by the officers, in which it was determined to return to Isle aux Noix, throw a boom across the channel, and erect works for its defence.

"In the meantime, a breastwork was ordered to be thrown up on the spot where we stood; and accordingly every one went to work with alacrity. While some were felling trees and preparing timber for this purpose, and others throwing up the earth to form a parapet, we were constantly annoyed by the shells thrown from the fort. This circumstance tended to retard our operations; for when a shell rose in the air, every one would stop working to watch its course, and ascertain if it would fall near him. I must confess that I felt no particular affection for these unwelcome intruders, but rather regarded them as 'messengers of evil;' still, however, notwithstanding the cold reception which I gave these warm-hearted visitors, I never thought of the fashionable expedient of 'not being at home,' (in other words, of 'dodging them,') until I heard some one exclaim, 'Look out!—take care, there!' when I looked up, and saw one descending towards the very spot where I was standing. I threw myself flat on the ground, and it just passed over me. 'A miss is as good as a mile' thought I, as I sprang from my recumbent posture, and resumed my labour. But after that, I kept one eye upon the enemy.

"Our general, however, gave us some instructions on this subject. He advised us never to change our position until the shell was directly over us; and if it should then appear that it had lost its projectile force, and was falling, 'it would be well enough to step on one side.' He was a noble fellow, that Montgomery.† Every soldier in the army loved him like a brother.

"When the breastwork was completed, which was in a much shorter

---

* Ramsay says, that "the British pickets were driven into the fort. The environs were then reconnoitred, and the fortifications were found to be much stronger than had been suspected. This induced the calling of a council of war, which recommended a retreat to Isle aux Noix." Mrs. Warren says, that "an unexpected attack from a large body of Indians obliged them to retreat to their former post, and await the arrival of reinforcements." The latter account is in strict conformity with Mr. Crosby's own statement. Both, however, may be correct.

† Montgomery was a warm-hearted Irishman; and war was his profession. He had been a captain of grenadiers in the 17th regiment of British troops, of which Moncton was colonel. In 1772, he bequitted his regiment, though in a fair way of preferment, because he disapproved of the sentiments of the ministry, and had imbibed an affection for America, which he viewed as the rising seat of arts and freedom. A sentiment of a still more tender nature might have had some influence in this transaction, as he soon afterward married the beautiful and accomplished daughter of Judge Livingston, of New York. His many amiable qualities had procured him an uncommon share of private affection, and his great abilities an equal proportion of public esteem. His name was mentioned in parliament with singular respect. The minister himself acknowledged his worth, while he reprobated the cause he had espoused. He concluded an involuntary panegyric, by exclaiming—"Course on his virtues! they have undone his country." When he embraced his amiable lady for the last time, on his departure for Canada, and bade her a tender farewell, his parting words were—"You shall never blush for your Montgomery." She never did—but a nation wept his untimely fall

"Yes, yes, I go," he whispered soft,
 "In freedom's cause my sword to wield,
Columbia's banner waves aloft,
 And glory calls me to the field."
Then foremost on the foe he prest,
 While war's rude tempest wildly roar'd,
Till, gushing from the hero's breast.
 The purple tide in torrents pour'd.

He fell, and oh! what fancies stole
 Through memory's vista, bright and warm,
Till one loved image o'er his soul
 Came like an angel in the storm.
But loudly swell'd the bugle's blast,
 His hand instinctive grasp'd the steel;
Again 't swelled—but all was past,
 The warrior's breast had ceased to feel.
    WOODWORTH.

time than might have been expected considering the circumstances under which we laboured, we prepared for a retreat; as this show of hostility was merely a finesse to divert the enemy's attention. As soon as night set in, and every object was shrouded in darkness, we were ordered to decamp with as little noise as possible. We accordingly took our boats, and returned up the river; leaving the enemy to wonder at our sudden and mysterious exit. On the following day, we reached Isle aux Noix, where we remained two weeks, waiting for reinforcements."

Soon after this event, an extreme bad state of health induced General Schuyler to retire to Ticonderoga, and the sole command devolved on General Montgomery. Immediately on the arrival of his expected reinforcement, this intrepid and enterprising officer returned to the vicinity of St. Johns, and opened a battery against it on the seventeenth day of September. "Ammunition, however, was so scarce, that the siege could not be carried on with any prospect of speedy success.

The General, therefore, detached a small body of troops, to attempt the reduction of fort Chamblee, only six miles distant. Success attended this enterprise; and, by its surrender, six tons of gun powder were obtained, which enabled the General to prosecute the siege of St. Johns with vigour. The garrison, though straitened for provisions, persevered in defending themselves with unabating fortitude.*

The severe duties of so arduous a campaign; the frequent skirmishes,

---

* Ramsay's American Revolution.

marches, and counter-marches, and constant exposure to sudden changes of weather, in the inclement month of October, were not without their effects on the health of the soldiers. Among others, Crosby was seized with a severe indisposition, and removed to the hospital at Isle aux Noix. But his impatience to share in the dangers and glory of the approaching contest, would not permit him to remain under the surgeon's hands but a few days, when he returned to the army, in direct opposition to the wishes of his medical adviser. In relating this incident, Mr. Crosby says:

"I returned against the surgeon's advise, and contrary to the expectations of my Captain; for as the time for which we had enlisted had nearly expired, he had no idea that any of us invalids would rejoin the army. As soon as he saw me, he accosted me in a tone of unaffected surprise; 'Halloo, Crosby! Have you got back? What induced you to return before your health was restored; I never expected to see you here again; so you might as well have gone home. You have not had time to get well; for you look more like a scarecrow than a soldier fit for duty.' I replied, that I wished to be with him; and that if I was not able to *fight*, I might at least *frighten* the enemy, as he thought I looked like a scarecrow. At this remark he laughed heartily, and told me, that if I wished so much to fight, that I should soon be gratified. Accordingly, in the course of the day we had a severe engagement, in which we proved victorious; and, to my great satisfaction, I was one of the number that marched into the fort to the tune of Yankee

Doodle, and took charge of the prisoners."*

Our invalid soon recovered his health, and continued in the service until the army took possession of Montreal, which they did, without resistance, on the 12th of November. His term of enlistment having now expired, he proposed to return, once more, to the tranquil scenes of his childhood. He was warmly solicited by his commandant to remain with the army, and even promised promotion if he would comply; but, being strongly impressed with the idea that a more extensive field for usefulness would soon be opened in the vicinity of New York, he persisted in his intention of leaving the army. In company with several others, whose term had also expired, (having enlisted for six months only,) he embarked in a small schooner for Crown Point,† where he arrived about the 1st of December.

"From thence, (says he,) our little party proceeded on foot to Ticonderoga, where we procured a small boat, and rowed up the river which connects Lake George with Champlain. On reaching the falls, however, we were compelled to draw our boat on shore, and drag it on the ground, across a neck of land about a mile in width. In this manner, with immense labour and fatigue, and suffering greatly from the inclemency of the season, we reached Sabbath-day Point,‡ in Lake George. Here, however, no friendly shelter awaited us; and though, almost perishing with cold, we could obtain no better quarters than an old pig-stye. This miserable substitute for a tent was soon filled with brush and straw; when, with wet feet and shivering bodies, (all of us being thinly clad,) we laid ourselves down to rest from the fatigues of the day."

---

* Major Preston, the commanding officer at St. John's, surrendered that fortress on receiving honourable terms of capitulation. "By those it was agreed, that the garrison should march out with the honours of war; that the officers and privates should ground their arms on the plain; the officers to keep their side-arms, and their fire-arms be reserved for them, and that the people of the garrison should retain their effects. About five hundred regulars, and one hundred Canadians became prisoners to the provincials. They also acquired thirty-nine pieces of cannon, seven mortars, and two howitzers, and about eight hundred stand of arms. Among the cannon were many brass field-pieces, an article of which the Americans were nearly destitute."

† On Lake Champlain, about 12 miles north of Ticonderoga. "The celebrated fortress of Crown Point, one of the best ever erected within the present territory of the United States, gave its name to this town, which contains the ruins of the fort. Along the lake, the surface is pretty level, but high mountains prevade the western part. The fort itself is on a point of land jutting far into the water northward, and washed by a considerable bay on the west, called West Bay. This fortress was first erected by the French, in 1731, and called Fort St. Frederick. In 1759, it was surrendered to the British troops under General Amherst, and was occupied by them until May 14, 1775, when it fell into the hands of the Americans, (as stated in a preceding note,) but was evacuated in 1776, and again fell into the hands of the British. The walls were of wood and earth, twenty-two feet thick, and sixteen feet in height. It was about fifteen hundred yards square, surrounded by a deep and broad ditch, cut in a solid granite rock, with immense labour. On the north is a double row of strong stone barracks, of a capacity to contain two thousand troops. On the same side was a gate, a strong drawbridge, and a covered way to the margin of the lake. The whole are now in ruins, and the outworks, of which there were some pretty extensive, are little else than heaps of rubbish, barely sufficient to revive remembrance."--*Spafford's Gazetteer.*

‡ So called from its having been the scene of a bloody massacre on the Sabbath day. A large party of whites had encamped there, without suspecting an enemy to be near them; but the Indians came upon them suddenly, and cut them off, almost to a man. Very few escaped to tell the disastrous story. We have often heard the tradition, but are not in possession of the particulars. Lake George, of course, could not have been attractive to our travellers in the middle of winter; but in any other season it is the most beautiful sheet of clear water in America, perhaps in the world. It is about thirty-three miles in length, and nearly two in breadth. Its northern extremity approaches within two and a half miles of Lake Champlain, and the outlet is little more then three miles long, where it is said to descend 157 feet. Lake George is surrounded by high mountains, and is excelled in romantic beauties by no similar waters of the world. Its water is very deep, the bottom so clean that neither winds or freshets render it turbid, and it abounds with the finest fish for the angler. Salmon trout are taken weighing twenty pounds and upwards, with a great variety of other fish.

At early dawn, on the following morning, this intrepid little party resumed their unpleasant journey; and, after several days of fatigue and suffering, without meeting any remarkable adventure, at length reached their respective homes in safety.

After a few weeks repose had restored Crosby to his usual health and strength, he resumed the peaceful occupation of shoemaking, in his former situation at Danbury. Here he continued until the 25th of January, 1776, when a sudden gloom was spread over the whole country, by the disastrous news that his beloved General, the brave and amiable Montgomery, had fallen before the walls of Quebec, on the last day of December. Even at this distant period, (1828,) Mr. Crosby cannot speak on this subject without emotion. The soldiers almost adored Montgomery; and there was scarcely an individual that had ever served under him, but shed tears for his untimely fate. Crosby was so much affected on first hearing of the melancholy event, that he found it difficult to pursue an occupation that gave so much opportunity for painful reflections; he, therefore, sought relief in change of scenery, and paid a visit to his friends in Kent, where we leave him for the present, while we take a glance at the state of the country, on the opening of the eventful year 1776. In doing this we shall discover the *causes* which prompted the subject of this memoir to assume a *new character* in the revolutionary drama—that of a Spy, on the "Neutral Ground."

CHAPTER IV.
THE TORIES.

Know, villains, when such paltry slaves presume
To mix in treason. if the plot succeeds,
They're thrown neglected by; but, if it fails,
They're sure to die like dogs, as you shall do.
                                    ADDISON.

The winter of 1775-6 passed tardily away, and no military movements of consequence were made on either side. The British troops remained shut up in Boston, under the command of General William Howe, the perfidious Gage having sailed for England. The continental army in the vicinity of Boston was rapidly decreasing by the expiration of the short period for which the soldiers had enlisted.* Although Congress had exerted all its energies to create a new army, still the recruiting service went on very slowly, and no active operations were attempted until the beginning of March, when a threatened bombardment, from the heights of Dorchester,† compelled General Howe to evacuate Boston, and thus relieved the suffering inhabitants from their distress and privations.‡ The British army was

---

* At the close of the year 1775. the continental army near Boston, was reduced to a very critical situation, being obliged to substitute new raised troops and militia, in the place of those who had been in service five or six months; and this exchange was made within musket-shot of the enemy's lines. During part of this period, their numbers were not sufficient to man the lines, nor was there powder enough in camp to furnish four rounds *a man!* They had only four small brass cannon, and a few old honey-comb iron pieces, with their trunnions broken off; and these were ingeniously bedded in timbers, in the same manner as that of stocking a musket. These machines were extremely unwieldy and inconvenient, requiring much skill and labour to elevate and depress them. Had the enemy in Boston been made acquainted with the situation of their besiegers, the consequences might have been unpleasant.—*Thacher's Journal*

† See Appendix, No. IV.

‡ The distresses of the inhabitants of Boston, during the memorable winter of 1775-6, exceed description. They had been promised permission to leave the town, if they would deliver up

hastily embarked on board the ships and transports then lying in the harbour, together with a host of *tories* and *refugees*, who claimed the protection of General Howe, and abandoned their bleeding country. The fleet proceeded to Halifax, where the loyal fugitives were landed, and where Howe determined to remain, until the arrival of his brother from England, with the expected reinforcements, which should enable him to pursue the year with vigour.

Immediately after this joyful event, Washington sent on the continental army, in detachments, to New York; and as soon as he had made some necessary arrangements for the future defence of the eastern states, he hastened on himself, and made every possible preparation for the reception of the expected enemy, who did not arrive at Sandy Hook until the 29th of June.

After waiting, at Halifax, two or three months, for the arrival of his brother Lord Howe, with his "motley mercenaries from Hesse, Hanover, and Brunswick," Sir William became impatient of delay, and set sail for New York, accompanied by Admiral Shuldham. Here, however, he found the continental army so strongly posted on Long Island and the island of New York, that he did not immediately attempt anything of consequence; but landed his troops at Staten Island, and there awaited the arrival of his brother.

In the meantime, the declaration of Independence was adopted by Congress, and published to the nation. Four days after its passage, it was read to the army at New York, by whom it was received with the most enthusiastic demonstrations of joy. A leaden statue of his Majesty George III, was immediately thrown down, and run into bullets, for the reception of Lord Howe, and his host of mercenaries, who arrived, four days afterwards, with a formidable squadron.

After amusing, or rather insulting, the American government with an inadmissible proposition of reconciliation, the enemy made preparations to act with vigour. Having been joined by "the repulsed troops from the southward,‡ and the broken squadron under the command of Sir Peter Parker; by a regiment from St Augustine, and another from Pensacola; also, by a few troops from St. Vincents, some small additions from other posts, and a considerable party of *tories* from New Jersey, and from the environs of Philadelphia and New York, which, by great industry, had been collected and embodied by Governor Tryon," the whole hostile army crossed the channel, and landed on Long Island, where they were posted, in detachments, on the south side, from one end of the island to the other; separated from the American army by a ridge of hills covered with woods.

---

their arms, which were accordingly deposited in Faneuil Hall, to the care of the select men. But no sooner were the citizens completely disarmed, then Gage violated his agreement, and refused to let them depart. Nor was general Howe, his successor, any more lenient; for he issued a proclamation, prohibiting all persons attempting to quit the town, without a written license, on penalty of *military execution*; and, if they escaped, they were to be proceeded against as traitors, and their effects to be forfeited. The consequences may be easily conceived. That ill-fated town was a scene of *famine* and distress. The inhabitants were almost in a state of starvation, for the want of food and fuel. Totally destitute of vegetables, flour, and fresh provisions, they were actually obliged to feed on horse flesh; while the pews of churches, old houses, and timbered wharves, were demolished for fuel.—*Thacher's Journal*.

‡ See first note, in Chapter VIII.

Tryon, it will be recollected, was the last governor who presided at New York, under the crown of England. He had formerly been governor of North Carolina, where his severities had rendered his very name universally detested. He, of course, entered with great zeal into all the measures of the British government; and endeavoured with art, influence, and intrigue, (of which he was perfect master,) to induce the city of New York, and the inhabitants under his government, to submit quietly, and not unite with the other colonies in their plans of opposition. Failing in this purpose, and becoming apprehensive for his own personal safety, he left the seat of government, and put himself at the head of a body of *tories*, whom he assisted in butchering their fellow countrymen, and committing the most shocking enormities on the defenceless inhabitants of New Jersey, and wherever else he could penetrate. He constantly held out such flattering inducements for these wretches to join him, that scarcely a day passed without his receiving recruits from some quarter.

At this period, the "Committee of Safety" for the colony of New York, consisted of Messrs. Jay, Platt, Duer and Sackett; gentlemen who have since held conspicuous situations in the government of their emancipated country. It, of course, became the policy of this committee to counteract, as far as in them lay, the arts and intrigues of the wily Tryon. For this purpose, they exercised the utmost vigilance to prevent the *tories* from joining the standard of the enemy; and felt perfectly justified in resorting to coercive measures to effect this desirable object. In fact, so daring had become their opposition and outrages, that any lenity extended towards them would have been cruelty to the friends of liberty, as the following facts will amply demonstrate.

A gang of these unprincipled wretches, who had associated in New York for the purpose of joining the British army, had even concerted a plan to assassinate Washington, and some other officers; and, while our army was engaged with the enemy, to blow up the magazines. The mayor of the city, and an armourer who was employed in making rifles for the *tories*, together with several others, were taken into custody, and committed to prison. The mayor, on examination, confessed that he had received money from Tryon to pay the armourer for the rifles. Two of Washington's body-guards were confederates in this nefarious scheme; but a third, to whom the secret was confided, honestly disclosed the information. Several of these miscreants were tried and convicted, and two or three were executed.

About the same time, a similar plot was brought to light in Albany by the confession of two *tories*. Their plan was to set the city on fire, and blow up the magazine. In consequence of this premature exposal, some of the conspirators were apprehended, and the meditated plot frustrated.*

But the most dangerous and culpable of these internal enemies, were those who had the effrontery and address to pass themselves off for whigs. One of these was Dr. Benjamin

---

* See Thacher's Journal, p. 64.

Church, who had long sustained a high reputation as a patriot and a son of liberty. He had been a member of the house of representatives of Massachusetts, and was afterwards appointed surgeon general, and director of the hospitals. Previous to the evacuation of Boston, however, he was detected in a traitorous correspondence with the enemy; tried, convicted, and expelled from the house of representatives, and ordered to be "closely confined in some secure jail in Connecticut, without the use of pen, ink, or paper; and that no person be allowed to converse with him, except in the presence and hearing of a magistrate, or the sheriff of the county." After all this, however, he was finally permitted to depart from the country. He and his family embarked for the West Indies; but the vessel foundered at sea, and all were lost.†

A man by the name of Ledwitz, who, by his own solicitation, had been appointed Lieutenant-colonel in the continental army, was also detected in a traitorous correspondence with the infamous Tryon. He intrusted his letter to one Steen, an honest German, to be conveyed to New York; but, considering it his duty to expose the perfidy, the messenger delivered it to Washington. By this criminal act the perfidious wretch had forfeited his life, according to the articles of war; but, on his trial by a court-martial, his life was saved by the casting vote of a militia officer, who pretended some *scruples of conscience!* He was, however, cashiered, and declared incapable of holding any military office in the American service.*

But it is unnecessary to multiply instances. Enough has been said to show that the *tories* were the most insidious, virulent, and implacable enemies, with which the friends of liberty had to contend in the fearful struggle which secured the independence of these United States. Internal secret enemies are always more dangerous than open avowed foes in the field; and it ought to be considered as a signal and remarkable interposition of divine providence, that their vile machinations were so frequently defeated. But Providence always operates by instruments; and among the most efficient, patriotic, disinterested, and successful agents, in counteracting the meditated treachery and machinations of internal secret enemies, was Enoch Crosby; as will be sufficiently shown in the following pages.

CHAPTER V.
SECRET SERVICES.

What is it that you would impart to me?
If it be aught toward the general good,
Set honour in one eye, and death i'the other,
And I will look on both indifferently;
For let the gods so speed me, as I love
The name of honour more than I fear death.
SHAKSPEARE.

The unfortunate battle of Long Island, the consequent retreat of the American army, and the subsequent occupation of the city of New York by the British, under General Howe, are events familiar to every reader. The first occurred on the 27th of August, 1776, and the last on the 15th of the following month. The affair at Kipp's Bay,† the contest at Har-

---

† See Thacher's Journal, p. 38.

* Ibid. p. 64.
† See Chapter VI, third paragraph.

laem Heights, and the landing of the enemy at Throg's Neck, in 'Westchester county, followed each other in rapid succession, and excited the most lively interest throughout the country.

It was during the occurrence of these important transactions, that Crosby determined to rejoin the standard of his country. Several months' repose had recruited his health and strength after the fatigue and sufferings of his northern expedition. He was now in the twenty-seventh year of his age, with every personal and mental qualification requisite for acts of enterprise, hazard, and address. In height, he was nearly six feet, with broad shoulders, full chest, and a liberal share of bone and muscle, but not a superabundance of flesh.‡ Active, athletic, and inured to hardships, he determined no longer to indulge in inglorious ease, while his brave countrymen were in arms in defence of their rights and liberties, and while persons of every age, sex, and condition, were cheerfully submitting to unexampled privations, for the sake of political freedom.§ He, therefore, resumed his knapsack, shouldered his musket, and, once more bidding adieu to the rural scenes of Kent, he bent his course towards the headquarters of the American army.

It was towards the close of a warm day, in the month of September, 1776, that he reached a wild and romantic ravine, in the county of Westchester.*

Here he fell in with a gentleman, who appeared to be travelling in the same direction, and with whom he soon entered into familar conversation. Among other questions, the stranger inquired, if Crosby was going "down below?"—to which he readily answered in the affirmative. The interrogator appeared pleased with this reply, and let fall some expressions which plainly indicated that he had "mistaken his man," supposing Crosby to be a loyalist, on his way to join the British army. The latter instantly perceived the advantage which might be derived from this mistake, and suffered his new companion to remain under the erroneous impression.

"Are you not aware," said the stranger, "that it is somewhat hazardous to go down alone? The rebels are on the alert, and you may meet with obstacles that will not be very pleasant."

"Indeed!" returned Crosby, with much affected concern. "What course would you then advise me to pursue?"

"I will tell you, sir. I reside but a short distance from hence; go with me, and make my house your home for a few days, when you can go down with a company that is now forming for that purpose."

"That is, indeed, a most fortunate circumstance," replied Crosby; "and I accept the hospitable invitation with as much cordiality as it appears to

---

‡ "In person, the pedlar was a man above the middle height; spare, but full of bone and muscle. His eyes were gray—sunken, restless; and, for the few moments that they dwelt on the countenances of those with whom he conversed, seemed to read the very soul."—*Spy, Vol. i.* p. 34.

§ See Appendix, No. V.

* Westchester county is situated on the east side of the Hudson, immediately above York Island. It is joined to Putnam county on the north, and Connecticut on the east; comprising about four hundred and eighty square miles. It enjoys a direct communication with the Hudson on the west, and with the Sound on the south-east. Its surface, in some parts, is rugged and mountainous; in others, beautifully undulating, and luxuriantly fertile: the whole well watered, and diversified with scenery that is truly picturesque and romantic. The centre of this county, lying between the two hostile armies, during the revolutionary war, was called the "Neutral Ground."

have been given. This arrangement will relieve my mind from a load of anxiety, and I shall feel myself under a weight of obligation to you."

"Not at all, sir; it is a pleasure to serve those who, in these trying times, retain their integrity, and remain faithful to his majesty. I am happy to know that many of my neighbors are of this class; and though the vigilance of Jay, Duer, Platt, Sackett, and their deluded instruments, compel my friends to be very circumspect in their movements, there is no doubt of their being able to complete their arrangements, and reaching the army without molestation. They will very gladly receive you as a member, and in their company you will be perfectly safe."

"I have no doubt of it," returned Crosby; "and am impatient to be introduced to their acquaintance."

"Yonder is my residence; and you need refreshment and repose. Rest yourself to-night, and in the morning your wish shall be gratified."

Crosby readily acceded to this proposal, and followed his new acquaintance into a small enclosure that led to a neat farm-house at a short distance from the road. Here he was received with a cordial welcome, and furnished with such refreshments as his situation required. After supper, the evening was spent in conversing on a variety of subjects, that naturally grew out of the critical state of the times at that period; such as may easily be imagined to have passed between a covert whig, anxious to obtain intelligence, and a real tory, who had no suspicion of the character of his guest.

Having had a comfortable night's rest, and a substantial breakfast, Crosby reminded the host of his promise to introduce him to such of his neighbours as were faithful to the royal cause; particularly those who were about forming a company to join the British army.

"I am anxious," said he, "to become acquainted with the agents, before I join in the enterprise. It is not every man of fair professions that can be safely trusted. I like to see and judge for myself."

The reasonableness of this request induced his kind entertainer to comply with it without delay. Crosby was accordingly introduced to a number of persons, on many of whom the shadow of suspicion had never before lighted, they having ever professed to be warm adherents of the American cause. Every one received him with cordiality, and conversed on political subjects without the least disguise or restraint, so completely had they been thrown off their guard by their confidence in the person who had recommended him. He found the whole of them to be most inveterate and virulent in their hostility to the friends of liberty, and was convinced that he could not render a greater service to his bleeding country, then by counteracting the machinations of her most dangerous (because most secret and insidious) foes.

Accordingly, at the expiration of three days, during which time he had made himself master of all the information in their power to communicate, (and some of them held secret correspondence with the enemy,) he told his host, that he felt too impatient to join the army, to wait any longer the dilatory movements of this company. He was, therefore, resolved to proceed alone, and to trust to fortune and his own address for protection. After vainly exhausting every argument to dissuade his guest from so hazardous a project, the other finally consented, and Crosby resumed his knapsack and musket, took leave of his entertainer, and was soon out of sight on the road to New York.

In this direction, however, he did not travel long; but took advantage of an abrupt angle in the road, to change his course; when, leaving the highway, he plunged into a thicket, and pursued his way, through a pathless tract of country, in a northwestern direction.

He had heard of a Mr. Young, who resided within eight miles from White Plains, and knew him, from reputation, to be a warm friend to the American cause. With him, therefore, he determined to consult on the proper steps to be taken with respect to the arrest of these traitors to their country. Owing, however, to the circuitous route he had adopted, to avoid the observation of his late associates, night had set in before his journey was half accomplished; and it was with extreme difficulty, that he "groped his darkling way" through the wild and broken region that lay between him and the object of his pursuit. Hills were to be climbed, thickets penetrated, and streams forded, before he could gain the road which was to conduct him to the mansion of Mr. Young.

All these difficulties, however, were at length happily surmounted; but it was near midnight when he reached the end of his journey. Fortunately, the master of the house was still up and alone, his family having all retired. Crosby was a stranger, and the hour unseasonable; but such circumstances were not unusual in those "stirring times." He was promptly admitted, and politely invited to take a seat; when Mr. Young, fixing on him a searching gaze, (as if anxious to penetrate into the secret recesses of his heart, and there to read his real character,) intimated that he was ready to learn the purport of his untimely visit.

Crosby was aware that the inhabitants in that section of the country, had lost much of their former confidence in each other, and knew not whom to trust; he, therefore, hastened to explain the object of his intrusion, and relieve his host from the evident embarrassment his suspicions had created.*

"I understand, sir," said Crosby, "that you are a friend to the 'upper party.'† Give me leave to ask if I have been correctly informed? Is it true?"

"Yes, sir," promptly replied the other; "it *is* true. I *am* a friend to my country; and am not afraid or ashamed to avow it, to friend or foe."

"I have always understood, sir, that such was your character, and rejoice to find that I am not deceived. Under this impression, I have taken the liberty to wait on you, for the purpose of communicating informa-

---

* "The county of Westchester, after the British had obtained possession of the Island of New York, became common ground, in which both parties continued to act for the remainder of the war of the revolution. A large proportion of its inhabitants, either restrained by their attachments, or influenced by their fears, *affected* a neutrality they did not always feel."—*Spy*, Vol. i. p. 2.

† As respects *location*, the Americans were always the "upper" party, in the vicinity of New York; for while they retained possession of the city, the British were still below them, at Staten Island. The same relative position continued on their retreat through the county of Westchester.

tion that may prove beneficial to the American cause."

"Go on, sir," returned the host, in a tone bordering on sternness, and without relaxing his features. "Proceed; I am all attention."

"Do you know, sir, that there are traitors around you?—that even some of your neighbours are secretly concerting plans to assist the common enemy in plundering and butchering their own brethren and fellow-countrymen?"

"I am well aware," returned Young, with a sigh, "that there are too many who feel secretly disposed to aid the cause of the enemy. But they dare not openly avow it."

"That is true, sir."

"O, that I knew them!" continued the host, with increasing animation, as he rose from his seat. "O, that I could designate them—point them out—name them! They should soon be linked together by closer and stronger ties than those which now connect them."

"Then, sir," replied Crosby, with confidence, rising on his feet, and approaching the other, "I have news that will interest you. I have just left a company of these wretches, after having spent three days with them, and know all their plans. Their intention is to join the 'lower party,' with whom they now hold a secret correspondence, and raise their parricidal hands against their bleeding country."

"Is it possible!"

"It is most true, sir. I know them all—have visited their families—attended their secret meetings—assisted them in maturing their nefarious plans."

"Indeed! Then you yourself——"

"Understand me," interrupted Crosby. "I have levelled this musket too often at the open and avowed enemies of my country, to be on terms of intimacy with her secret foes, except for the purpose of discovering and preventing their contemplated treachery."

Here Crosby gave a particular detail of the circumstances connected with his introduction to the members of this hopeful confederacy; particulars with which the reader is already acquainted; and, as he proceeded, the countenance of his auditor gradually brightened. As soon as he had finished, the latter seized him eagerly by the hand; and, with sparkling eyes, exclaimed—

"Is this true, upon the honour of a man?"

"It *is* true, by Heaven!" returned the other; "and if you will assist me with your advice and co-operation, eight-and-forty hours shall not elapse until you are convinced by the testimony of your own eyes."

"Come on, then, my good fellow!" exclaimed Young, seizing his hat. "The Committee of Safety are at White Plains, and thither we must proceed immediately. Follow me quickly, and I will be your pilot."

Crosby was not backward in complying with this injunction, though already much fatigued by his recent journey; but promptly followed his hasty guide, on this midnight excursion. Fences, rocks, and streams, were but slight impediments

"To hearts resolved, and limbs inured to toil,"

and, before two o'clock, they found themselves at the end of their journey, in the village of White Plains, and in the presence of the honourable John Jay, one of the most vigilant of these watchful guardians of the public safety.

This gentleman being made acquainted with the foregoing particulars, dismissed his informant with a request that they would remain near at hand, for further instructions, as he intended, at early dawn, to convene the committee, and hold a consultation on the important subject.

Were we writing a romance, instead of an authentic narrative of events which actually occurred, and could we command the descriptive pen of our inimitable Cooper, here would be the place to introduce a series of incidents which attended, (or might have attended,) the subsequent movements of our nocturnal adventurers. Their difficulty in procuring comfortable quarters for the remainder of the night; a description of the village inn, where they finally succeeded in rousing the lazy landlord from his slumbers; the motley group which lay snoring on the floor of the bar-room; a portraiture of the florid-faced landlady, and the various incidents resulting from this unexpected interruption of her arrangements for the night, would, all together, form sufficient materials for an interesting chapter. But as nothing of the kind has been promised in our title page, the reader must rest contented with a plain unadorned narrative of such facts as our hero can actually remember at the advanced age of seventy-eight.

The committee were convened at an early hour on the following morning, when Crosby was summoned before them, to recapitulate the particulars of his recent adventure. After hearing his statement, and consulting on the most proper steps to be taken in the business, Crosby was requested to hold himself in readiness to accompany a detachment of Rangers,* (on the ensuing night,) to the place where his recent associates were in the habit of holding their secret cabals.

The enterprise was crowned with complete success. Without dreaming of molestation, these vile conspirators found themselves suddenly surrounded by a troop of horse, and compelled to surrender. Thus, in less time than our hero had specified, his friend Young had the satisfaction of seeing the whole cavalcade, linked together in pairs, safely conducted to prison, to the tune of the "Rogue's March."

The successful result of this enterprise, induced the committee to believe that the cause in which they had so zealously embarked, might be highly promoted by engaging a person of Crosby's acuteness and address in similar secret services. The proposition was accordingly made to him at a confidential interview.

"It was your intention," said the chairman, "again to serve your country as a private in the ranks. Such a resolution, in a person of your character and abilities, could only have originated in motives of the purest patriotism. But you must now be convinced that much greater services may be rendered by pursuing a different, though certainly not a less hazardous, course. There is a sufficient number of brave fellows to repulse our open and avowed enemy. The greatest danger which now

---
* These rangers were a company of mounted men, reserved expressly for exigencies of this kind, whenever they should occur, and to go wherever the Committee should direct.

threatens this suffering country, is from her internal foes; those secret enemies who, in their midnight cabals, are plotting our destruction. He who succeeds in bringing such wretches to justice, deserves infinitely more of his country, than he who fights her battles. Are you willing to engage in such service?"

"I am willing to encounter any danger, and make any sacrifice, (my honour only excepted,) in the service of my country."

"It cannot be disguised that, in the service now proposed to you, even honour, in the general acceptation of that term among men, must also be sacrificed; but not so in the eye of that Being who reads the secret thoughts of the heart, and judges the motive instead of the act. He will approve, though man may condemn."

"It is, indeed, a hazardous part you would have me play. I must become a Spy."

"In appearance only. Our bleeding country requires such service at this momentous crisis. We must fight our secret foes with their own weapons; and he who will magnanimously step forward as a volunteer in that service, will merit a rich reward —and receive it, too, from Heaven, if not from man. If he falls, he falls a martyr in the glorious cause of liberty."

"I will be that man," replied Crosby, with firmness.—"I have counted the cost, and am aware of the danger. I know that I must be content to endure reproach, obloquy, and detestation; to cover my poor doating parents with shame and misery, and incur the hatred of those I dearest love. Perhaps to suffer an ignominious death, and leave a name of infamy behind. I know it all, and yet I will not shrink from the task. I will encounter all—risk all—suffer all, if I can thereby serve my country. But there is one condition ——If I *do* fall in the discharge of this duty, you must pledge yourselves to do justice to my memory. It would be dreadful to die, and leave such a name behind me."

"Of that rest assured," replied the chairman, not a little affected by the solemn earnestness of this appeal; "but we hope and trust that the melancholy duty will not be soon required at our hands. We will furnish you with a pass for your protection; but it must never be exhibited save in the last extremity. Should you be arrested as an emmissary of the enemy, you shall be secretly furnished with the means of escape. But the secret of your real character must go no farther. Your dearest friend must not be intrusted with it."

After furnishing their new agent with every necessary instruction, together with the promised *pass*, the committee adjourned, and Crosby immediately set about making arrangements for his new undertaking. His musket was laid aside; and instead of a knapsack, he furnished himself with a large *pedlar's pack*,* containing a complete set of shoemaker's tools. Thus equipped, he sallied forth in quest of adventures. His ostensible object, (in order to avoid suspicion,) was searching for employment; or what the sons of St. Crispin, at that period, termed "whipping the cat;" but, in

---

* "Harvey Birch had been a pedlar from his youth; at least, so he frequently asserted."—*Spy, Vol. i. p.* 31.

more modern times. we believe it is called "cutting a stick." Whatever be the genuine classical appellation, however, we must leave our intinerant to pursue his peregrinations in the interior of Westchester county, while we take a peep at the army below.

CHAPTER VI.
THE SPY AND THE HAYSTACK.

"Our foes shall fall, with heedless feet,
Into the pit they made;
And tories perish in the net
Which their own hands have spread."

Immediately after the battle of Long Island, the retreat of the Americans, and the barbarous execution of the brave and unfortunate Hale,* the enemy made prompt dispositions for attacking the city of New York. It was a serious question with Washington, whether that place was defensible against so formidable a force; it was finally decided, however, in a council of war, that it had become not only prudent, but necessary, to withdraw the army.

Several of the enemy's ships of war having passed up the Hudson, on the west side of York Island, and also up the East river, on the opposite side, Sir Henry Clinton embarked at Long Island, at the head of four thousand men; and, proceeding through Newtown Bay, crossed the East river, and landed, (under cover of five ships of war,) at Kipp's Bay, about three miles above the city. Works of considerable strength had been thrown up at this place, to oppose the landing of the enemy; but they were immediately abandoned by the troops stationed in them. Terrified at the fire of the ships, they fled precipitately towards their main body, and communicated their panic

† See Appendix, No. VI.

to a detachment which was marching to their support.

Washington, to his extreme mortification, met this whole party retreating in the utmost disorder, and exerted himself to rally them, but, on the appearance of a small corps of the enemy, they again broke and fled in confusion! The General, who was not only mortified and distressed, but actually enraged at their cowardice, drew his sword and snapped his pistols to check them; but they continued their flight without firing a gun!

For a moment, the feelings of Washington got the mastery of his reason. "Are these the men with which I am to defend America?" exclaimed he, in a tone of bitterness. as he gazed after the recreant fugitives; then, turning his horse's head to face the advancing enemy, he remained for some minutes exposed to their fire, as if wishing, by an honourable death, to escape the infamy he dreaded from the dastardly conduct of troops on whom he could place no dependence. His aids, and the confidential friends around his person, by indirect violence compelled him to retire.

Nothing now remained but to withdraw the few remaining troops from New York, and to secure the posts on the heights. The retreat was effected with very inconsiderable loss of men; but all the heavy artillery, and a large portion of the baggage, provisions, and military stores, were unavoidably abandoned.

Major-General Putnam, at the head of three thousand five hundred continental troops, was in the rear of the retreating army. In order to avoid any of the enemy that might be advancing in the direct road to the city, he made choice of a rout parallel with, and contiguous to, the North river, till he could arrive at a certain angle, whence another road would conduct him in such a direction as that he might form a junction with the main army. It so happened, that a body of about eight thousand British and Hessians were, at the same moment, advancing on the road, which would have brought them in immediate contact with Putnam, before he could have reached the turn into the other road.

Most fortunately, the British Generals, seeing no prospect of engaging the Americans, halted their own troops, and repaired to the house of a Mr. Robert Murray, a quaker, and a whig. Mrs. Murray treated them so hospitably with cake and wine, that they were induced to tarry two hours or more, during which time Tryon was frequently joking her about her American friends.

By this happy incident, Putnam escaped a rencountre with a greatly superior force, which must have proved fatal to his whole party, as one half hour would have been sufficient for the enemy to have secured the road at the turn, and entirely cut off Putnam's retreat. Dr. Thacher, in relating this circumstance, adds: "It has since become almost a common saying, among our officers, that Mrs. Murray saved this part of the American army."

The enemy immediately took possession of the city, for the defence of which he left a suitable detachment, and then advanced towards Harlaem, in pursuit of Washington. The Americans now occupied Kingsbridge, at the northwestern extremity of York Island, both sides of which had been carefully fortified; they were also in considerable force at M'Gowan's Pass, and Morris's Heights. A strong detachment was also posted in an intrenched camp, on the heights of Harlaem, within a mile and a half of the enemy.

On the day after the retreat from New York, a considerable body of the enemy appearing in the plain between the two camps, Washington ordered Colonel Knowlton, with a corps of Rangers, under Captain Townsend, and Major Leitch, with three companies of Virginians, to get in their rear, while he amused them by making apparent dispositions to attack them in front. The plan succeeded. A skirmish ensued, in which the Americans charged the enemy with great intrepidity, and gained considerable advantage.

Knowlton was killed, and Leitch badly wounded; but their men behaved with great bravery, and fairly beat their adversaries from the field. Most of these were the same men who had disgraced themselves the day before, by running away from an inferior force. Struck with a sense of shame for their late misbehaviour, they had offered themselves as volunteers, and requested the commander-in chief to give them an opportunity to retrieve their honour.

In the mean time, Crosby was earnestly pursuing his new vocation; traveling about the country; and, with his characteristic acuteness,* becoming "all things to all men," in order to elicit such information as

---

* "Harvey Birch possessed the common manners of the country, and was in no way distinguished from men of his class, but by his acuteness—and the mystery which enveloped his movements.—*Spy*, Vol. I. p. 31.

would enable the committee of safety to discriminate between their real friends and their secret foes. Through his intimacy with the latter, (who, of course, hailed him as a kindred spirit,) he obtained regular information of the movements of the enemy below, and privately transmitted the same to his employers.

As may readily be supposed, the committee, at this time, were trembling for the safety of the American army; and their well-grounded apprehensions were hourly increasing, when a secret communication from their new agent informed them, that the contest on the heights of Harlaem had fully retrieved the tarnished honour of the American arms; that their good conduct, at this second engagement, had proved an antidote to the poison of their example on the preceding day; and demonstrated that Americans only wanted resolution and good officers to be on an equal footing with their enemies. The committee were thus inspired with hopes, that a little more experience would enable their countrymen to assume, not only the name and garb, but the spirit and firmness of soldiers.

In one of Crosby's reconnoitering excursions, the approach of evening, and some fatigue of body, reminded him that it was time to look out for comfortable quarters for the night. There was no public house of entertainment within several miles, and only a few poor farm-houses, thinly scattered, within the whole circumference of his vision. To one of these, therefore, he determined to apply, for supper and lodgings. He accordingly struck off into a foot-path which led to the nearest; and, bending beneath the weight of his pack, advanced to the door, and knocked for admittance.

A rosy-cheeked girl, of about fifteen, just budding into maturity, of rustic appearance, and bashful demeanour, at length appeared, with visible reluctance, to answer to his summons. On being made acquainted with his wishes, the timid maiden hesitated, stammered, and then suddenly retreating; saying, as she closed the door, "I will ask mother, sir."

In a few minutes, however, she again made her appearance, and bade him walk in. He did not wait for a second invitation; but followed his fair conductor into an apartment that served at once the two-fold purpose of parlour and kitchen. Here he repeated his request to a middle-aged female, who sat in a corner of the capacious fire-place, very busily employed with her knitting-work.

"Lodging, did you say?" exclaimed the good woman, surveying her weary guest over the top of her spectacles. "We don't keep lodgings, sir."

"I am very much fatigued, madam; and would be very grateful for permission to stay in your house till morning."

"O well, I don't know," returned the old woman, rising from her seat and approaching the stranger to examine him more particularly "There's some strange works, now-a-days, and I don't like to keep anybody for fear of something. What, in mercy's name, is that great bag there?"

"That, Madam, is my shop. I am a shoemaker, by trade, and am in search of work; with my shop upon my back. Will you give me leave to dismount it?"

"Well, I don't care if you stay long enough to make our John a pair of shoes, for he is going over east, to see some men that are going down to the army next week."

"Are they going to *our* army?" asked Crosby, as he disencumbered himself from his ponderous pack.*

"I 'spose you mean the lower army; don't you, sir?"

"O, yes, madam; certainly," answered Crosby, helping himself to a chair. "I mean the royal army, a large detachment of which is now at Throg's Neck. The rebel army has run away from York Island, and is now moving towards White Plains. But Howe will soon overhaul them, and give a good account of them, too, or I miss my guess."

"Here, Sally!—Where are you?— Get this man something to eat, for his good news; and then see if the best bed-room is put to rights, and make him as comfortable as you can."

As a good loyalist, Crosby was now made welcome to the best the house afforded. While he was thus refreshing himself, and chatting with his loquacious landlady, the good man of the house himself came home, to whom she eagerly introduced her guest as a warm adherent of his Majesty, and a sworn enemy to the rebels. This assertion was abundantly confirmed by the remarks of Crosby himself, during a long and interesting conversation on the subject of that wicked rebellion against the mother country.

---

* "At first sight his strength seemed unequal to manage the unwieldy burden of his pack; yet he threw it on and off with great dexterity, and with as much apparent ease as if it had been feathers."—*Spy*, Vol. i. p. 84.

In the course of this conversation, Crosby learned that a company was forming, about three miles east of that place, for the purpose of joining the British army. On his intimating a desire to become a member of this corps, his host readily agreed to introduce him to the Captain, in the course of the following day. He then conducted his guest to the best bed in the house; and, wishing him a pleasant night's repose, left him to his own meditations, to dream of plots and counterplots, or any other subject that fancy might conjure up.

Whatever might have been the character of his dreams, however, our adventurer arose the next morning completely refreshed and invigorated; and, after partaking of a hearty breakfast, he accompanied his host to the residence of the tory Captain before mentioned. On being introduced, by his attentive guide, as a loyalist, who was desirous of serving his Majesty, Crosby was most cordially received, and politely invited to stay to dinner, and to spend the remainder of the day and the coming night at the Captain's house.

This invitation was readily accepted; and, in the course of the evening, Crosby was made acquainted with many interesting particulars relative to the plans and intentions of the Captain and his confederates.

On the following morning, at breakfast, the subject was again introduced, when Crosby was asked if he was ready to enter his name on the muster roll.

"I have not yet entirely made up my mind," replied he. "Such a step will necessarily be attended with considerable danger; for, in case I should be taken by the Americans, and my name known, they would hang me as a traitor."

"Were there any solid grounds for such an apprehension," replied the other, "you would only incur that risk in common with us all. But the rebels dare not resort to such extremities, for fear of a terrible retaliation."

"It may be so," returned Crosby. "But I think I should rather go down without entering my name on the roll; unless, indeed, I could first examine, and see if there are any names of my acquaintance on it.'

"That privilege shall be cheerfully granted you," said the Captain, producing a long roll of signatures, and handing the same to his visitor, who ran over them with a satisfaction which he took good care to conceal; for he readily perceived, to use his own expression, that there was a "fine haul for his net." After attentively examining every name, he rolled up the list, with an air of disappointment; saying, as he returned it to the Captain,

"I shall beg to be excused, sir. They are all strangers to me; and it is not impossible that this roll may one day fall into the hands of the Americans. Besides, I can just as well go down without enrolling my name."

"Well, sir," replied the Captain, "I have a safer way yet, for those who are influenced by similar apprehensions with yourself. I put five or six names on one slip of paper, which I then conceal beneath a large stone in my meadow. I have several such deposits. Come along with me, and say what you think of the plan."

So saying, he arose from the table, and, accompanied by his guest, sallied out into a large meadow, at some distance from the house. After visiting several spots where these secret muster rolls were deposited, he directed the attention of his companion to a hay-stack of enormous dimensions, and asked him what he thought of it.

"I think it would prove a *great* temptation to a rebel foraging party,' answered Crosby, after a short silence, and with some covert humour which cost him an exertion to conceal.†

."It probably would," observed the other, "were such parties abroad. But it would be difficult for the best mathematician among them to determine its solid contents by measuring its superficies. It is a mystery worth penetrating into. Let me instruct you."

With these words, the speaker lifted up the hay, on one side of the huge edifice, and discovered a small opening which led to the interior of the excavated pile. Fond of adventure, Crosby entered without hesitation, and found himself in a most ingenious hiding place, of sufficient capacity to contain forty or fifty men, comfortably seated.

"What think you of that?" asked the proprietor of the hay, as his guest emerged from its interior. "Would the rebels ever think of looking for you there?"

"I think not," replied the other, with an inward chuckle, as he surveyed the exterior of the premises

---

† "When engaged in his ordinary business, the intelligence of his face appeared lively, active, and flexible, though uncommonly acute; if the conversation turned on the ordinary transactions of life, his air became abstracted and restless; but if, by chance, the revolution and the country were the topic, his whole system seemed altered—all his faculties were concentrated—he would listen for a great length of time without speaking, and then would break silence by some light and jocular remarks, that were too much at variance with his former manner, not to be affectation."—*Spy, Vol. i. p. 34.*

very attentively. "I should as soon think of searching for a needle in a haymow."

The Captain smiled with much self-complacency at this brief approval of his invention, and then renewed his solicitations for Crosby to enroll his name. The latter, however, still hesitated, but promised to give a definite answer on the following day. With this assurance the other remained satisfied, and the remainder of that day was devoted to making further arrangements for the contemplated expedition.

Night soon returned, and Crosby was still the Captain's guest. At the usual hour, he retired to his bed, where he lay, listening attentively to every movement in the house, until he felt perfectly assured that the family were safely locked in the arms of sleep. When "every sound was hushed, and all was still," he cautiously arose, dressed himself, and stole out of the house, without giving any alarm. Before midnight he was consulting with his employers at White Plains.

Such arrangements were immediately adopted by the Committee of Safety as were considered, by all parties, appropriate to the emergency. Their informant then took his leave; and, before daylight, was again snoring in his bed, at the house of the loyal Captain.

On the following morning, he informed his entertainer that he had made up his mind as to the subject of their recent conversation. He was willing and anxious to become a member of the company; and would hold himself in readiness to march with them at a moment's warning; but should decline signing his name to the muster-roll until they had safely arrived within the British lines. The Captain appeared satisfied with this arrangement, and expressed a hope that every thing would be prepared for their departure on the following day.

"Would it not be advisable, then," asked Crosby, "to call a general meeting of the company this evening?— There is much to do, and it is necessary that we act in concert. When we are all together, our plans can be better digested, as we shall have the opinion and advice of each individual. Such a meeting is indispensable before we go down, and there is certainly no time to be lost."

"The idea is a good one," replied the Captain; "and every man shall be notified to meet here this evening, when we will complete our arrangements, and be off to-morrow. You must assist me in calling them together."

Crosby readily consented to exert himself on this occasion; and went about the business with such cheerful alacrity, that, before nine o'clock in the evening, the whole company were assembled in the Captain's parlour, with the exception of the lieutenant, who had gone from home on some temporary business.

By ten o'clock the business of the meeting was nearly all completed; and the usual refreshments were about being introduced, when the attention of the party was suddenly arrested by the loud trampling of horses.

The lights were instantly extinguished; and they all sat in breathless silence; every heart palpitating with fearful anticipations of some unpleasant adventure, until they were aroused to action by a voice at the door exclaiming—

"Surrender! or you are all dead men!"

At that instant the door was thrown from its hinges, and the apartment was filled with the American Rangers, all heavily armed.

"Surrender! I demand it in the name of the continental congress!" exclaimed the leader of these unwelcome intruders. "Resistance is useless, and escape impossible, for the house is surrounded. You are our prisoners."

Words are inadequate to depict the general consternation produced by this alarming salutation. Some flew to the attic; others retreated as precipitately to the cellar; and almost devoutly wished themselves in the bowels of the hay-stack, as there was nothing to hope from the bowels of their captors. Several attempted to throw themselves from the windows; but were soon convinced that there was no chance for escape in that direction.—The secret, but unsuspected cause of all this confusion and dismay, made a feint of concealing himself in a closet; but was quickly dragged forth, and compelled to share the fate of his companions, who were manacled together in pairs, and marched, like felons, to the village of White Plains.

CHAPTER VII.
THE ESCAPE.

———————————To be the mark
Of smoky muskets! O you leaden messengers,
That ride upon the violent speed of fire,
Fly with false aim.——— ———
　　　　　　　　　SHAKESPEARE.

The historic events connected with the name of White Plains, will long live in the pages of American history; and if the readers have patience to accompany us through a few more chapters, he will acknowledge that there is sufficient cause for this lasting celebrity. At present, we merely wish to introduce him to the scene of so many important transactions.

Bronx river, a beautiful stream of water that rises just on the south line of Newcastle, in the county of Westchester, holds its course nearly due south to the village of West Farms, from whence it empties into the East river, between Morrissania and Throg's Neck. A few miles east of this stream, and nearly parallel with it, is another called Mamaroneck creek, which empties into Long Island Sound, near a village of the same name.

Between these two little rivers, and near the head of the latter, is the township of White Plains, comprised in an area of about eight and a half square miles; with Northcastle on the north, Harrison on the east, Scarsdale on the south, and Greensburgh on the west. On a fine plain, near the centre of the town, stands the flourishing little village, of the same name, which has been the theatre of so many revolutionary incidents. The reader will recollect that we left our prisoners on the march to this place, under a strong escort of Townsend's Rangers.

On arriving at the village, where the Committee of Safety were still in session, awaiting the result of the enterprise, each of the prisoners underwent a partial examination, which resulted in their being ordered to Fishkill, there to await a more formal investigation. Our hero was privately reminded that he must still continue to support the character he had assumed, until his arrival at their place of destination, when some means should be provided by which he might effect his escape, without awakening any suspicions as to his real character.

On the following morning, the whole party resumed their journey, in the same order as before. After a march of about twenty-five miles, they arrived at Peekskill, a small village on the eastern bank of the Hudson, where they took boats, and crossed the river to Fort Montgomery.* Here the prisoners were permitted to remain a short time, for rest and refreshment. And here our hero encountered the most distressing incident that he had ever yet experienced.

On entering the fortress, the first person he recognized was his former tutor, the worthy gentleman of whom a brief notice was taken at the conclusion of our first chapter. The recognition was mutual; but the circumstances under which the meeting took place, rendered it peculiarly painful to both parties.

The worthy preceptor started with terror and astonishment, on beholding his favorite pupil, the son of his dearest friend, manacled like a felon, and dragged to prison, with a gang of unprincipled wretches, under the ignominious charge of treason to their country! He gazed for a moment, as if unwilling to believe his senses; then, advancing to the prisoner, and seizing him by the hand, he exclaimed, with an emotion that it was impossible to conceal,

"Enoch Crosby!—It cannot be possible!—Explain this horrid mystery! —How is it that I see *you* in this situation?"

Crosby instinctively returned the friendly pressure of his tutor's hand; then casting his eyes on the ground, he meekly replied,

"You see me as I am. I have no explanation to offer."

"Good God! Is it then true that you have turned traitor to your country, and are now a prisoner to her brave defenders! It cannot be. There must be some dreadful mistake. Speak, and relieve me from this fearful suspense. Have *you* been concerned in the secret plots for which these men are now in custody?"

"Were it not so," replied Crosby, with a slight tremor in his voice, "we should both have been spared the pain of this interview."

"O, who shall tell your poor old father this!" exclaimed the other, dropping his pupil's hand, and clasping both his own together in agony, while the big tears coursed each other down his furrowed cheeks. "What will be the feeling of your doating parents, when they learn that the son to whom they looked as the pride and prop of their declining age, has proved unworthy of the care and affection which have been so freely lavished upon him! That he has forgotten the precepts of his father—the lessons of his teacher—and is a convicted trator to his country! The news will break their hearts."

For the first time, Crosby now felt the full weight of the cross to which he had voluntarily lent his shoulder. He felt—and it almost crushed him. But it was too late to recede; he had put his hand to the plough, and dared

---

* "This fort was tolerably situated on the western bank of the Hudson, to annoy shipping going up the river; the works were pretty good on that side, but were not so, nor fully completed on the back side."—*Heath's Memoirs*, p. 129.

not look back. With a groan of anguish, he lifted up his manly form beneath the load. The effort was desperate, but it was successful.

"Spare me," he faintly articulated, as he brushed a truant tear from his eye, and turned to accompany his fellow-captives to their quarters. "There is *one* who knows—who judges—who approves. He will comfort my parents. Farewell."

So saying, he departed with the rest, leaving his good old tutor to lament an apostacy as unexpected and inexplicable as it was mortifying and distressing. The old gentleman immediately despatched a letter to the elder Crosby, in which he communicated the afflicting intelligence with as much caution, delicacy, and gentleness, as possible. It was a blow for which the parents were not prepared; but it is not our province to portray their feelings on the occasion. We must accompany the son.

From Fort Montgomery, the prisoners were again embarked, and proceeded up the river, through the lofty and sublime scenery of the Highlands, and between those Herculean pillars of the Western world, which are supposed to have been once united in an adamantine barrier across the present course of the majestic Hudson. Leaving West Point and Butter-Hill on the left, and the Collossean break-neck,* St. Anthony, on the right, a beautiful campaign country opened at once upon their view. Here the pleasant villages of New Windsor, Newburgh, and Fishkill, with the smiling landscapes beyond them, presented a charming contrast to the rude scenery which our voyagers had just left behind them.

On reaching the mouth of Fishkill creek, on the east side of the Hudson, nearly opposite Newburgh, the prisoners were landed; and from thence proceeded on foot, under their former escort, along the delightful valley, then thickly studded with trees, through which that stream pursues its sinuous course to the river. A march of five miles brought them to the beautiful little village which was to terminate their journey.

Here the captive loyalists were committed to prison; or, rather, conducted to church, for such was the edifice which the peculiar circumstances of the times had converted into a strong hold for the safe keeping of prisoners of war. It was a low antiquated building, in the Dutch style of architecture, with enormous thick walls of rough stone, pierced with two rows of arched windows. The main building was an oblong square, with a square tower attached to the eastern extremity, from the top of which arose a modest Gothic steeple, surmounted by a ball and weathercock. The principal entrance was in the centre of the south side, fronting the road which led from the village to the river.

Instead of the sepulchral yew, with which romance has invariably embellished such consecrated ground, a number of luxuriant willows here cast a melancholy shade among the rustic memorials of departed worth. Here it was that little groups of villagers were wont to assemble on a Sabbath morning; and, while they awaited the appearance of their pious clergyman, reverently discuss the local news and politics of the day.

---

* See 4th note in Chapter IX.

OLD REFORMED DUTCH CHURCH, FISHKILL, N. Y.,

IN WHICH *CROSBY* WAS IMPRISONED.

[*See Pages 46 and 145.*]

But, alas! even the hallowed rites of the sanctuary must sometimes give place to the blighting footsteps of ruthless war! That roof which had so often resounded with the language of "peace, and good will to man," was now re-echoing with the curses of disappointed malevolence. The stone church had become a prison, as its more humble neighbor (a wooden church without a steeple) had, for similar reasons, been converted into a hospital. for the sick and wounded. If this be sacrilege, of what was that British General guilty, who protituted an elegant church in Boston to the purposes of a stable! But this is digression. Our present business is at Fishkill.

This pleasant little village (situated in a township of the same name), is in the county of Dutchess, north of the Highlands, and about five miles east from the Hudson. It consists of a handsome collection of neat white farm houses, with here and there a mansion of more ample dimensions and showy exterior. These buildings are principally on a semi-circular street, a little north of a corresponding bend in the stream before mentioned; and in the midst of them, on a little plain, are the two churches, rising with modest dignity above the elevation of the humbler mansions around them.

The first appearance of this village, in approaching it from the south, is picturesque in the extreme. After toiling, for fifteen miles, among the rugged hills and shapeless rocks, between which the road winds its serpentine course; when there appears no prospect of a speedy termination to the traveller's fatigue; and when his impatience begins to despair of relief; at that moment, the village and plains of Fishkill suddenly open upon his view with the effect of enchantment, affording an ample compensation for all his previous anxiety and perplexity.

Although this is the oldest village in the county of Dutchess, it was but thinly populated at the time of which we are writing. The Marquis de Chateleux, who visited it four years afterwards, when it had become the principal depot of the American army, says: "There are not more than fifty houses in the space of two miles." He adds, however, that the American magazines, hospitals, workshops, &c., "form a little town of themselves, composed of handsome large barracks, built in the woods at the foot of the mountains." It is well known, that Fishkill possessed all the qualities necessary for a place of military depot, at this critical period; being situated on the high road from Connecticut, near the river, and West Point, that "Gibraltar of America;" and protected, at the same time, by a chain of inaccessible mountains, which occupy a space of more than twenty miles between the Croton river and that of Fishkill.

But whatever local advantages, or rural charms, this village might have boasted in the year 1776, they were all lost on the wretched inmates of the stone church. The Committee of Safety had arrived from White Plains, and were now in session, at a farm house within a few rods of their prison. Thither were the newly-arrived captives conducted, one by one, to undergo a second private examination. The muster-roll, and other papers, found on the person of their leader, were considered as a sufficient testimony of their traitorous intentions; they were, therefore, remanded to prison to await a more formal investigation before a competent tribunal.

Crosby, in his turn, was also placed at the bar of this military inquisition. On entering the apartment where his employers were seated in all that magisterial dignity which surrounds, or is supposed to surround, the stern arbiters of life and death, he affected such extreme reluctance to advance, as rendered it necessary for the officer in attendance to compel him to proceed. With clanking chains, and an aspect of vacant despair, he at length approached the awful bar, and tremblingly awaited the pleasure of his judges. A lurking smile was visible in each of their visages; but the prisoner appeared to be too much agitated with terror to observe it.

As soon as the officer had resumed his station on the outside of the door, however, and Crosby was left alone with the Committee, the characters were changed; for they at once lost the gravity of judges, and laughed outright at a scene which so nearly approached the ludicrous. When their merriment had a little subsided, they highly commended Crosby for the effective manner in which he had performed his part, and the important service he had thereby rendered to his country. They then consulted with him on the best mode of making his escape; and requested him, when that was effected, to repair, with all possible diligence, to Wappinger's Creek, and call upon Mr. * * * *, who would furnish him with further instructions, as "*there was business for him on the other side the Hudson.*"

Crosby signified his readiness to continue in this hazardous and disreputable service; but suggested the propriety of his assuming a different name, in order to prosecute it with greater effect. The Committee approved the idea, and it was finally understood between them, that all communications from their secret agent would, in future, bear the signature of "JOHN SMITH."

As soon as these preliminaries were all duly adjusted, the Committee resumed their former stern deportment, and Crosby his fictitious character. The officer re-entered, and, in obedience to orders, led his trembling prisoner back to the church.

On the approach of night, a competent number of soldiers were detailed for the prison guard, some of whom were stationed in the basement of the tower, to guard the eastern entrance of the building. On the outside, four armed sentinels were posted in as many different positions, corresponding to the four cardinal points of the compass. The remainder of the little force then in the village were in barracks, at a short distance from the church.

In entering and leaving his prison, Crosby had hastily reconnoitred the premises without; and after his attendance on the Committee, he lost no time in making his observations within. He soon ascertained that there was only one avenue through which an escape could be attempted with the least probability of success; and that was a window at the extreme northwest corner, which was partially obscured by the thick foliage of a large willow that grew near it.

Screened from observation by the friendly gloom of this tree, he thought it practicable to pass the sentinel, and clear the church-yard in safety. Or, should he not be able to elude the vigilance of the guard, still the uncertainty of his aim in that shadowy position, would leave little to apprehend from the discharge of his musket. At all events, he determined to make the experiment.

Harassed in mind, and fatigued in body, the prisoners soon availed themselves of such indifferent accommodations as their situation afforded; and, before the "noon of night," there were few, besides Crosby, who were not fast locked in the arms of sweet forgetfulness. But, as Hamlet says,

Some must watch, while others sleep,
So runs this world away.

When every sound was hushed, save the discordant nasal chorus of the unconscious performers around him, Crosby arose from his counterfeit slumber, and cautiously approached the window, from which he had previously succeeded in removing the fastenings. Without noise, he raised the sash,

"And, that they might not clank, held fast his chains."

In the next moment, he was safely seated on the soft mould of a newly covered grave, busily employed in divesting his limbs of their iron bracelets. When this was accomplished, he cautiously raised himself upon his feet; and, knowing that a thick swamp lay within one hundred rods, northwest of the church, he started in that direction with as much speed as the uneven surface of a burying ground would permit.

He had not proceeded fifty paces, however, before he was suddenly challenged by a sentinel on his right. Hesitation would have been fatal. The swamp was before him—the path had become plainer—he darted forward with the celerity of a deer. The whizzing of a bullet and the report of a musket saluted his ear at the same moment; but he considered the salutation merely as a friendly warning not to relax his speed. The race was for life or death; for the alarm was given, and "the chase was up." Three or four more leaden messengers,* each as harmless as the first, passed him in quick succession; and, as if emulating their velocity, he pursued them with accelerated swiftness. The pursuers were behind—but the friendly swamp was in front, extending its bushy arms to receive him. One more effort—He is safe!

CHAPTER VIII.
THE MOUNTAIN CAVE.

Honour and policy, like unsevered friends,
I' the war do grow together.—*Shakspeare.*

WHILE the foregoing events were transpiring in the vicinity of the Highlands, transactions of higher importance and on a much larger scale, were going forward forty miles below. It was an important object with Washington to secure the roads and passes that communicated with the eastern states; to prevent which Howe had left New York, with the greater part of the royal army, by the way of Hurlgate, and landed, as before mentioned, at Throg's neck, in Westchester county. It was evidently the determination of the British General,

---
* "Fifty pistols lighted the scene instantly, and the bullets whistled in every direction around the head of the devoted pedlar.l'—*Spy*, Vol. i, p. 138.

either to force the Americans from their position on York Island, or to enclose them in it.

Aware of his design, Washington removed a part of his troops from York Island to join those at Kingsbridge; and, at the same time, detached some regiments to Westchester. It still appeared to be his intention, however, to retain that part of the island which he now occupied; and there was certainly a prevailing disposition among the officers generally to do the same. But the gallant Lee, who had just returned from a successful expedition at the south,* gave such convincing reasons for evacuating the island altogether, that it was immediately resolved to withdraw the bulk of the army.

He also urged the expediency of evacuating fort Washington;† but in this he was opposed by Greene, who argued that the possession of that post would divert a large body of the enemy from joining their main force; and in conjunction with fort Lee, on the opposite side of the river, would be of great use in covering the transportation of provisions and stores, up the Hudson, for the service of the American troops. He added further, that the garrison could be brought off at any time, by boats from the Jersey side of the river.

Unfortunately for the cause, the opinion of Greene prevailed. Though the system of evacuating and retreating was generally adopted, an exception was made in favor of Fort Washington, and near three thousand men were assigned for its defence. An unfortunate error, as will appear in the sequel; for, as Adjutant-General Read afterwards said, in a letter to Lee, "If a real defence of the lines was intended, the number was too few; if the fort only, the garrison was too numerous by half."

In retreating from York Island, the American leader was careful to make a front towards his enemy, from Eastchester almost to White Plains, in order to secure the march of those who were behind, and to defend the removal of the sick, the cannon, and the stores of the army. In this manner, the Americans formed a line of small, detached, intrenched camps, on the several heights and strong grounds, from Valentine's Hill, near Kingsbridge, on the right, to the vicinity of the White Plains, on the left: the whole, of course, fronting eastward.

In the mean time, the enemy was not idle; although he had, apparently, been so, for several days after his landing at Throg's Neck—which is a kind of mole or point, connected with the main by a long causeway, through a marshy tract of considerable extent. His spies, however, had been on the alert; and the first movement of Washington was the signal for Howe to commence his favourite scheme of circumvention.

---

* Some time previous to the evacuation of Boston, Sir Henry Clinton had been sent southward, to the assistance of Governor Martin and Lord William Campbell, Governors of the two Carolinas. As soon as this was known in Cambridge, Lee was ordered to set forward and observe his movements, and prepare to meet him with advantage, in any part of the continent he might think proper to visit. On reaching New York, with his detachment from Cambridge, Lee put the city in a state of defence, and proceeded south with such haste, that, to the astonishment of Clinton, Lee was in Virginia before him. But as the object of the British armament was still further south, Lee, with uncommon celerity, traversed the continent, met Clinton in North Carolina, and was again ready for the defence of Sullivan's Island, near Charleston, in South Carolina, before the arrival of the British troops, under the command of Clinton. The Americans were triumphant, and the discomfited enemy was glad to retire to the general rendezvous before New-York.

† This fort was situated on the bank of the Hudson, in the vicinity of Kingsbridge.

Flushed with his recent victory on Long Island, the British General ardently longed to grapple, once more, with his discomfited opponent. But Washington wisely considered that the prize at stake was of too much value to be risked on the fortuitous result of a single contest, under his present disadvantages of numbers and discipline. He, therefore, cautiously avoided a general engagement, while his troops were daily acquiring confidence and experience by skirmishing with their enemies.

After several unsuccessful attempts to pass the causeway before mentioned, which was strongly guarded by the Americans, the British crossed to the other side of Throg's Neck, embarked on board their boats, crossed over the cove, and re-landed on a place called Pell's Neck. From thence they commenced a brisk movement towards New Rochelle.‡ Three or four American regiments were immediately sent forward to annoy them on their march.—These took a good position behind a stone fence; and when the advance of the enemy had approached sufficiently near, poured such a well-directed fire upon his columns, as caused many of his finest troops to bite the dust. This unexpected assault not only checked, but even caused the advancing party to fall back; but, being immediately supported, they returned vigorously to the charge. For a short time, the action was sharp, and well supported; but the Americans were finally obliged to give way to superior force, and the enemy pursued his march almost to New Rochelle, where he halted.

‡ New Rochelle is about five miles south of White Plains, and is washed on one side by the waters of the East river, or Long Island Sound.

Shortly after this affair, Howe removed the right and centre of his army two miles farther north, on the road to White Plains. During this movement, a skirmish took place between two hundred of Lee's men and three hundred Hessians, in which the latter suffered considerably. The British then moved on, in two columns, and took a position with the Bronx river in front;* upon which Washington assembled his main force at White Plains, behind intrenchments.

Thus, like two skillful chess-players, did these able Generals manœuvre their men; while the theatre of their movements, like an immense chess-board, was crossed with lines, and chequered with redoubts, and intrenchments. But an important crisis in the game was now evidently at hand; one more move must, apparently, decide it. Heaven grant that it may be "checkmate to the king."

But while these two gallant opponents are thus sternly looking defiance at each other, both eagerly watching for an opening to strike, it is our duty to return to the fugitive whom we left in the swamp, near the village of Fishkill.

Crosby remained secure in his place of concealment, until every sound of alarm and pursuit had ceased; he then proceeded, with no little difficulty, to grope his way through bushes and brambles, quagmires and morasses. He doubtless reasoned with himself, on this occasion, as Æsop's fox is said to have done, under similar circumstances: "For the sake of the good, let me bear the evil with patience; each bitter has its sweet; and these brambles,

* See Chapter VII, 2d paragraph.

though they wound my flesh, preserve my life from danger."

After much exertion and fatigue, he succeeded in emerging from the thicket; and, fortunately, on the side opposite to where he entered. He then pursued his course northward, with the speed of one who is sensible that every step removes him farther from danger.

In less than two hours he found his course impeded by a stream, which he rightly conjectured to be Wappinger's Creek, the boundary line between Fishkill and Poughkeepsie.†

Agreeably to the instruction he had received from the Committee, he now turned to the left, and a short half hour brought him to the residence of Mr. ****.

To be suddenly aroused from bed, by some hasty messenger, at any hour of the night, had become so common an occurrence, since the commencement of hostilities, that this gentleman evinced no symptoms of surprise or alarm, when he appeared at the door, in his night gown and slippers, to answer to the knock of his untimely visitor. A few brief sentences, exchanged in a low voice, convinced both that they were treading on safe ground. Crosby was, therefore, requested to enter and be seated, while the other retired to resume such habiliments as were better adapted to the purposes of business.

On the return of his host, Crosby was informed that his coming had been anxiously waited for, as the Committee had intimated that he might be expected before midnight. Refreshments were then introduced;

† This name is said to have been derived from the Indian word *Apokeepsing*, signifying "safe harbour."

and while the weary traveller was diligently employed in appeasing the cravings of a voracious appetite, his entertainer proceeded to "open the business of the meeting."

It appeared, that Mr. ***** had received certain information that an English officer was privately enrolling a company, on the other side of the river. This fact he had communicated to the Committee of Safety, on their arrival at Fishkill; and they had agreed to send him an agent with whom he might concert some feasible plan for seizing the officer, and making prisoners of his men.

This being a business in which Crosby, to use his own expression, felt himself "perfectly at home," he readily entered into the scheme, and undertook to see it accomplished by his own ingenuity and address. This proposition was gladly acceded to by his host, who gave him such instructions as would tend to facilitate the project; and, before daylight, our hero was safely landed on the western bank of the Hudson, in the town of Marlborough, a little north of Newburgh.

Agreeably to the directions he had received, Crosby immediately struck into the country, in a southwestern course from the river; and, after proceeding about twelve miles, applied at a farm-house for refreshment. Here a comfortable breakfast was cheerfully prepared for him; and, while partaking of it, he received such topographical information, as convinced him that he had reached the right spot to commence operations.

After finishing his repast, therefore, he began to make himself known as an itinerant shoemaker, in pursuit of work; and intimated a wish of being employed to make shoes for the farmer or his family.

"I wish to do something to pay my way," added Crosby, with an honest simplicity, which he well knew how to assume; "as I don't like to be beholden to any one for a meal's victuals, or a night's lodging."

"That's all very right," returned the farmer; "every honest man would wish to live by his own airnens."

"Well, don't you think that you could give me something to do for a few days? If you are not in want of shoes, I wouldn't care to turn my hand to anything."

"Why, yes," replied the other, after a little reflection; "I rather guess that I should like to have you work for me a day or two. It is true, I have no shoemaking to do at present; but if you can help me on the farm, in killing hogs, and sich like, I should like to have you, and my wife shall assist you."

Crosby readily consented; and, as there was no cavil on the score of wages, the bargain was soon struck. He accordingly went to work with that characteristic diligence and assiduity which was always certain to win the approbation of his employers.

But though his whole time and attention appeared to be devoted to the duties of his new vocation, his grand object was never lost sight of. At every fitting opportunity, he strove, by sundry indirect, and apparently indifferent, inquiries, to elicit some information from the family, that might assist in the prosecution of his ulterior designs. For two days he was unsuccessful; but, on the third, he was indebted to accident for what his ingenuity had been vainly exerted to obtain.

It was a mild morning, near the close of October, that Crosby and his employer were making some arrangement for the business of the day, when their attention was arrested by a sound that resembled distant thunder. It came from the southeast, from whence a light air was breathing; but neither cloud nor rack appeared in that quarter.

"Can that be thunder?" asked Crosby.

"I should rather guess not," replied the other: "we seldom have it so late in the fall. It is more likely the two parties are skrimmaging below."

"They must be skirmishing to some purpose," observed Crosby. "That is the language of artillery, and not of the smallest caliber. 'And yet," continued he, in a soliloquizing tone, "they cannot be above the Plains." Then, turning to his companion, he inquired if he thought the report of cannon could be heard so far.

"Why, yes, I should say so." replied the other. "From here to White Plains is only about forty miles, in a straight line; and in the last French war, when General Abercrombie was beat at Ticonderoga, the cannon was heard at Saratogue, which is over fifty miles, as plain as we hear these."

The sounds still continued, without much intermission, while both remained silent, and listened with interest. At length Crosby ventured to observe—

"They must have warm work below. Both parties must loose blood whichever gains the day."

"Ah! these are awful times!" sighed

the other.—"There's no telling how it will end."

"What do you think of all this business?" asked Crosby, in a tone that did not indicate much interest in the question.

"Why, really, I don't know what to think," replied the other, evasively. "Sometimes I think it is a very doubtful case with us; and then, again, I almost think, If I had a good chance, and no family to support, that I would just go down to the lower party. But, you know, it won't do for me to say so."

"Perhaps you couldn't get down there safe, if you felt ever so much disposed to go," said Crosby, in a tone that might be considered interrogatory or not, as the auditor pleased.

"O, yes, I could," returned the other, with a significant leer, that intimated the speaker knew more than he was at liberty to communicate.

Like a keen pointer, Crosby had now scented the game, and was determined to persevere in the pursuit, he, therefore, promptly answered—

"Well, I wish that *I* could; for I believe that I might do better *there* than by staying here."

The other turned on him a look of cautious scrutiny; but, reading nothing in his countenance to excite suspicion, he ventured to observe—

"I can tell you, if you promise not to expose me, how you can get there if you wish."

"Of course, I will not expose you; for how *can* I, without exposing myself? I will be much obliged to you if you will assist me in going down, so that I may not be detected by the rebels."

"Well, then I *will* tell you," returned the other, with renewed confidence; at the same time looking cautiously around, in every direction, to ascertain that no listeners were near. "Do you see yonder mountain? On the west side of it is a curious little cave, that's been dug o' purpose; but you might pass it a hundred times without knowing there was such a thing there. In that cave, an English Captain keeps himself concealed; and we, who are in the secret, supply him with every thing that heart can wish. He is recruiting among the Highlands, and has nearly got his company filled."

"I will offer myself immediately," exclaimed Crosby, with a sudden animation, that might have excited suspicions in the mind of a keener observer than his companion; who, without noticing it, immediately replied—

"Well—I will tell you just where you can go to find him; or, wait till after dark, and I will go with you."

"That will be the very thing," returned our hero, inwardly chuckling at the success of his manœuvre. "By joining his company, I can go down in safety."

"No doubt of it. But we must be very cautious. In these times, every one is watching his next neighbour."

"You may depend upon my prudence," returned Crosby. "I have no inclination to get into the hands of the rebels again; it was at the hazard of my life that I escaped from them at Fishkill."

"What! have you really been taken by them? Why, how in nature did you get away?"

Crosby here recapitulated the particulars of his escape from the stone church, and then added—

"They are obstinate dogs, for, you hear, they are at it yet."

"Let the riglars get them at close quarters, with the baggonet, and the rebels will stand no chance," replied the other. "They must be at long shot now, or the skrimmage would not last so long."

Here the conversation ended; and, separating to pursue their respective avocations, they met no more till supper time. After which they set out, according to agreement, to seek an interview with the military hermit in the "cave of the mountain."

On arriving at the western side of the lofty eminence which our hero's conductor had pointed out to him in the morning, they paused near a clump of dwarf cedars which grew at its base. In front of them was a dark looking object, which proved to be a huge rock, cleft in twain by some concussion of the elements, or by a precipitate descent from the dizzy steep above it. With a heavy stick, which the farmer carried with him, he struck several blows, in quick succession, on the flat surface of the rock; and, in a short time, a bright ray of light darted from behind it, and gradually increased in brilliancy. In the next moment the object of their visit stood before them, with a small lauthern in his hand, by the aid of which he took a critical survey of his visitors without speaking. He then bid the farmer welcome, who promptly introduced his companion as "John Smith, a faithful friend to his majesty," and instantly disappeared.

The Captain received Crosby very cordially; and after numerous inquiries, to all of which he received plausible and satisfactory answers, he at length exclaimed—

"Well, sir, you appear to have limb and muscle, and would make a devilish good looking soldier. I should like to have you in my corps of Highlanders, which have just been collected. Come, what say you?"

"I have not the least objection," replied Crosby; "and as I have no fixed home, or place to go to, I should like to stay with you; for if the rebels catch me again, they will show me no mercy."

"Agreed!" exclaimed the Captain, after eyeing him sharply for a few moments. "You are a d——d honest looking fellow, and I'll try you. Come, sir; see if you can double up that gigantic carcass of yours so as to get into that hole," pointing to the mouth of an artificial excavation in the mountain, just behind the cloven rock, which Crosby had not before observed.

The new recruit instantly obeyed the orders of his superior, and found himself in a small, comfortable, well-furnished apartment, with seats, and other conveniences, suitable for two or three persons. In the centre of the floor, stood a small round table, liberally supplied with a great variety of cold meats, pastry, bread, butter, cheese, and every other kind of eatables that the neighbouring farmhouses could furnish. But what the occupant of the cave most earnestly commended to the attention of his guest, was a large jug, or rather its contents, which he swore was as fine Madeira as had ever graced the table of Sir Harry, or even his lordship himself.

"Come, my good fellow, help yourself," said the hermit, pushing the jug to his new proselyte, after filling his own goblet to the brim. "D—n me, but you shall live like a fighting cock, for the few days longer that I have got to burrough in this hole. A health to his Majesty, and success to the good cause."

"With all my heart," exclaimed Crosby, and drained the goblet.

As our hero now appears to be very comfortably situated, in a strong hold, with plenty of provisions for the garrison, we will venture to leave him there for a few days, while we revisit the scene from whence proceeded those "sounds of war," which gave rise to the conversation that ultimately brought about the present change in his circumstances.

CHAPTER IX.
CHADERTON'S HILL.

This day hath made
Much work for tears in many an English mother.
Whose sons lie scattered on the bleeding ground;
Many a widow's husband groveling lies
Coldly embracing the discoloured earth.
SHAKS. KING JOHN.

We left the two hostile armies, in front of each other, at White Plains, with souls "in arms, and eager for the fray." On the morning of the 28th of October they still retained the same position, sharply watching each other's motions.

In the mean time, a commanding eminence, on the southwest of the American camp, had caught the attention of Washington; who, knowing the importance of strengthening his position, resolved to reconnoitre the ground immediately. He, accordingly, ordered such of his general officers as were not on duty, to attend him, and rode to the spot; but, on examination, found it not so suitable for his purposes as he had anticipated.

"Yonder," said Lee, pointing to another eminence on the north, "is the ground we ought to occupy."

"Let us, then, go and view it," replied the commander-in-chief; and away they posted as fast as their mettlesome steeds would carry them.

They had not proceeded far, however, when a light horseman was seen coming up, on full gallop, his steed almost out of breath. Hastily saluting the General, he exclaimed—

"The British are on the camp, sir!"

"Then, gentlemen," said Washington, "we have other business than reconnoitring. Follow me!"

So saying, he put spurs to his prancing charger, and galloped to the camp, swiftly followed by his well-mounted Generals, Lee, Heath, and the rest. On arriving at head quarters, the party were met by the Adjutant General, the Gallant Bead, who hastily addressed his commander

"The guards, sir, have been all beat in, and the whole army are now at their respective posts, in order of battle."

Washington, on hearing this, turned coolly to his officers, and dismissed them with this brief order—

"Gentlemen, you will repair to your respective posts, and do the best you can."*

Here they separated, each officer repairing to his own division, which he found in the lines, firmly awaiting the charge, which had already commenced on the right of the Americans. by a column of Hessians, the forlorn hope of the British army. They were commanded by General de Heister and Colonel Rhal, who di-

---
* See Heath's Memoirs.

rected their first attack against the Americans that were posted on an eminence called Chaderton's Hill, commanded by General M'Dougall.

The cannonade now become brisk on both sides. Suddenly, the enemy's right column, consisting of British troops, under the command of General Leslie, appeared in the road leading to the court-house, in front of Heath's division, on the American left. This advancing column was preceded by about twenty light-horse men, in full gallop, brandishing their swords, as if they intended to decapitate every Yankee they could reach.

Without hesitation, they leaped the fence of a wheatfield, at the foot of the hill on which the brave Malcolm's regiment was posted; of which circumstance the cavaliers were not aware, until a shot from a field-piece struck in the midst of them, and uphorsed one of the party without ceremony.

This being a hint that the gentlemen could not well misunderstand, they wheeled short about and galloped out of the field as as fast they came in; nor did they slacken their speed until a friendly hill left nothing but the tips of their plumes for Malcolm to waste his fire on.

Whether it was owing to this circumstance, (the precipitate flight of his horse,) or to previous arrangement, it is certain that the British column advanced no farther up the road, but suddenly wheeled to the left, by platoons, as fast as they came up;-and, passing through a bar or gateway, directed their head towards the troops on Chaderton's Hill, already engaged with the Hessians.

The appearance of this column of well disciplined troops, the flower of the British army, was truly imposing. Their brightly polished arms, bristling with bayonets, glittered in the sunbeams with almost a dazzling lustre.---What a contrast to their undisciplined opponents, the American militia, who, with rusty muskets, irregular accoutrements, and scarcely a bayonet to a platoon, stood before them undismayed, and (even when vanquished) unsubdued!

The cannonade still continued brisk across the Bronx; the Americans firmly retaining their position on the hill, and the enemy directing all his energies to dislodge them. Convinced, at length, that long shot would never effect the object, preparations were made to come to closer quarters.

For this purpose, a part of the enemy's left column, composed of British and Hessians, forded the river, and marched along, under cover of the hill, until they had gained sufficient ground to the left of the Americans; when, by facing to the left, their column became a line parallel with their opponents. In this order they ascended the hill with a quick movement.

The fire from the British artillery now ceased, of course, in order not to endanger their own men, who were bravely advancing to charge the Americans on the summit of the hill; but the fire of the musquetry between the two parties was so rapid and incessant, that it was impossible to distinguish the sounds.

The Americans finally gave way before superior discipline, and moved off the hill in as good order as could have been expected. The British ascended the hill very slowly, but in that close compact order for which their infantry are so justly celebrated. There is no doubt, however, that every man felt glad when he had reached the summit, where they formed and dressed their line, without evincing any disposition to pursue their retreating foe.

The fact is, both parties felt perfectly willing to rest awhile after the fatigues of the day. It is true, that obtaining possession of the contested eminence gave the British great advantage over their opponents; but, feeling too sore to pursue this advantage, they were content to let things remain as they were for the present.

During this action, which ought to be called the "Battle of Chaderton's Hill," several hundreds fell on both sides. It was a waste of lives, without much advantage to either party. In the midst of the engagement, however, the American baggage and stores were moved off in full view of the British army.†

Washington soon after changed his front, by drawing back the right and centre of his forces to some hills in his rear, and leaving the left wing in its former position; thus forming a line nearly east and west, fronting his enemy on the south. In this eligible position he expected and desired an action; but the enemy did not see fit to make the attempt. He afterwards withdrew the whole army to the heights of Northcastle, about five miles above White Plains, near the Connecticut line, where his position was so strong that Howe found it necessary to adopt an entire new plan of operations.

In the mean time, Crosby was enjoying ease and luxury in the "cave of the mountain," which was regularly supplied with provisions by several farmers who secretly favored the royal cause. He found the Captain to be a good-humoured jovial fellow, somewhat coarse in his manners, but not a disagreeable companion. As he and Crosby lived and messed together, they were, of course, on the most familiar terms of intimacy; it will, therefore, be readily conceived, that the latter soon made himself acquainted with every particular of the other's plans.

"In three days, my lad, we shall cross the Highlands," said the Captain, gaily, as he folded a letter which had just been handed him by our hero's late employer.

"In three days," repeated the other. "Let me see—that will be Tuesday, as this is Saturday."

"Yes, this is Saturday, and tomorrow will be Sunday, when your motely psalm-singing rebel army will be chaunting hallelujahs through their noses; that is, if our cavalry didn't shave off those vocal appendages at White Plains."

"According to the letter you have just read to me, it would seem that some of the royal cavalry have been even closer shaved by the rebels in Heath's division," returned Crosby, with a slight indication of humour in his countenance.

"By Heaven!" exclaimed the Captain, "you look and talk as if you were glad of it."

"I should be glad to have been in their situation," said Crosby, drily.

"Where?—Behind the hill?"

---

† "The brunt of this battle," says Sballus, "was sustained by the American General M'Dougall, posted on the right of the American army, who nobly sustained his post with six hundred men, against the British army, though basely deserted by four regiments of militia, who fled on the approach of two hundred and fifty light horse."

'No—I would have cleared the hill, and made for the *Heath*."

"Good by ***! If the flash of your musket be like that of your wit, you will be an honour to the corps."

"Wit sometimes wounds a friend."

"Then there the comparison ends, for your musket will only be levelled at the rebels. But come; let's to business. Do you know where the little heap of earth stands which the Yankees call Butter Hill?"*

"Yes—at the north entrance of the Highlands, opposite St. Anthony's face."†

"True—and were that break-neck rock a real living saint, and the opposite hill composed of genuine Goshen butter, d—n me, but the saint's mouth would water. But, as I was saying, on the western side of that mountain, (for so we would call an eminence of fifteen hundred feet in England,) is a lonely barn, belonging to a good loyalist, and a d——d fine fellow. To that barn we must all go on Tuesday evening; and, after taking an hour's rest in the hay-mow, pursue our course to the royal lines. To-morrow you and I will bid good-bye to this cursed hole, as my friend S**** has generously offered to accommodate the whole of us, until we march."

Having nothing to oppose to this arrangement, Crosby made no objection; and Sunday evening saw the whole corps (about thirty) assembled at the house of Mr. S****.

But how was the Committee of Safety to be made acquainted with these circumstances? This was a question that, for some time, baffled the ingenuity of our hero; as he was aware that he could not absent himself a moment without exciting suspicions. At length, however, he hit upon a plan, and hastened to put it into execution.—Taking the Captain apart, he thus commenced it:—

"I am apprehensive, sir, that our being here altogether may turn out to be bad policy."

"Your reasons Jack, your reasons," said the other, with a dramatic air. "The devil's in't if we are not retired enough; there's not a neighbor within a mile."

"It is just such retired situations that Townsend's Rangers are always searching. They seldom seek for organized companies of loyalists in populous villages."

"D—n Townsend's Rangers! They are over the river."

"That's not certain. They are everywhere by turns, and nowhere long. But let us suppose the worst. If the rebels should discover us, and surprise us altogether, the whole corps is at once annihilated. But if we disperse until the hour of marching, they can only pick up one or two, and the main body will remain safe."

"D--n me, Jack, but you shall be my orderly. Your advice is good, and we will separate immediately. No one shall know where another sleeps, and that will prevent treachery. There's an improvement of my own, Jack. Go—choose your own

---

* This is a high cobble hill, on the west side of Hudson river, opposite Breakneck Hill. These are the northern hills of the Highland chain.

† St. *Anthony's Face* is on the south side of Breakneck Hill, at the north entrance of the Highlands, sixty miles from the city of New York. Its name is derived from a ludicrous resemblance of a Colossal human face, as seen from the river. The rock which has this appearance, exhibits a good profile of a face of thirty-two feet, aided by a little fancy, and a relish for the marvellous. A tree which grows upon the chin, just reaches the height of the eyes, and kindly spreads its branches for the eye-brows of the saint. There is another promontory, opposite the site of Fort Montgomery, five miles below West Point, which is called St. Anthony's Nose, but the resemblance is less remarkable.

lodgings; and you need be at no loss in this *bundling* country of yours. But recollect, here we all muster at seven o'clock, on Tuesday evening."

With these words they separated; when Crosby lost no time in repairing to the house of a man whom he knew to be a warm friend to the country, and desired him to saddle his horse instantly, and carry an express to the Committee of Safety, at Fishkill. The other complied without hesitation; and, while he was preparing for the journey, our hero wrote the following communication:

"*To the Committee of Safety :*

"Gentlemen—

"I hasten this express to request you to order Captain Townsend's company of Rangers' to repair immediately to the barn, situated on the west side of Butter-Hill, and there to secrete themselves until we arrive, which will be to-morrow evening, probably about eleven o'clock; where, with about thirty tories, they may find,

"Your obedient servant,
"JOHN SMITH."

Monday evening, Nov. 4, 1776.

As soon as this express was despatched to Fishkill, Crosby repaired to the house of his former employer, where he remained until the hour appointed on the following evening; when (his messenger having returned with an answer), he rejoined his company, which was now assembled at the house of Mr. S****. Every thing being arranged for their departure, they took leave of their loyal host, and cautiously proceeded across the country, to Cornwall, where they forded Murderer's Creek, and soon reached the solitary barn where they contemplated to rest in safety.

Completely jaded by their long and rapid march, every one was eager to secure a snug berth in the hay, in order to snatch an hour's repose before they resumed their journey. Our hero nestled down with the rest, close to the side of the building; and, in a few minutes, he was the only individual awake.

In about an hour he heard some one cough on the outside of the barn. This, being the preconcerted signal, was immediately answered by Crosby, through an opening between the boards; and, in the next moment, the building was filled with armed men, headed by Captain Townsend, accompanied by Colonel Duer, one of the Committee of Safety, who had given the signal before mentioned.

"Surrender!" exclaimed Townsend, in a voice that startled every drowsy slumberer from his rustling couch. "Surrender! or, by the life of Washington, you have taken your last nap on this side of the grave!"

No resistance was attempted, for none would have availed against such fearful odds. Some gave up without hesitation, while others endeavored to conceal themselves in the hay; but they were soon dragged forth, and mustered on the barn floor, where several of the Rangers were stationed with lanterns.

"Who commands this band of heroes?" demanded Townsend.

"I do," answered the Englishman, promptly and proudly. "I have the honor to bear his majesty's commission, and demand your authority for this arrest and detention."

"The authority of the continental congress, whose commission I have the honor to bear," answered Townsend: "I shall, therefore, trouble

THE WHARTON HOUSE, FISHKILL, N. Y.

[See pages 61 and 147.]

you for such papers as you may have in your possession; we pledge ourselves, however, that nothing of a private nature shall be detained."

The Englishman reluctantly complied with this military usage, and at Townsend's request, proceeded to call his own men by the muster-roll. At the name of Enoch Crosby no answer was returned.

"Search for him with your bayonets!" exclaimed Townsend, and fifty blades were instantly plunged into as many different sections of the hay mow. Our hero now began to think it high time to show himself, and ask for quarter.

On descending to the floor, the first person he recognized was Col. Duer, a member of the Committee, who had accompanied the party for the express purpose of affording Crosby an opportunity to escape; but this generous intention was completely frustrated by the zeal of Townsend, who instantly knew the prisoner, and seized him with an arm as muscular and sinewy as his own.

"Well met, again, old comrade!" exclaimed the Ranger, with a smile of triumph. "You showed us a light pair of heels at Fishkill; but if I do not see them made sufficiently heavy this time, may I never be a Major."

"Who is he?" inquired Duer, affecting ignorance of the prisoner's person.

"Enoch, the patriarch," returned Townsend, smiling at his own conceit. "He who disappeared from the church in Fishkill, almost as mysteriously as his ancient namesake is said to have done from the earth."

"It is true, he did play us a slippery trick," observed Duer, who thought it necessary to say something. "But we cannot blame the poor fellow for consulting his own safety."

"Poor!" echoed Townsend. "If he be poor, John Bull must pay him ill."

"Yes, indeed," said the Lieutenant, who felt his own honor a little piqued at Crosby's former escape: "King George owes him a dukedom."

"And Congress a halter," added the Captain, as he resigned the silent subject of these sarcasms to two men, who soon shackled his limbs in such a manner as to prevent the possibility of his again giving them the slip.

As soon as the prisoners were all secured, the party were ready to march; and, "to shorten a long story," as Crosby quaintly expressed it, not many hours elapsed, before he found himself in full view of the stone church at Fishkill.

But Crosby, it appears, had forfeited the protection of the church; for while the other prisoners were conducted into that friendly asylum, he was compelled to march a mile further, to a farm house on the east side of the plain, which lies in front of the village.

Here he was permitted to halt; and soon discovered that it was not only the temporary headquarters of Captain Townsend, but the permanent residence of Mr. Jay, chairman of the Committee of Safety. This circumstance, however, was not likely to operate in his favor, as Townsend immediately adopted such prompt measures to prevent the escape of his prisoner, as evinced the deep interest that officer felt in his detention. Crosby was placed in a room by himself, and a guard detailed for his se curity, comprising some of the most vigilant members of the corps.

All men must eat at times, and Captain Townsend had fasted for the last twelve hours. Under such circumstances, it is not surprising that he awaited the preparations for supper with no little degree of impatience. This feeling, however, was frequently beguiled and diverted by the frank, free, and insinuating address of a rosy-cheeked lass, who, on this occasion, officiated in the capacity of house-maid. The Captain was no anchorite, and the maid appeared to be scrupulously attentive to his most trifling wants; until he became so completely absorbed with love, wine, and broiled chickens, that he forgot there was such a man as Enoch Crosby in the world.

But Miss Charity was too liberal in her opinions of right and wrong to

"Feast the rich, and let the humble starve."

She very considerately reflected that the sentinel at Crosby's door, might probably be as sharp set as his Captain; and, under this impression, without consulting the superior, prepared him another chicken, which she accompanied with a bottle of Jay's best old French brandy. How the ranger relished the joke was never accurately ascertained; but one thing is certain, that, owing either to the quality or quantity of the liquor, he actually fell asleep on his post.

About midnight, our hero was aroused from an unquiet slumber, by a gentle shake of the shoulder. On opening his eyes, he beheld the figure of a female bending over him, with a dark lantern in her hand.

"Follow me, without speaking," said she in a whisper; "and hold fast by them ugly things, that they don't make a noise."

Crosby instinctively obeyed in silence, and followed his fair conductor from the apartment. For a moment he paused to gaze at the snoring sentinel, while Charity carefully closed and locked the door. She then led the way through a small garden, in the rear of the house, and pointing to the West Mountain, against the side of which the moon was pouring a stream of mellow radiance, she bid him haste to seek a shelter amidst its almost impenetrable fastnesses.

"But how have you effected this?" asked the bewildered and astonished prisoner; "and what will be the result to yourself, and that careless sentinel?"

"Fear nothing, for either," hastily replied the girl; "but hasten to the mountains. I shall instantly return the key to Townsend's pocket, who is himself snoring on the sofa. Dr. Miller's opiates are wonderfully powerful when mixed with brandy. Now, fly for your life! The sentinel shall be on his feet when the relief comes. You have not a moment to lose. I shall be at Hopewell by the time the alarm is given. Not another word—I want no thanks—Jay is your protector—Fly!"

With these words she disappeared in the house.

The heavy shackles with which our hero's limbs were encumbered, allowed him to move but slowly. The coast was perfectly clear, however, and the moon illumined the whole of the plain before him. No obstacle appeared to oppose his progress to the mountain, which, rising like a huge pyramid, seemed to invite his approach. He advanced with confidence, but with tardiness and fatigue, until he reached a little thicket on the left, where he determined to stop, and, if possible, free himself from his fetters. This object being effected, after much exertion, he bounded forward with a heart as much lightened as his heels, until he found himself beyond the possibility of pursuit, among the intricate passes of that gigantic eminence.

On the following morning, Townsend found himself refreshed, the key in his pocket, and a trusty sentinel before the door of his prisoner's apartment. There was no other outlet to the room except a window, closed with a strong shutter, and guarded by another sentinel on the outside. No alarm or noise had been heard by any one during the night, and what doubt could there be of the prisoner's safety?

But words are inadequate to a description of Townsend's feelings, when, on taking the key from his pocket, and unlocking the door, the apartment was found evacuated and without a tenant. The guard were all summoned, but every one protested his ignorance and innocence of the prisoner's escape; and all united in expressing their surprise that a man in irons could creep up the chimney. But there was no other alternative; if he did not escape that way, in which way could he have made his egress from the apartment?

Captain Townsend could not forgive this second deception. He felt that his honour, as an officer, was implicated; and inwardly swore that if Enoch Crosby became his prisoner again, a very summary process should put an end to his career.*

CHAPTER X.

THE SECRET PASS.

We must find
An evident calamity, though we had
Our wish, which side should win: for either thou
Must, as a foreign recreant, be led
With manacles through our streets, or else
Triumphantly tread on thy country's ruin.
Shaks. Coriolanus.

As soon as our hero considered it prudent to leave his place of concealment in the West Mountain, which was not until the following night, he cautiously descended in a southern direction; and being, by this time, well acquainted with every pass through the Highlands, knowing where the ravines might be penetrated, and where the streams were fordable, he proceeded with silent celerity, and increasing confidence. For several hours he pursued his course without interruption, carefully avoiding such spots as he knew to be inhabited; sometimes plunging into thickets, at others finding it necessary to ascend hills that appeared to be almost inaccessible.

About sunrise he ventured to descend into the highway, where he continued to travel until fatigue and hunger compelled him to seek for a habitation where he might safely apply for refreshment

At this juncture, he found himself within a quarter of a mile of a farm house, the owner of which he knew to be a tory, and would doubtless supply his immediate wants. He directed his steps accordingly, and soon received a cheerful welcome from the mistress of the family, her husband being absent from home. He told his story, or as much of it as was proper to be related, and his loyal hostess could not find language to ex-

---

* See the Spy, Vol. I., Chap. V., three concluding pages.

press her commiseration of his sufferings, and her indignity at the wrongs he had received at the hands of the abominable rebels! In short, she treated him like a son; and insisted upon his making her house his home, for as long a time as he thought it prudent to remain. On his departure, she loaded him with provisions and clothes, with a capacious new pack to contain them.

Being well aware that patrols were scouring the country in every direction, who, if they recognized him, would be sure to retake him, he felt the necessity of being very cautious in his movements. It is true, that he might meet a cordial welcome from those who secretly favored the British cause; but at a period when so many were induced by circumstances to disguise their real sentiments, it was difficult to discriminate between friends and foes. Every whig would have thought it a duty he owed his country to deliver up the fugitive to the vengeance of her violated laws; while many, who felt interested in *his* safety, were deterred from affording him protection by a prudent regard for their own.

Under such circumstances, our hero soon found himself placed in a very unpleasant dilemma; while every succeeding day seemed to increase the gloom, which, like a portentous cloud, hung over his untoward destiny. Hunted like a beast of the forest by one party—suspected and avoided by the other—he felt himself, at times, an outcast in the world—a houseless wanderer, without a country or a home!* While looking at this side of the picture, it exhibited a cheerless, dreary scene of desolation, at the contemplation of which his heart sickened within him. But when he recollected the *object* for which he had voluntarily submitted to this living martyrdom—when he reviewed the *motive* of the sacrifice—a ray of peaceful tranquillity, emanating from a self-approving conscience, stole over his mind, which he would not have exchanged for the crown and sceptre of England.

It was near the close of a toilsome day's wandering, in the cheerless month of November, that he called at an indifferent looking farm-house, and requested to be accommodated for the night. This request was cheerfully granted; and, throwing off his pack, he sat down, with a thankful heart, to rest from the fatigues of the day.

He had not remained in this situation long, when two large men, armed with muskets, entered the apartment. One of them started on seeing our traveller; and, in a low voice, said something to his companion, to which the other apparently assented.

Crosby remained silent, watching the movements of these men with the deepest interest, as he suspected them to be volunteer scouts, numbers of which were constantly on the lookout for such persons as were suspected of toryism.

In a short time they advanced to our hero, and, after surveying him attentively, one of them accosted him—

---

* "Most of the movements of the pedlar through the country, were made at the hours which others allotted to repose. His approaches to the American lines were generally so conducted as to baffle pursuit. Many a sentinel, placed in the gorges of the mountains, spoke of a strange figure that had been seen gliding by them in the midst of the evening."—*Spy. Vol. i.*, p, *149*.

"I think, sir, that I have seen your face before."

"Very possibly, sir," resumed Crosby, cooly; "though I cannot say that I have the pleasure of recollecting yours."

"Probably not. But, if I mistake not, I saw you conducted to Fishkill prison a short time since, in company of a number of tories, arrested by Townsend's Rangers."

"O, yes, it is he," exclaimed the other; "I could swear to him among a thousand."

"So, you have made your escape, sir, it seems," continued the first speaker. "But under our escort you will not find it so easily done again. To-morrow morning you shall accompany us to Heath's head-quarters; and, if the provost marshal does his duty, your plots and escapes will soon be terminated. The Committee of Safety will not take the trouble of trying you again."

"It is a serious subject for jesting," observed Crosby, throwing an unquiet eye around, as if in search of some avenue of escape.

"You will find it no jest," returned the other. "Jay and Duer are determined to make an example of you. A tory they can pardon and pity. But a traitor, who, after bearing arms in the good cause, basely turns those arms against his countrymen, has forfeited all claims to protection. Mercy to such a wretch would be a cruelty to our country."*

"And think you that *Jay* would pronounce *me* a traitor?"† asked Crosby, with earnestness.

"How could he do otherwise?" returned the other. "What have you to urge in your own defence?"

Notwithstanding his reliance on the secret protection of the Committee, our hero felt a strong repugnance to become a prisoner again so soon; especially, as the exasperated Rangers (at a time when the civil law, but little regarded by the soldiery) might feel themselves justified in inflicting a summary punishment, without the ceremony of a trial. Weakened and fatigued as he was by toilsome marches, he could not contend against such odds with any hope of success. Having weighed all these circumstances in his mind, he concluded that he would be justified in appealing to the last resort: his present situation being one of extremity. He, therefore, drew a small folded paper from a secret place within the lining of his vest, and presented it to his interrogator.

"Read that, sir," said he proudly, "and learn how easy a thing it is to mistake a man's real character; and how prone we are to suspect the innocent."

The two strangers perused the paper in silent astonishment; and, for a moment, appeared unwilling to credit their own senses. At length, however, he who appeared to be principal, returned the paper, saying,

"I am satisfied, sir, that we have been mistaken in your real character, for those signatures I know to be genuine; and the writers certify that you are actually engaged in the service of

---

* "Dark and threatening hints began to throw suspicion around his movements, and the civil authority thought it incumbent on them to examine narrowly into his mode of life. His imprisonments were not long, though frequent; and his escapes from the guardians of the law comparatively easy, to what he endured from the persecution of the military."—*Spy*, Vol. 1, p. 34.

† "Will Washington say so, think you?" said Birch, with a ghastly smile. "No—no—no— Washington would never say, 'lead him to a gallows.'"—*Spy*, Vol. 1, p. 249.

your country. But how is the mystery to be explained? Why were you imprisoned by the orders of those very men?'

"Ask me no further questions, if you please," replied Crosby, as he returned the pass to its secret depository. "Be content to believe me a true whig, and in the service of my country. But, above all, I most earnestly request you, as you wish well to the cause, never to disclose what you have now learned to any human being."

So saying, he re-shouldered his pack; and, after evasively answering the numerous questions with which they assailed him, he bade both a hasty "good evening," and left them to wonder at the strangeness of the adventure. He now felt convinced that it would not be prudent to remain there for the night, as he had at first intended; and being somewhat refeshed by the short respite he had enjoyed, he travelled onward, in search of a more eligible asylum.

After proceeding more than two miles farther, he ventured to apply at another cottage, and renew his request for accommodation; which, after much solicitation on his part, was, at length, reluctantly complied with by the woman of the house. Here again he disencumbered himself of his pack, and sat down. much fatigued with his prolonged journey.

While inwardly congratulating himself on the happy termination of that day's labours, and fondly anticipating a comfortable night's rest, his attention was caught by the particular and suspicious manner with which he found himself regarded by a man who had just entered, and taken a seat by the fire. Crosby felt confident that he had somewhere seen him before; but could not recall to mind the place or circumstances; and began to feel somewhat alarmed at the closeness of his scrutiny. At length, Crosby spoke —

"Somewhat cool, this evening, sir."

Without noticing this sagacious remark, the other started on his feet, and exclaimed, with a bitterness of tone that well corresponded with the ghastliness of the grin that accompanied it,

"Now I know you! I thought I could not be mistaken. You are the very d——d rascal that betrayed us to the rebel Committee, and caused our company to be taken and confined in jail. Now, sir, if you don't make yourself scarce pretty d——d quick, I will call one of my neighbours, who swears that, if ever he can lay eyes on you again, he will take every drop of your heart's blood!"

Crosby made several efforts to reply, during the delivery of this philippic; but the other refused to hear a word he had to say, and thus continued —

"You shall leave this house immediately, sir; but not till I have had the satisfaction of pounding you!"

"Come on, sir," said our hero, rising cooly from his seat, and elevating himself to the full height of his manly stature; while that of his antagonist appeared to dwindle in the same proportion. "Come on! sir;" repeated he, deliberately rolling up his sleeves, and displaying a pair of muscular arms and bony fists, of the most formidable dimensions. "Come on — I am ready to try you a pull."

But, from some cause or other, the host had suddenly changed his mind, and appeared a little more inclined to the side of mercy; for, in a less elevated tone he replied,

"I believe I will let you off this time, if you will leave my house immediately, and never set your foot in it again."

Tired and jaded as he was, Crosby thought it best to comply; and travelled another mile before he succeeded in procuring lodgings for the night; but there he learned a fact which induced him to change his plans immediately.

He had long been anxious to obtain a private interview with the Committee; but dared not venture to Fishkill, while Townsend remained in the village with his vigilant Rangers. He now ascertained, however, that the corps was on the other side of the river,* and resolved to profit by the circumstance on the following morning. This determination he put in execution, and arrived at Duer's residence, on the succeeding evening, without interruption or molestation.

After a long consultation, that gentleman advised him to repair privately to a retired residence, on Wappinger's Creek; the farm house of an honest old Dutchman, and there work at his trade for the family, and keep himself concealed from observation, until further orders.

Being furnished with a complete set of tools for the purpose, he shouldered his pack, and proceeded to the designated place; where he soon found himself very comfortably situated, in the family of the friendly old Dutchman, who had feet enough in his family to keep the shoemaker in constant employment. It is true, a large majority of them were the property of females; but Crosby soon found, by actual admeasurement, that the *understanding* of a plump round face, rosy-cheek, country Dutch lass, is not such a *trifling* appendage, as the same article appears to be among our modern city belles; for, at the period of which we are writing, the doctrine of Dr. Sitgreaves most generally prevailed, that "the wider the base, the more firm is the superstructure."

In this tranquil asylum he had continued but two days, when a letter from Duer, desiring his immediate attendance on the Committee, at Fishkill, was handed him on his seat, by a messenger sent express for that purpose.

The good old Dutchman, as well as every member of his family, evinced much curiosity to know the purport of this communication; which they knew, by some expressions that had fallen from the messenger, must have come from high authority; and our hero immediately rose, in their estimation, at least one hundred per cent. Could he have conversed with Mynheer, in the mother-tongue of the latter, there is little doubt that he might have "taken his pick" among the daughters, with a good farm into the bargain.

"Mine Cot!" exclaimed the Dutchman, knocking the ashes from his pipe; "you know tee shentlemen of tee army? Vat for tey rite you?"

"I suppose they want shoes for the soldiers," replied Crosby, rising from his seat, and taking off his leather

---

* "Once when a strong body of the continental army held the Four Corners, for a whole summer, orders had been received from Washington himself, never to leave the door of Harvey Birch unwatched; the command was rigidly obeyed, and during this long period, the pedlar was unseen. The detachment was withdrawn; and the next night Birch re-entered his dwelling."—*Spy*, Vol. 1., p. 150.

apron, which he carefully spread over his unfinished work and tools. "I understand that the poor fellows are all barefoot, and there's a cold winter at hand. At all events, I must go and see; but will probably return time enough to finish Catrine's shoes for Sunday."

"Now, don't you disappoint me," cried the smiling girl, with sparkling eyes, and one of her sweet insinuating tones. "If you do, you'll be sorry."

"Tevil take tee shoes!" exclaimed the father, [filling his pipe again. "Vy you botter tee shentlemen mit shoes, ven he got bishness mit tee army? You know Gitty ish sick pon tee ped, and vont vant hern till Christmas. But, dunder and blixem, man! You vont trudge to Vishkill mit Shank's mare. Here, you Hauns! Puckle tee pest shaddle on Valdecker, and pring him to tee horse-plock, tirectly—you hear!"

Crosby was not very strenuous in declining this polite arrangement of his friendly host; but was soon mounted, and waving a farewell to the whole groupe, who had assembled in the yard to witness his departure, he struck his pony into a gallop, and was soon out of sight.

On reaching Fishkill, he immediately waited on Duer, to learn the pleasure of the committee; who reminded him that it would be extremely unsafe for him to remain in that place long enough for the committee to hold a consultation; he therefore directed him to leave the village as secretly as he entered it, and travel about three miles, in a north-east direction, to a place called Hopewell; there to inquire for Dr. Miller, who kept a small retail druggist shop, where one of the committee would meet him in the course of the afternoon.

In compliance with these instructions, Crosby again mounted his Dutch pony, and soon found the residence of the Doctor, who happened to be absent from home, and not expected back until evening.

This information was communicated by a sprightly smiling female, whose voice and figure struck Crosby as not being entirely new to him; while some marked peculiarity in her manner of addressing him, evinced, on her part, a reciprocal recognition. But it was in vain that he tasked his recollection to elucidate the mystery; until, with an arch smile, and an emphasis of much meaning, she said—

"If you wish any article from the shop, sir, I think I can wait upon you to your satisfaction. Dr. Miller's opiates, you recollect, are wonderfully powerful when mixed with brandy. They have been known to put even the vigilant Rangers to sleep."

"Is it possible!" exclaimed Crosby. "Are you then the ——"

"Hush! Not a word on that subject, for your life!" returned the damsel, in a low voice. "These men by the fire are not Rangers; but it might not be safe to expose your real name in their hearing." She then added aloud, "You had better take a seat by the fire, Mr. Brown; as the Doctor will not be home till dark."

Several of the neighbours were, as usual, collected round the fire, at one end of the shop, discussing the news and politics of the day. Crosby ventured to mingle with the groupe; and, not being personally known to either, had the satisfaction to hear his own adventures related, and descanted on, with all those embellishments, variations, and exaggerations, that ever accompany the verbal disposal of retailed wonders.

"There can be no doubt," observed one, "that Sir Henry Clinton obtained that information from Crosby. How else would Knyphausen, and his d——d Hessians, have known the way to Spiten-devil Creek?"*

"Aye, and how the d——l, without the assistance of some spy, could the regulars have known on which side to attack the post on Laurel Hill †" demanded another, looking round him with an expression of triumph that challenged contradiction. "The Dutchman's left column, you know, bore all the brunt of the battle, and were pretty decently peppered."

"Well, well." said a third, with a self-complacent smile, and a knowing toss of the head; "every dog has his day. But if Townsend ever gets the traitor in his clutches again, he will soon dangle in the air, without judge or jury."

"What sort of a fellow is this Crosby?" asked our hero, addressing the last speaker. "Have you ever seen him?"

"O yes, I saw him at Fishkill. He is a little slender artful looking fellow, of about five feet three. There's no confining him; for he'll creep out of a knot-hole, and I have no doubt that all our late disasters may be attributed to his secret intercourse with the enemy."

"It is shrewdly suspected," said Crosby, dryly, "that this fellow was at the bottom of the affair at Kipp's Bay."

"Very probably," said the other, forgetting the nature of that affair;‡ wherever there is a tory plot, you may swear that Crosby is head-devil in the business."

"Whether at the head or tail," observed a third, "his intrigues have given an unfortunate turn to our affairs. Fort Washington and Fort Lee are both in the hands of the enemy.§ The American army is retreating through the Jerseys, and Howe is close upon their heels."

"But didn't Gooch do the neat thing?" exclaimed the first speaker.

"Gooch! Who the d——l is he?" asked his friend.

"Who is he! A full-blooded yankee, from Boston, and a captain in Heath's division. During the attack on Fort Washington, which was bravely defended by Colonel Magaw, the commander-in-chief, who was across the river, on the high bank at Fort Lee, was a spectator of the whole affair. He wished to send a message across to Magaw, and Gooch offered to be the bearer of it. He ran down to the river—jumped into a small boat—pushed over in style——landed under the bank—ran up to the fort, and delivered the message—came out—ran and jumped over the broken ground—dodged the Hessians,

---

* Near the site of Fort Washington, in the vicinity of Kingsbridge.

† This hill was bravely defended by the Americans, during the attack of Fort Washington. It is supposed that over twelve hundred of the royal troops were killed or wounded. After being twice summoned, the commandant, Colonel Magaw, was compelled to surrender, with 2870 Americans.

‡ See Chapter VI., 3d paragraph.

§ Soon after the reduction of Fort Washington Lord Cornwallis, with a large force, conjectured to amount to about six thousand men, crossed over the North River, to attack Fort Lee, on the opposite Jersey shore. On the intelligence of their approach, the first determination of the Americans was to meet and fight them; but it was soon discovered that the contest would be too unequal, and the garrison was saved by an immediate evacuation, under the able guidance of General Greene.

some of whom struck at him with their pieces, while others attempted to thrust him with their bayonets. But he escaped through the whole—got into his boat, and returned to Fort Lee."*

"Was that message a recommendation to surrender?" asked Crosby.

"So it is presumed," replied the other. "Magaw had been summoned to surrender; but requested that he might be allowed to consider until 9 o'clock the next morning, before he gave a decisive answer. Only two hours were granted, and Magaw replied that he would defend the fort to the last moment. After receiving Washington's message, however, the fort was surrendered; and it would have been a useless waste of lives to hold out any longer."

"Was our loss great?" asked Crosby.

"Not in killed and wounded;" returned the other; "but the loss in prisoners was a serious blow indeed. It is said they were marched to the city, and crowded into prisons and sugar houses, where they are now dying off by dozens; so that probably very few of the poor fellows will ever get home again."

At this stage of the conversation, a gentleman entered the shop; and, without noticing the speakers, advanced to the counter, and ordered a phial of medicine. In this new comer, our hero instantly recognized the person of Jay, who had ridden from Fishkill on an elegant horse, which was standing at the door. While the shopman was waiting upon his customer, Crosby slipped out, and pretended to be admiring the noble animal, until his owner approached to remount. Our hero politely held the stirup, while Jay seized that opportunity to whisper in his ear—

"It will not do; there are too many observers in this place. Return to the Dutchman's, and there wait for further orders."

He then mounted; and was soon out of sight, on the road to Fishkill.

On re-entering the shop, which he did without being perceived, Crosby discovered that his own person had been the subject of remark, by the loungers present.

"His conversation and manners bespeak the gentleman," observed the principal speaker. "I wonder who he is, and what his business can be with Dr. Miller?"

"He appears to be acquainted with Jay," said another; "for I saw them whispering together at the horse-block."

On overhearing these remarks, Crosby began to feel apprehensive, that if he remained much longer, these village politicians might become more inquisitive than he could wish. He therefore told the shopman that he would call in the evening; then mounted his horse, and soon found himself on the banks of Wappinger.

His host met him in the yard, in front of the cottage, with his inseparable companion, the pipe, in his mouth.

"Vell, ten, sho you cot pack," said he, puffing a huge volume of curling vapour from his mouth.

"O yes," replied Crosby, dismounting. "There is no difficulty in getting back, on such a horse as yours, when his head is once turned toward home."

"O yaw, Valdecker vill ride any potty right to mine house. Here,

---

*"See Heath's Memoirs.

Haunse! Take off tee shaddle, ant rup him town mit a visp of shtraw; ant, to ye hear, Haunse! tont let him trink till he coutch'd coold."

"O there is no danger," returned Crosby; "I have not rode him hard. But how are the girls, and poor Gitty?"

"Vell, she complains as she is leetle petter; but she stood up, ven tinner vosh ready, pon tee ped, and ate pred, mit putter by it."

By this time they had entered the house, where Crosby was met by the smiling Catreen, who kindly welcomed him back, and again reminded him of her Sunday shoes. These he promised to attend to immediately; and, after visiting Gitty in her room, resumed his seat, and pursued his usual vocation.

CHAPTER XI.
LIGHTS AND SHADOWS.

————— Why then, you princes,
Do you, with cheeks abashed behold our works:
And think them shames, which are, indeed,
nought else
But the protractive trials of great Jove,
To find persistive constancy in men.
Shakspeare.

The political intelligence which Crosby gathered from the conversation at Hopewell, proved, alas! to be too true. Forts Washington and Lee *had* fallen into the hands of the enemy; and the Americans *were* retreating across the Jerseys, closely pursued by the British; so closely, "that the rear of the army pulling down bridges, was often within sight and shot of the van of the other, building them up."

At Newark, Washington asked Col. Reed—"Should we retreat to the back parts of Pennsylvania, will the Pennsylvanians support us?"

"That may depend upon contingencies." replied the Colonel. "If the lower counties are subdued, and give up, the back counties will doubtless do the same."

"My neck does not feel as though it was made for a halter," returned Washington, passing his hand over it. "We must repair to Augusta county, in Virginia. Numbers will be obliged to repair to us for safety, and we must try what we can do in carrying on a predatory war; and, if overpowered, we must cross the Allegany mountains."

To increase the gloom which now shrouded his future prospects, the hero, about this time, was deprived of one of his most able coadjutators and active generals. The veteran Lee, while leading on his division to join the main army, incautiously took up his lodgings at a house 3 or 4 miles from his troops. This circumstance was immediately communicated, by some unprincipled tories, to Colonel Harcourt, of the Britsh light-horse, who resolved to attempt his capture. Accordingly, with a detachment of dragoons, he speedily surrounded the house; made Lee his prisoner; and, not permitting him time to take his hat and cloak, mounted him on a horse, and conveyed him to New York.

In the meantime, Carleton's army in Canada, after driving the Americans from post to post, had made their appearance before Ticonderoga. A naval engagement had also taken place between the two fleets on Lake Champlain, which continued about four hours, and then resulted in the defeat of the Americans. The enemy, soon afterwards, established himself at Crown Point, and strengthened the fortifications; while Gates, with a corresponding ardor, continued to increase the works of defence at Ticonderoga, determined to give his neighbour a warm reception, if he honored him with a visit.

During the development of the foregoing transactions, the Committee of Safety felt very anxious respecting the state of affairs on the northern frontier. Frequent instances had been reported to them, of persons, in that quarter, being detected in enlisting soldiers for the tory regiments in New York. It had been already decreed, that every person of this description, who might fall into the hands of the Americans, should be tried by court-martial; and, if found guilty, executed as a spy.* Some had already suffered death under this law, and still the nefarious practice was continued. Under such circumstances, the Committee determined to send Crosby to the north.

Our hero was still a member of the Dutchman's family. Gitty had recovered her health, and the Sunday shoes of Catreen had been once displayed at church.

It was a cold morning, near the close of December, and at a very early hour, that Crosby received a communication from the Committee of Safety, on the subject of this northern excursion. He had just resumed his seat on what has been not unaptly termed St. Crispin's fiddle; for, in the present instance, it not only resembled that instrument in form, but also in tone, as its unstable joints squeaked in unison to the music of the hammer and lapstone. Such as it was, however, it was the manufacture of Crosby's own hands; exhibiting another evidence of that Yankee ingenuity which has since become proverbial in the production of horn flints, wooden nutmegs, and artificial pumpkin-seeds.

He had just taken his seat, and was attempting to soften a roll of wax by the warmth of his own breath, when, casting his eyes to the window, he saw a horseman at the gate, in the act of dismounting from a white steed, of superior form and dimensions.

The unusual clatter of an old iron knocker, which ornamented the front door of the building, soon announced a message of more than ordinary import; on being admitted, however, the messenger appeared to have forgotten the object of his journey amid the more important concerns of blowing his fingers, and warming his feet. But as soon as such matters were perfectly arranged to his mind, he took a letter from his pocket, and inquired for Jacob Brown.*

"I answer to that name, for want of a better," quaintly observed Crosby, waxing his thread.

"Then you are the man into whose hand I am directed to deliver this letter. An answer is expected by those who sent me."

Crosby broke the seal, perused the epistle, and then wrote a brief reply, with which the messenger departed on foot. This done, our hero repaired to the sleeping room of his host, who was yet in bed, and informed him that he was under the necessity of leaving him immediately; being ordered to the north, on busi-

---

* One Daniel Strong was found lurking about our army at Peekskill, and, on examination, enlisting orders were found sewed in his clothes. He was immediately tried as a spy from the enemy, sentenced to suffer death; and was executed accordingly.—*Thacher's Journal.*

* This was the name by which Crosby was known in the Dutchman's family.

ness that would admit of no delay, and that a swift horse had been sent for the express purpose of expediting his journey.

"Mine Cot!" exclaimed the other, starting up in his bed. "Ten you vill not shtay mit us all tee Christmas holidays."

"Not an hour," replied Crosby.

"Vell, den, shtay till I kit up, and Catreen kit tee breakfast py tee table. You must not ride pon your pelly empty in tee coldt."

The whole family were soon mustered: and, by the time Crosby had completed his own preparations for the journey, the table was loaded with hot buckwheat cakes, fried sausages, and every other substantial argument with which a Dutch farmer's larder is always liberally supplied. During breakfast, our hero expressed his gratitude to every member of the family, for the kindness and hospitality which he had uniformly received at their hands.

"Nonesense, man! nonesense!" exclaimed the generous Dutchman. "Who vouldn't do tee same, ish no petter ash nobody."

After taking an affectionate leave of every member of the family, and slily saluting Catreen as he stooped to assist her in buckling his portmanteau, which she had liberally furnished with necessaries, Crosby left the hospitabe mansion, and mounted his horse. He then inquired of his host, who had followed to the gate, the most direct road to Sharon.

"To Sharon? Val, you see dat roat pon de hel?—pointing in a northeast direction.

"O, yes, I see it.'

"Val, you musht not take dat roat. You see dis roat py tee colabarak?"

"Yes, sir."

"Val, dat ish not tee roat But you musht go right straight py tee parn, and vere you see von roat dat crooks just so—see here"—bending his elbow, and describing it at the same time—"and ven you kit dere, keep right along; and you musht mind to come pack, and shtay all night mit me, and make done our Hannse's shoes." †

In due time Crosby found himself in the right road, and mounted upon an excellent horse. But the dreary season of the year, and the consequent inclemency of the weather, rendered the journey extremely unpleasant. In speaking of this excursion, Crosby says—

"I travelled as far as Bennington,‡ in Vermont, a distance of one hundred and twenty-five miles, and suffered much from the cold and severe storms I encountered, and from riding on horseback, contrary to my usual habits. Had it not been for expediting my journey, I should rather have trusted to my legs."

The object of his journey, however, was accomplished; for, besides detecting a number of secret enemies to the country, in that quarter, whom he caused to be apprehended and brought to justice; he obtained such information, also, as enabled him ul

---

† This direction of the worthy Dutchman reminds the writer of the following story: "A Yankee, travelling through a Dutch settlement, in the State of New York, and, *guessing* that he was near his place of destination, thought he would ascertain the fact by inquiring of a man who was hard at work in a field of potatoes. He was answered in the following manner: "Val, den, you vill turn de potato patch round, de pridge over, and de river up stream, and de hel up; and tirectly you see mine prother Haune's parn, shingled mit straw: dat's his house vare mine brother Schnyven lives. He'll tell you so petter as I can. And you go little further, you see two roats—you must not take bote of 'em."

‡ Bennington is about thirty-six miles from Albany in a northeast direction, and is famous for General Starke's victory over the Hessians, on the 16th of August, 1777.

timately to surprise a company of them much nearer home.

In the meantime, while Washington, with the main body of the American army, was retreating through the Jerseys, closely pursued by the enemy, General Heath, with his division, remained to fortify and defend the Highlands, on both sides of the river. While attending to this arduous duty, assisted by Lincoln, Wooster, Scott, and Ten Broeck, he received agreeable intelligence that Washington, who had previously retreated over the Delaware, into Pennsylvania, had suddenly turned upon his pursuers with the most complete success.

Such an event was totally unexpected by the enemy, who were reposing in confident security in Trenton, and other parts of New Jersey. They had been celebrating the festival of Christmas with unusual satisfaction, occasionally mingling in their libations some bitter sarcasms against the flying Yankees. The mercenaries of Hesse, Waldecker, and Hanover, who were posted at Trenton, were particularly elated on this occasion, as they fondly believed that their labors were now over, and the promised reward ready for their acceptance. They imagined that they had at length succeeded in driving the rebels from their country, and that their houses and lands were to be immediately divided among the Hessians—for such had been the delusive tale with which they had been flattered by their false-hearted employers.

Under such impressions, they celebrated the birth of the Saviour with unusual demonstrations of joy; and feasted, and drank, and laughed, and sang, until the night was far spent. It was the Hessians' Christmas banquet. But like the impious feast of Belshazzar, its termination was to be fatal. The handwriting was already on the wall of their air-built castle of success and security. In the morning watch, the hero of Liberty came upon them like a thief, and few escaped. After a contest of half an hour, those who had not fallen, surrendered to the victorious chief, and his gallant little band of barefooted heroes.*

The news of this affair was like the first ray of sunshine after a long dismal storm. It rejoiced the Committee of Safety, elated and encouraged the army, and revived the drooping hopes of Americans in every section of the country.

In the midst of their congratulations on this auspicious event, the same gallant band stole a march upon the British who were posted at Princeton, over whom they obtained another complete victory.†

The tide of success which had so long flowed in favour of the enemy, had now turned against them; while the Americans, suddenly aroused from a state of despondency, had become elated with joy; and, in their turn, pursued their invaders with as much rapidity as they had recently fled before them. Washington had always been popular; he was now the idol of the army—the acknowledged saviour of his country.

In order to take advantage of the general consternation which these events had produced in the ranks of the enemy; and, if possible, to drive them entirely out of the Jerseys,

---

* See Appendix, No. VII.   † Ibid, No. VIII.

Washington sent an express to Heath, whose headquarters were at Peekskill, directing him to draw his forces from the Highlands (excepting a sufficient guard), and march them down through the "neutral ground," towards New York, as if he had a design upon the city. This manœuvre had the desired effect. The enemy became alarmed for the safety of the city, and withdrew his forces to protect it.

Heath advanced down as far as Kingsbridge, where a battle took place without much advantage on either side. He then retired to the fortresses of the Highlands, where he retained the command until Washington ordered him to take that of the eastern department, and hold his headquarters at Boston.

Several other events of interest occurred about this period. General Dickinson, with four hundred militia, and fifty Pennsylvanian riflemen, defeated a British foraging party of equal numbers, taking nine prisoners, one hundred horses, forty wagons, besides a number of sheep and cattle. Shortly after this affair, Colonel Neilson, of New Brunswick, with a party of militia, defeated the British Major Stockton, killed four of his men, and captured fifty-nine, together with their commander.

Every such incident produced a beneficial effect on the reviving hopes of America; and tended, not a little, to lessen the mortification arising from several concomitant disasters; such as the enemy taking possession of Rhode Island; and also, their destroying some stores at Peekskill.

This latter affair, however, was of trifling import. Heath had gone to Boston; and McDougall, who commanded the post at Peekskill, finding it prudent to retire, on the approach of the enemy, the object of their expedition was partially accomplished. But the gallant Willett, then Lieutenant-Colonel, with only sixty men, came upon the enemy by surprise, and compelled them to retire with great precipitation, on board their vessels in the North river, after having suffered a considerable loss.

CHAPTER XII.

QUAKER HILL.

Do you confess, 'twas not a thirst of honour
Drew you thus far: but hopes to share the spoil
Of conquered towns, and plundered provinces?
Fired with such motives, you do well to join
With Cato's foes, and follow Cæsar's banners,
ADDISON.

While the prospects of the American army were the most gloomy, and the hopes of the people at the lowest ebb, the two Howes, flushed with the rapid successes of the royal troops, had availed themselves of the occasion, and put forth a second proclamation, granting *pardons* to all those who should, within sixty days, subscribe a declaration to remain peaceable, not to take up arms, nor encourage others to act against the king's authority. At the same time, they charged and commanded all who were assembled in arms, against his majesty, to disband; and all legislative assemblies, committees, &c., to desist from their treasonable practices, and relinquish their usurped power, within sixty days from the date of the proclamation.

In order to convince the friends of England that Crosby was in the employment of Howe, the Committee of Safety, previous to his journey to the north, had furnished him copies of the foregoing proclamation, together with Howe's former declaration, offering rewards to such Americans as would assist him in subjugating their fellow-countrymen.

By exhibiting these documents to such as were too wary to avow their real sentiments, our hero was certain to gain their confidence, which was all that was requisite to secure their ultimate detection. It was not always easy to determine who were genuine whigs, as hundreds assumed that mask to conceal their real characters. But there was little difficulty or danger in denouncing the cautious and the wavering as tories. In a cause where the liberties of the whole nation, and the lives and property of thousands, are all at stake, "he who doubts is damn'd." He that is not for his country, is virtually operating against it. It was to such persons that Crosby exhibited the British proclamations, and always with success.

But there were not wanting occasions of detecting the blustering pretenders also. Crosby had sufficient discernment, and had seen enough of human nature, to know that hypocrisy is apt to overact its part. Under this impression, he frequently set his trap for some of the most violent brawlers in the cause of liberty —and always with the same result— for the mask of patriotism was instantly thrown off, while the wearer would secretly confess to the bearer of Howe's proclamation, that he was at heart a partizan of Britain.

On his return from this excursion, while on his way to Fishkill, our hero ascertained that a company of loyalists was about being formed and organized at Pawling, a small town in Dutchess county, near the Connecticut line, and not many miles distant from the scenes of his boyish days.

To Pawling, therefore, he immediately repaired; where, in the course of a fortnight, he succeeded in winning the confidence of the recruiting officer; and, as usual, agreed to become a member of the company.

In the centre of this town is an extensive valley, bounded by high hills on the east and west; and in the midst of the valley is a great swamp, where Croton river, Fishkill creek, and some other streams, take their rise. On the east side of the valley, a well-known eminence, called Quaker-hill, rears its gigantic height, on which stands a large old-fashioned Quaker meeting-house

It was at a retired habitation, in the vicinity of this building, that the newly formed company of tories were in the habit of holding their secret meetings. Our hero, accordingly, made his arrangements to have the whole corps, himself included, taken into custody. Unwilling, however, to trust himself again in the hands of the rangers, and aware that his absence at the time of the capture, would awaken the suspicion of his less fortunate comrades, he applied to Colonel Morehouse, who resided in the vicinity, and requested his co-operation. This gentleman had no immediate command, but promised to assemble and arm a sufficient number of men for this particular occasion.

Accordingly, at the time appointed, the tories being all collected at their usual rendezvous, two of the members hastily entered, with some degree of consternation depicted in their faces, one of whom addressed the captain—

"Sir, there is a company of armed men collecting at Colonel Morehouse's. What can be their object?"

"Are we betrayed!" exclaimed the Captain, looking sternly round upon the company. "Can it be possible that we have any traitors among us?"

"O no;" replied the Lieutenant. "The probability is, that the lower party are coming up to drive the d——d rebels off; and that Morehouse has collected this company to oppose them."

"Some of you go out and reconnoitre," said the Captain; "and if there be any appearance of danger, give us timely notice."

Five or six immediately, sallied forth, while their comrades remained in anxious suspense for their report. This suspense, however, was not of long duration; for the challenge of "stand! surrender!" soon saluted the ears of the whole party, and threw them into a state of consternation, dismay, and confusion, which it would be difficult, if not impossible, to describe. Some sprang from the windows, and attempted to conceal themselves by plunging into snowbanks; others ran to the top of the building, and secreted themselves under the eyes of the roof. Crosby retreated to an adjoining room, and crept under a bed; but was soon dragged out, when he learned, to his secret joy, that scarcely one of the party had succeeded in making good his escape. Seing his fellow-captives undergoing the process of being bound, our hero was seized with such a severe lameness in one of his limbs, as rendered it utterly impossible for him to walk.

"I beg that you would not bind me," said he to the Colonel: "for in attempting to escape I have sprained my leg in a most shocking manner, and am not able to move a step."

"Go you shall!" exclaimed the Colonel, preparing to mount his horse. "Lame, or not lame, dead or alive, to prison you go with the rest. If you cannot walk, you shall be carried; here's a good horse, that will carry double, and you shall be tied to the crupper."

So saying the Colonel mounted, and ordered two of his men to raise up Crosby and seat him, straddle, on the crupper behind him. The men instantly obeyed, without much tenderness for the sprained leg, of which the prisoner bitterly complained.

The whole cavalcade, horse and foot, now took up the line of march, with their prisoners tied together in pairs. On approaching the place of confinement, the Colonel dropped in the rear, and in a whisper gave Crosby the necessary directions for escaping. The escort halted in two lines, between which the prisoners marched into the building. While every eye was fixed upon the procession, Crosby slipped from the Colonel's horse and disappeared; nor was his absence noticed for several minutes; so that all search for the fugitive was rendered unavailing*

From Pawling Crosby made his way to Patterson, a few miles further south; but "finding no game in that quarter," he concluded to repair to Fishkill for further orders. On reaching that place, and obtaining a private interview with the Committee of

---

* "Why the rebels suffer him to escape so easily, is more than I can answer," returned the Captain, "but Sir Henry would not permit a hair of his head to be injured."
"Indeed!" cried Frances, with interest; "is he then known to Sir Henry Clinton?"
"At least he ought to be," said the Captain, smiling significantly.—*Spy, Vol. i., p. 62.*

Safety, they informed him that the service on which they next wished to employ him, would expose him to the danger of taking the small-pox, which then prevailed in various sections of the country. They therefore wished him to repair to Dr. Miller's to receive the disorder by inoculation; to which proposition he very readily assented. Being furnished by the Committee with a letter of introduction, together with the necessary funds, in "continental," he immediately waited on the Doctor for that purpose. The process was so favorable, that the patient was confined but a few days.

As soon as he was pronounced fit for duty, the Committee requested Crosby to visit the city of Albany, and the town of Claverack,† upon special business with Colonel Van Ness. Of the purport of this mission, or the time it occupied, we have not been informed; but during the absence of their agent, the Committee of Safety was dissolved,‡ and two Commissioners appointed in their stead; viz., Captain M. Smith, and a Mr. Benson.

At Claverack, Crosby remained some time, acting as an agent, in transferring the property, which had been left by those tories who had joined the enemy, into the hands of such as had abandoned their own property, in order to escape from the British. "This course," says Crosby, "had a very beneficial effect; as the tories soon became tired of leaving their property to the enjoyment of other people."

On returning to the vicinity of the "Neutral Ground," our hero resumed his former vocation of ferreting out such tories as were concocting plans to aid the common enemy, and causing them to be brought to justice. But such was the result of his ingenuity and address, that his plans were always so contrived as to leave an impression on the minds of his victims, that he was one of their warmest adherents. He was frequently taken and imprisoned with the rest; but always escaped, and in such a mysterious, inexplicable, wonderful manner, as occasionally elicited from some good old Dutch matron, a dark hint, or an "ambiguous giving-out," that Crosby had entered into a solemn covenant with a certain being whose name shall not sully our pages.

Through the medium of the tories, whose confidence in our hero's loyalty was every day strengthened by the risks he ran to serve their cause, he obtained much valuable intelligence respecting the contemplated movements of the lower party. This he always found means to communicate to the Commissioners, who as regularly transmitted the same to headquarters.

The year 1777 was distinguished by many events, highly interesting to those who were engaged in the glorious struggle for American freedom; and there is little doubt that in the development of several, the unseen

---

† Claverack is about thirty-five miles south of Albany, on the eastern side of the Hudson. It was settled at a very early period by the Dutch, and their descendants still occupy a large proportion of the rich lands in its vicinity.

‡ Jay was afterwards sent as an envoy to the court of Spain. "His capacity was equal to the business; he was well received, and his public character acknowledged; yet his negotiations were of little consequence to America, while he resided in Spain. Perhaps, apprehensive that the spirit of freedom and revolt might extend to her own colonies, Spain chose to withhold her assistance." "The highest favor he could obtain was, the trivial loan of four or five thousand pounds. A short time afterwards, however, Spain declared war against England."—*Warren's Revolution.*

agency of Crosby produced the most auspicious results.

Among the fortunate incidents of the year, may be enumerated, the brilliant success of Colonel Meigs, at Sag-Harbour, on Long Island;§ the capture of the British General Prescott, by Colonel Barton, of Providence, R. I.;† Colonel Willett's successful sally from Fort Stanwix, since called Fort Schuyler;‡ General Stark's victory, at Bennington;§ Colonel Brown's success at Lake George and Ticonderoga;‖ the battles of Saratoga and Stillwater;¶ the defeat of the Hessians at Red Bank, by Colonel Greene;** and, finally the surrender of General Burgoyne, with his whole army.††

But this life, alas! is a chequered scene, and the current of human affairs seldom runs smooth. As a set-off to the foregoing, the Americans had to deplore a series of disasters. The most important of these were, the unsuccessful battles of Brandywine and Germantown;‡‡ Wayne's defeat at Paoli;§§ Warner's defeat at Hubbardstown, in Vermont;‖‖ Herkimer's defeat, while marching to the relief of Fort Stanwix,*a* the plundering and burning of Danbury, in Connecticut, and the consequent battle, in which General Wooster was mortally wounded, and a number of Crosby's old friends and fellow-soldiers slain;*b* the occupation of Philadelphia by the enemy; the capture of Fort Montgomery;*c* and the wanton conflagration of the continental village of Esopus, and Livingston's manor

CHAPTER XIII.

THE SPY UNMASKED.

Fictitious characters aside are thrown,
And epilogues are given in their own.
PLAYER'S MANUAL.

Intrigue and stratagem in war, are not only justifiable, but absolutely necessary; and he who proves the greatest adept in these, will eventually pluck the laurel from the brow of his opponent. But that man must possess more art, ingenuity, and address, than generally falls to the share of an individual, who can support a fictitious political character for months, and even years, without being compelled sooner or later to throw off the mask, and to stand exposed in his own proper person.

---

* On the 24th of May, Colonel Meigs made a successful attack on the British store at Sag-Harbour; destroying twelve brigs and schooners, together with great quantities of hay, corn, &c. He sustained no loss, and brought off with him ninety prisoners.

† See Appendix No. ix. ‡ See Appendix No. x.

See Appendix No xi.

‖ On the 18th of September, the Americans, under Col. Brown, attacked and defeated the British, on the north end of Lake George, and Ticonderoga. They took 293 prisoners, released 100 Americans, and retook the continental standard left there on its evacuation, July 6, 1777.

¶ See Appendix, No. xii.

** See Appendix, No. xiii.

†† See Appendix, No. xiv.

‡‡ See Appendix, No. xv.

§§ On the 21st of September the British, under General Gray, surprised the American General Wayne, about one o'clock in the morning, at Paoli. Of the Americans about three hundred were killed or wounded with the bayonet, and about seventy or eighty prisoners taken, including several officers.

‖‖ Colonel Warner commanded the rear guard of General St. Clair, consisting of twelve hundred men, on their march from Ticonderoga to Hubbardstown, in Vermont. They were pursued by a detachment from Burgoyne's army, under General Fraser, who overtook them near Hubbardstown, where a close and severe engagement took place, in which the brave Colonel Francis fell, with other valuable American officers. American loss, 324 killed, wounded, and prisoners. British loss, 133 killed and wounded.

a Fort Stanwix, since called Fort Schuyler, was, early in August, invested by a body of Britons, Canadians, tories, and Indians, and Herkimer was on his march to disperse them. See Appendix, No. x.

b See Appendix, No. xvi.

c See Appendix, No. xvii.

Such, at length, proved to be the destiny of our hero. The mysterious and inexplicable *exits*, by which he uniformly eluded the fate and penalties of his less fortunate companions, began to excite suspicions, which were not long in receiving confirmation. The loyalists naturally concluded that there was something more in this than mere chance and good luck, if their philosophy could only find it out; and by consulting on the subject, collating circumstances, and comparing notes, they at length came to the conclusion that Enoch Crosby, instead of being what he pretended, a friend to the king, was in fact an American Spy; and unanimously resolved to take summary and exemplary vengeance on the delinquent.

Aware of the threatening storm, Crosby thought it prudent to retreat from its fury. He had a brother-in-law in the Highlands, to whom he had lately imparted the secret of the part he had been playing, for the purpose of relieving his parents from the burden of anxiety under which they had so long labored. He therefore concluded to retire to the Highlands, and remain with this relation, until he could procure a respectable situation in the army of Washington.

But he was watched, by his new enemies, more closely than he had anticipated; and, on the second day of his retirement, was fired at through a window, by some person in ambush on the outside of the house. The ball just grazed his neck, and lacerated the collar of his coat; it then buried itself in an opposite wainscot, where the perforation is still to be seen. But, on the strictest search, no traces of the assailant could be discovered.

Our hero was now compelled to be very circumspect and guarded in his movements; seldom venturing to show himself on the outside of the dwelling, and constantly sleeping in a retired back room, with a loaded musket at hand. But what precaution can elude the subtlety of determined vengeance?

"A few nights subsequent to the foregoing incident," says Crosby, in relating this circumstance to the compiler, "an armed gang came to the house of my brother-in-law, burst open the door, dragged him from his bed, and demanded where I was to be found. On his refusing to tell them, they commenced beating him until they had almost killed him. Perceiving that there was no alternative left him, but either to die under their hands, or to inform them where I slept, he directed them to my room, which they entered with the fury of demons.

"I now awoke, out of a sound sleep, when the first object that met my view was a large hideous looking fellow, coming at me, with a light in one hand, and a drawn pistol in the other. I immediately sprang from my bed; but, before I could reach my gun, he discharged his pistol at me—happily without effect. I instantly returned his fire; but, being in a scuffle, my aim was imperfect, and the shot, of course, ineffectual. I then grappled with him, and soon had him on the floor, completely at my mercy.

"At this moment, however, finding myself, amidst the smoke and confusion, assailed by three others, I was obliged to relinquish my fallen enemy, who sprang upon his feet, while

I was defending myself against this formidable reinforcement. Two of them at length succeeded in making themselves masters of my hands and arms, which they held extended, while a third presented a pistol to my breast, with the manifest intention of blowing me through the body. But this was prevented by the *humane* interference of him who had just recovered his feet,

"'Don't shoot the d——d rascal!' exclaimed he. 'Let us pound him to death!'

"And sure enough, at it they went; and soon found that I had hands and feet as well as themselves. More than one of them was saluted with a kick in the windchest that shortened his breath; and, notwithstanding their superior numbers, several of them got a flooring, from a pair of fists that had seen some service.

"But they finally proved too powerful for me; when, exhausted with exertion and loss of blood, I fell on the floor in a state of insensibility."

Supposing that they had now consummated their bloody purpose, these merciless marauders left their senseless victim weltering in his gore, and returned to the apartment of his brother-in-law, who was not in a much more enviable situation; while the shrieks of women, and the cries of children, added to the distress and confusion of the scene.

The villians then proceeded to plunder the house. They broke open every drawer and closet they could find; and not a single portable article, of the most trifling value, was left behind. Among other things, they took the clothes and musket of our fallen hero, together with a sum of money belonging to his brother-in-law. They then departed with their booty, leaving the family in a situation that baffles description.*

But these midnight assassins had happily thought more of their plunder, than of their personal safety. The report of fire-arms had alarmed the neighbors, who hastily assembled and pursued the retreating ruffians, whom they finally overtook on the bank of the Croton. They were considered outlaws, undeserving of quarter. Those who escaped the fire of their pursuers, were driven into the river, and several of them drowned! On the fall of the stream, in the ensuing spring, the musket of our hero, with some other articles, were found and restored.

Crosby recovered slowly from his wounds and bruises, so that it was several months before he was fit for active duty of any kind. The health of his brother-in-law was much more speedily restored; but the event itself was one of too much consequence to every individual concerned, to be easily forgotten.

In the mean time, through the influence of the Marquis LaFayette, an alliance had been formed between France and the United States of America. This event gave a new and brighter aspect to affairs; and was soon followed by the active co-operation of a French army and fleet. Lafayette himself had been appointed a major general, by Congress, at an early period of the war; but, as yet, held no separate command. He had, however, distinguished himself, in several engagements, by the side of Washington; and, at the battle of

---

* Robbery of Harvey Birch by the Skinners, bears some resemblance to this affair.—*See the Spy, Vol. i. p 455.*

Brandywine, received a severe wound. While posted at Barren Hill, in Pennsylvania, with a detachment of two thousand five hundred men, an attempt was made by General Grant, at the head of seven thousand troops, to surprise him. But the Marquis defeated his design by a masterly retreat, which did him much honor. He also acted a conspicuous part at the battle of Monmouth,* where victory perched on the standard of freedom.

Time rolled its ceaseless course, and the great contest was continued with various success; dame Fortune sometimes smiling on one party, and sometimes on the other. While the enemy could boast of his successful depredations at Rhode Island, Egg-Harbour, Nantucket, New Haven, and various other places, the Americans could congratulate themselves on Wayne's glorious victory at Stony-Point;† the enemy's repulse at Rhode Island, by General Sullivan;‡ and on the success of Major Lee, at Pawles Hook.§ Although they had to deplore the unfortunate surprise of Col. Baylor, at Tappan, by the British General Gray, who ordered no quarter to be given to the Americans; yet they had the consolation of several brilliant achievements, on their own part, which were unsullied by a single act of inhumanity, or a drop of needless blood.

The history of our hero furnishes no event of interest, since the midnight assault of his enemies, until we find him holding a subordinate command in the elegant corps of the Marquis La Fayette.

Two brigades had been selected from the different regiments in the main army, by Washington himself, as a compliment to his gallant young friend, and fellow-laborer in the glorious cause of liberty. When duly organized, they were paraded and reviewed by the commander-in-chief, with all his general officers, who were unanimously of the opinion that the whole army could not furnish a more excellent corps of light infantry. They were then presented, in form, to the young marquis, who was so delighted with his command, that he immediately equipped them, at his own individual expense, in a style of superior elegance. To every officer he presented an elegant sword, and the privates were clothed in a beautiful uniform. "He infused into this corps a spirit of pride and emulation, viewing it as one formed and modeled according to his own wishes, and as deserving his highest confidence. *They* were the pride of *his* heart—*he* was the idol of *their* regard. They were constantly panting for an opportunity of accomplishing

---

* In this affair the enemy left four officers and 245 men dead on the field of battle, who were buried by the Americans; they also left four officers and forty men wounded. Several died on both sides from the excessive heat of the weather, it being the 28th of June, and thermometer at 96.

† Gen. Wayne took Stony Point, by assault on the 16th of July, 1779, Lieut.-Col. Johnson, commandant, and five hundred and forty three men were taken prisoners. The enemy lost sixty-three killed, and the Americans fifteen, with eighty-three wounded, thirty of them very badly. Wayne was wounded in the head with a musket ball.

‡ In this affair the enemy lost 38 killed and 210 wounded; 12 missing; total loss, 260. The American loss was much less.

§ On the 19th of July, 1779, Major Lee, of the Virginia cavalry, surprised the enemy's post at Pawles' Hook. Major Sutherland, who commanded the fort, with a number of Hessians, escaped; thirty of the garrison were killed, and seven officers and 150 men taken. The American loss was only six killed and wounded. Lee, according to his orders, retreated immediately. A large British force being in the vicinity prevented his destroying the barracks and artillery. Lee was a man of chivalric spirit and enterprise, and commanded the finest corps of cavalry that Washington could boast of. This active officer and amiable gentleman distinguished himself on many occasions during the war, and is, no doubt, the "Major Dunwoody" of Cooper's Spy.

some signal achievement worthy of his and their character, and their wishes were, ultimately gratified."

A detachment from this corps, commanded by Colonel Van Cortlandt, was stationed on the east side of the Hudson, to manœuvre on the "Neutral Ground," where the inhabitants were now continually exposed to the ravages and insults of refugees and tories. One company of this detachment was commanded by Crosby, during the absence of his captain to the north; and was not unfrequently engaged in some interesting affair with the enemy's outposts and patroles.

The situation of the "Neutral Ground," at this period, was painfully interesting to the patriot as well as the philanthropist. The country was rich and fertile, and the farms appeared to have been advantageously cultivated; but it now wore the marks of a country in ruins. A large proportion of the proprietors having abandoned their farms, the few that remained found it impossible to harvest the produce. The meadows and pastures were covered with grass of a summer's growth, and thousands of bushels of apples and other fruit were ripening on the trees, for no other purpose than to fall and rot on the ground!

The even mead that erst brought sweetly forth,
The freckled cowslip, burnet, and green clover,
Wanting the scythe, all uncorrected, rank,
Conceives by idleness: and nothing teems,
But hateful docks, rough thistles, kecksies, burs,
Losing both beauty and utility,
And as our vineyards, fallows, meads, and hedges,
Defective in their natures, grow to wildness.
SHAKS., HEN. V.

Those of the inhabitants of the "Neutral Ground" who were tories, had joined their friends in New York; while the whigs had retired into the interior of the country. Some of each side had taken up arms, and were now the most cruel and deadly foes. Within the British line, were hordes of banditti, consisting of lawless villains, who devoted themselves to the most rapacious pillage and robbery among the defenceless inhabitants between the lines, many of whom were dragged off to New York, after witnessing the plunder of their houses and farms. These shameless marauders were known by the name of *cow-boys* and *refugees;* who, by their atrocious deeds, had become a scourge and terror to the people.

In the vicinity of the American lines, was another class of robbers, equally unprincipled, but still more criminal, because they committed their depredations under the mask of patriotism. These were called *skinners*, and professed to be whigs; while the *cow-boys* claimed the title of *loyalists.* The lust of plunder alone was the governing impulse of each.

Numerous instances occurred of these miscreants subjecting defenceless persons to cruel tortures, to compel them to deliver up their money, or to disclose the places where it had been secreted. It was not uncommon for them to hang a man by the neck till apparently lifeless;* then restore him; repeat the experiment, and leave him for dead.

While Crosby was on duty in the vicinity of Teller's Point, where the waters of the Croton empty into Tappan Bay, a British sloop of war came up the river and anchored in the stream, opposite the Point. With

---

* In Cooper's description of the preparations for hanging a Skinner, by a leader of the Refugees, he says, the Skinner "had so often resorted to a similar expedient to extort information or plunder, that he by no means felt the terror an unpractised man would have suffered, at these ominious movements."—*See Spy. Vol. ii. p.* 254.

an unconquerable predilection for stratagem, our hero immediately concerted a plot, for the sole purpose, as he says, of affording "a little sport for his soldiers." He accordingly, proceeded down to the Point, accompanied by six men; five of whom, besides himself, concealed themselves in the woods, which grew a short distance from the shore, while the other paraded the beach, so as to display La Fayette's uniform in so conspicuous a manner as to attract the notice of the officer on board the vessel.

The enemy swallowed the bait; and a boat soon put off from the sloop of war, manned with eleven men, under the command of a lieutenant, to make a prisoner of this one yankee, who precipitately fled into the woods, as the barge approached the shore. The Englishmen followed, threatening to shoot the fugitive unless he stopped and surrendered.

As soon as the pursuers had passed his own little party, which were scattered in various directions, Crosby exclaimed—

"Come on, my boys! Now we have them!"

At this signal every man sprang up in his place, with a shout that made the welkin ring; making, at the same time, such a rustling in the bushes, that the British, thinking themselves surrounded by a superior force, surrendered without resistance. On the next day they were marched to Fishkill, and confined in the old Dutch church.

Van Courtlandt's detachment was small; but by a well-managed finesse, he often succeeded in deceiving the enemy, as to its real numbers. He would occasionally approach the British lines; and, posting his men in scattered positions, among the hills, cause each squad to beat to arms successively. They would then show themselves to the British, and manœuvre in such a manner as to appear like reinforcements coming down to join the main body. This *ruse de guerre* often deterred the enemy from pursuing his predatory excursions against the defenceless inhabitants of the "Neutral Ground."

Van Cortlandt's detachment, however, was at length ordered to West Point, and from thence to the main army at Tappan, in New Jersey; where Crosby remained until his stipulated term of service had expired. In the meantime, the following incident occurred, for the authenticity of which we have the testimony of Van Cortlandt himself; although the particulars, it is believed, have never before been published :

A young man, of Peekskill, by the name of John Paulding, while serving his country in the Westchester militia, was taken prisoner, and sent to New York city. Whether he was confined in a sugar-house, or the *provost*,† as it was then called, we have not been informed; nor do we know the length of time he remained a captive. It was in the summer of 1780, however; about the period that a celebrated satirical poem was published in New York, entitled the "Cow-Chase,"‡ from the pen of John Andre, adjutant-general in the British army.

---

† The present debtor's jail.

‡ This bitter satire, the reader will doubtless recollect, was directed against the American Brigadier-General Wayne, the hero of Stony Point: whom the poet accuses of stealing cattle for the use of the American army. The poem concludes with the following *prophetic* stanza:

"And now I close my epic strain,
　I tremble as I show it,
Lest this same warrior-drover Wayne
　Should ever catch the poet."

Though vigilantly watched, Paulding was allowed the liberty of his prison-yard, a capacious enclosure, surrounded by a strong high fence. By bribing a colored woman, who lived in the vicinity, to furnish him with a ladder, he one night effected his escape from the yard; and, after remaining concealed some time in her cellar, succeeded in reaching the North River, undiscovered. Here he found a boat, and finally landed in safety, on the Jersey shore, near Hoboken. He then made the best of his way to the American army at Tappan, where he related his adventure to his fellow townsmen, Colonel Van Cortlandt, whose assistance he solicited, in proceeding to Peekskill. Van Cortlandt, accordingly, supplied him with money, furnished him with a pass, and procured him a passage across the river.

After landing on the eastern side of the Hudson, Paulding directed his course homeward; but had not proceeded far, when he met two of his former companions in arms, David Williams and Isaac Van Wart; who hailed his return with joy, and heartily congratulated him on his fortunate escape. After some conversation, they prevailed upon Paulding to relinquish his intention of going directly to Peekskill, and to accompany them on an excursion down the "Neutral Ground," towards the British lines, where they were going, they said, "to have some fun with the cow-boys." Young and enterprising, Paulding readily acceded to the proposal; and, after providing himself with a musket, and other requisites, he accompanied his reckless associates to Tarrytown, where they achieved an adventure that immortalized their names, and saved their country from inevitable ruin.

CHAPTER XIV.

THE SPY AND THE TRAITOR.

——————Is there not some chosen curse,
Some hidden thunder in the stores of heaven,
Red with uncommon wrath, to blast the man
Who owes his greatness to his country's ruin!
ADDISON.

About the middle of September, the commander-in-chief, attended by Generals LaFayette and Knox, with a splendid retinue, left the American camp in New Jersey, and proceeded to Hartford, in Connecticut, for the purpose of holding a conference with the commanding officers of the French fleet and army, which had lately arrived at Rhode Island. In the meantime, the command of the American army devolved on Major-General Greene, whose head-quarters were at Tappan, where the corps to which Crosby was attached, was now stationed.

A week had elapsed since the departure of Washington, and no incident of importance had occurred. Greene had learned, through the medium of his spies, that some secret expedition was on foot, at the city of New York; but of its nature and direction, he could not obtain the smallest hint. On the ninth day, however, at three o'clock in the morning, an alarm was spread through the American camp; and, in a few minutes, all were under arms. A detachment, consisting of two regiments, was immediately ordered to march to West Point, with all possible expedition; and the rest of the troops were directed to hold themselves in readiness to march at a moment's warning.

While every one was pondering in

his own mind the probable object of this sudden movement, and vainly endeavoring to conjecture the cause, a general order was promulgated, which soon explained it to the whole army, filling every breast with astonishment and indignation. The following communication, in the orders of General Greene, was read by the Adjutants to their respective regiments.

"Treason, of the blackest dye, was yesterday discovered. General Arnold, who commanded at West Point, lost to every sentiment of honor, of private and public obligation, was about to deliver up that important post into the hands of the enemy. Such an event must have given the American cause a dangerous, if not a fatal, wound. Happily the treason has been timely discovered, to prevent the fatal misfortune. The providential train of circumstances, which led to it, affords the most convincing proofs that the liberties of America are the object of Divine protection. At the same time that the treason is to be regretted, the General cannot help congratulating the army on the happy discovery. Our enemies, despairing of carrying their point by force, are practicing every base art to effect, by bribery and corruption, what they cannot accomplish in a manly way.

"Great honor is due to the American army, that this is the first instance of treason of the kind, where many were to be expected from the nature of our dispute. The brightest ornament in the character of the American soldier is, their having been proof against all the arts and seductions of an insidious enemy.

"Arnold has made his escape to the enemy; but Major Andre, the Adjutant-General of the British army, who came out, as a spy, to negociate the business, is our prisoner."

The particulars of Andre's arrest and trial are familiar to every reader.* Lieutenant-Colonel Jameson was then the commanding officer on the American lines, above the neutral ground; and to him was Andre conducted by his incorruptible captors, Paulding, Van Wart, and Williams; whom, in our last chapter, we left on their way to Tarrytown. The prisoner immediately requested Jameson to inform Arnold, by letter, that John Anderson was taken on his way to New York, with which request the Lieutenant Colonel immediately complied. Arnold received the letter about ten o'clock in the morning, while at breakfast. Two of Washington's aids. Major Shaw and Dr. M'Henry, had just arrived, and were at breakfast at Arnold's table. His confusion was visible, but no one could divine the cause.

Struck with the pressing danger of his situation, momentarily expecting Washington's return from Hartford, the traitor called instantly for a horse.

"A horse!" exclaimed he, as he started from the table. "Any one— even if a wagon horse!"

He then bade a hasty adieu to his wife, and enjoining a positive order on the messenger not to inform any one that he was the bearer of a letter from Colonel Jameson, he repaired to his barge, and ordered the coxswain, with eight oarsmen, to proceed down the river, to the sloop-of-war Vulture, which he reached in safety, under the

---

* See Appendix, No. XVIII.

protection of a flag, and which immediately set sail for New York.

Washington arrived at Arnold's quarters in two hours after the traitor had escaped. Not finding Arnold at home, and being informed that he had gone to West Point, Washington passed over the river to view the works at that post; but not finding Arnold, he returned, in the hope of meeting him at his quarters. But here he was again disappointed, for no person could account for his absence.

Mrs. Arnold was now in her chamber, in great agitation and distress, deprived of her reason, and Dr. Eustis in attendance. At a lucid interval, she requested to see Washington; but by the time he reached the chamber, her distraction returned, and she knew him not. He then withdrew, and, repairing to the dining-room, sat down to dinner, but soon arose again with apparent agitation. He then took Colonel Lamb aside, and expressed to him his suspicion that Arnold had deserted to the enemy. In less than two hours it was ascertained that the conjecture was too well founded; for a despatch arrived from Colonel Jameson, with an account of the capture of Andre, accompanied by his own letter of confession. The prisoner was conducted to West Point, and from thence to headquarters at Tappan, where preparations were made for his trial by a court-martial.

Washington immediately proceeded to the camp, at Tappan; and, the moment he arrived, sent for Major Lee, who was posted, with the Virginia light-horse, some distance in front. "This officer repaired to headquarters with celerity, and found the General in his marquee alone, busily engaged in writing. So soon as Lee entered, he was requested to take a seat, and a bundle of papers, lying on the table, was given him for perusal.

"In these papers, much information was detailed, tending to prove that Arnold was not alone in the base conspiracy just detected; but that the poison had spread; and that a Major-General, whose name was not concealed, was certainly as guilty as Arnold himself.

"This information had just been received by Washington, through his confidential agents in New York; and Lee immediately suggested the probability that the whole was a contrivance of Sir Henry Clinton, in order to destroy that confidence between the commander and his officers, on which the success of military operations depend.

"'The suggestion,' replied Washington, 'is plausible, and deserves due consideration. It early occurred to my own mind, and has not been slightly regarded. But the same suggestion applies to no officer more forcibly than a few days ago it would have done to General Arnold, now known to be a traitor.

"'I have sent for you, sir, in the expectation that you have in your corps individuals capable and willing to undertake an indispensable, delicate, and hazardous project. Whoever comes forward on this occasion, will lay me under great obligations personally; and, in behalf of the United States, I will reward him amply. No time is to be lost; he must proceed, if possible, this night. My object is to probe to the bottom the afflicting intelligence contained in the papers you have just read, to seize Arnold, and, by getting him, to save Andre. They are all connected. While my emissary is engaged in preparing means for the seizure of Arnold, the guilt of others can be traced; and the timely delivery of Arnold to me, will possibly put it into my power to restore the amiable and unfortunate Andre to his friends.'" *

Lee readily undertook to find a member of his corps capable of executing this hazardous service, but doubted whether he would consent to engage in an enterprise, the first step to which was desertion. The person he selected was the Sergeant-Major of the corps, Champe by name, and a Virginian by birth; who, after much persuasion, consented to undertake it. He that night deserted to the enemy; and, though closely pursued, reached Pawles' Hook in safety, and was taken on board a British galley, which conveyed him to New York, where he was closely examined by Sir Henry Clinton, who gave him a letter of introduction to Arnold, who immediately appointed him one of his recruiting sergeants.

In the meantime, the interposition of Sir Henry Clinton, who was extremely anxious to save his much-loved aid-de-camp, still continued; and it was expected that the examination of witnesses, and the defence of the prisoner, would protract the decision of the court of inquiry, which assembled on the twenty-ninth of the month, and give sufficient time for the consummation of the project committed to Champe, from whom information had just been received that gave some hopes of his success. But a complete disappointment took place from a quarter unforeseen and unexpected. Andre disdained defence, and prevented the examination of witnesses, by confessing the character in which he stood. He was consequently declared to be a spy, and condemned to suffer accordingly.

Washington approved the sentence, and ordered his execution to take place on the first day of October. at five o'clock in the afternoon. In this decision he was warranted by the very unpromising intelligence contained in another letter from Champe, which he had just received; by the still existing implication of other officers in Arnold's conspiracy; by a due regard to public opinion; and by real tenderness to the prisoner himself.

Neither Congress nor the nation could have been, with propriety, informed of the cause of the delay, had any been interposed; and without such information, it must have excited in both, alarm and suspicion. The secret was known to none but Washington, Lee, Champe, and a confidential agent in New York. Andre himself could not have been instrusted with it; and would, consequently, have attributed the unlooked-for event to the expostulation and exertion of Sir Henry Clinton, which would not fail to produce in his breast expectations of ultimate relief; to excite which would have been cruel, as the realization of such expectation depended only on a possible, but improbable, contingency.

On the first day of October, at the hour appointed, a large concourse of people assembled to witness the execution of the gallant and unfortunate young officer. The gallows was erected, and the grave and coffin prepared; but a flag of truce arrived

---

* See the Memoirs of Major Henry Lee.

with a communication from Sir Henry Clinton, making another and further proposals for the release of Major Andre; in consequence of which the execution was postponed until twelve o'clock on the following day.

This flag was accompanied by the British General Robertson, with Andrew Elliott and William Smith, Esquires, for the purpose of pleading for the release of Major Andre, the royal army being in the greatest affliction on the occasion.

Elliot and Smith, not being military officers, were not permitted to land; but General Greene was appointed, by the commander-in-chief, to meet Robertson, at Dobb's ferry, and to receive his communications. He had, however, nothing material to urge, but that Andre had come on shore under the sanction of a flag, and therefore could not be considered as a spy. But this plea was contradicted by Andre's own confession.

"Having failed in this point, Robertson requested that the opinion of disinterested persons might be taken; and proposed Generals Knyphausen and Rochambeau, as proper persons. This proposition could not be acceded to.

"Robertson then had recourse to threats of retaliation, on some people in New York and Charleston; but he was told that such conversation could not be heard nor understood.

"He next urged the release of Andre on motives of humanity, saying he wished an intercourse of such civilities as might lessen the horrors of war, and cited instances of Sir Henry Clinton's merciful disposition; adding that Andre possessed a great share of that gentleman's affection and esteem, and that he would be infinitely obliged if he was spared. He offered, that if his earnest wishes were complied with, to engage that any prisoner in their possession, whom Washington might name, should be immediately set at liberty."*

But all intercession was fruitless; and least of all availed a letter to Washington, of which Robertson was the bearer, from the traitor Arnold, filled with threats of retaliation, and the accountability of Washington for the torrents of blood that might be spilt, if he should order the execution of Andre! It is difficult to say which created the most astonishment in the breast of Greene—that Arnold should have the consummate effrontery to write such a letter; or that Robertson should consent to be the bearer of it.

Nothing, of course, was effected by this interview, and the messengers returned in despondency to New York. Andre, in the meantime, during his confinement, trial, and condemnation, evinced a composure and dignity of mind, that enlisted the sympathies of all in his favor. Not a murmur escaped him; while the civilities and attentions bestowed on him, were gratefully and politely acknowledged. Having left a mother and two sisters in England, he was heard to mention them in terms of the tenderest affection; and in his letter to Sir Henry Clinton, he recommended them to his particular attention.

Crosby assures us that, though every one acknowledged the policy of the sentence, there was scarcely one that spoke of his approaching fate

---

* See Thacher's Journal, p. 271.

without evincing the deepest emotions of sympathy. The principal guard officer, who was constantly in the room with Andre, informed Crosby that when the fatal hour arrived, and the prisoner was summoned to attend, he heard and complied without any visible emotion; and while all present were more or less affected, he retained a serene countenance, with calmness and composure of mind.

The prisoner walked from the stone house in which he had been confined, between two subaltern officers, arm in arm. A large detachment of troops was paraded, and an immense concourse of people assembled, to witness the awful ceremony. As the situation of Crosby, in the procession, was not so convenient for observation, we will give the remaining particulars in the language of Dr. Thacher, to whose excellent journal we have already acknowledged ourselves largely indebted.

"During the solemn march to the fatal spot," says the Doctor, "I was so near as to observe every movement, and participate in every emotion, which the melancholy scene was calculated to produce. The eyes of the immense multitude were fixed on the prisoner; who, rising superior to the fears of death, appeared as if conscious of the dignified deportment which he displayed. He betrayed no want of fortitude, but retained a complacent smile on his countenance, and politely bowed to several gentlemen whom he knew, which was respectfully returned.

"It was his earnest desire to be shot, as being the mode of death most comfortable to the feelings of a military man, and he had indulged the hope that his request would be granted. At that moment, therefore, when suddenly he came in view of the gallows, he involuntarily started backward, and made a pause. 'Why this emotion, sir?' said an officer at his side. Instantly recovering his composure, he said—'I am reconciled to my death, but I detest the mode.'

"While waiting, and standing near the gallows," continues Dr. Thacher, "I observed some degree of trepidation; placing his foot on a stone, and rolling it over, and choking in his throat, as if attempting to swallow. So soon, however, as he perceived that things were in readiness, he stepped quickly into the wagon; and, at this moment, he appeared to shrink; but, instantly elevating his head with firmness, he said, 'It will be but a momentary pang;' and taking from his pocket two white handkerchiefs, the provost marshall, with one, loosely pinioned his arms; and, with the other, the victim, after taking off his hat and stock, bandaged his own eyes, with perfect firmness, which melted the hearts and moistened the cheeks, not only of his servant, but of the throng of spectators.

"The rope being appended to the gallows, he slipped the noose over his own head, and adjusted it to his neck, without the assistance of the awkward executioner. Colonel Scammel now informed him that he had an opportunity to speak, if he desired it. He raised the handkerchief from his eyes, and said—'I pray you to bear me witness that I meet my fate like a brave man.' The wagon being now removed from under him, he was suspended, and instantly expired. It proved, indeed, 'but a momentary pang.'

MEMOIRS OF ENOCH CROSBY.

"He was dressed in his royal regimentals and boots; and his remains, in the same dress, were placed in an ordinary coffin, and interred at the foot of the gallows; and the spot was consecrated by the tears of thousands."*

The enterprise of Champe was well concerted, and would probably have succeeded but for an unforeseen accident. On the day preceding the night fixed upon for the execution of the plot, Arnold removed his quarters to another part of the town; and Champe, with all Arnold's new recruits, were transferred from their barracks to one of the transports. He was thus compelled to proceed with Arnold to Virginia, where he made his escape, and rejoined the American Army soon after it had passed the Congaree, in pursuit of Lord Rawdon.

CONCLUSION.

Now are our brows bound with victorious
  wreaths,
Our bruised arms hung up for monuments;
Our stern alarms changed to merry meetings,
Our dreadful marches, to delightful measures;
Grim-visaged war hath smooth'd his wrinkled
  front.   SHAKESPEARE.

A few weeks after the foregoing events, intelligence was received of a very brilliant exploit of the militia in North Carolina, under Colonels Campbell, Cleveland, Shelby, and Sevier; who, with about three thousand volunteers, attacked and defeated Major Ferguson, at the head of a large force of refugees and tories. Ferguson, with one hundred and fifty of his men, were killed, and eight hundred and ten taken prisoners, of whom one hundred and fifty were wounded. They also took fifteen hundred stand of arms. Of the Americans, Colonel Williams was mortally wounded; about twenty killed, and a number disabled. Ten of the prisoners were immediately hung as traitors. This is called the Battle of King's Mountain.

But few incidents occurred in the vicinity of New York, during the ensuing winter and spring. In July following, the French and American armies formed a junction at White Plains, from whence they proceeded to New Jersey. After some ingenious manœuvering to deceive the British with respect to his real designs, Washington suddenly marched to the south, with the combined armies, leaving Sir Henry Clinton under the apprehension of an immediate attack on the city of New York.

The result of this southern expedition is well known. Cornwallis surrendered his army at Yorktown, and the ministry of England gave up the contest in despair. Our independence was acknowledged, peace restored, and the smiles of joy scattered over the long afflicted country.

Crosby remained, with the division of the army which was left under the command of Heath, for the defence of the posts in the Highlands, until the period of his engagement had expired. He then retired to Southeast, where his father died shortly afterwards; and there he has since resided up to the present day.

He cultivates a small farm, the product of his own industry, since the peace of 1783; having received, for all his revolutionary services, only the trifling pittance of two hundred and fifty dollars.† He has had

---

* In the autumn of 1821, the remains of Major Andre were disinterred, and transported to England.

† "Never!" said Birch, speaking out; "was it for money I did all this."—*Spy, Vol. ii. p.* 274.

two wives, the last of which was the widow of Colonel Greene; and he is the father of four children, two sons and two daughters, who are grown up, and settled in the county of Westchester. For twenty-eight years he was justice of the peace in the town of Southeast; and for the last fourteen years he has held the office of deacon in the Presbyterian church. He has likewise held that of deputy-sheriff for the county. He is uni- versally respected by his neighbors, acquaintance, and fellow-citizens generally; and now enjoys a "green old age," which, we trust, will be succeeded by a happy immortality; for Enoch Crosby was, "for years, a faithful and unrequited servant of his country. Though man does not, may God reward him for his conduct."*

---

* See the concluding paragraph of the "Spy."

OLD TRINITY CHURCH, FISHKILL.
[See Page 143.]

APPENDIX.

Note I.—Page 21.
DESTRUCTION OF THE TEA IN BOSTON HARBOR.

The Americans, determined to oppose the revenue system of the English parliament, in every possible shape, considered the attempt of the East India Company, to evade the resolutions of the colonies, and dispose of teas in America, as an indirect mode of taxation, sanctioned by the authority of parliament. Several public meetings were held on the subject, particularly in the town of Boston. At one of these meetings, while the assembled multitude were in quiet consultation, on the safest mode to prevent the sale and consumption of an herb, *noxious* at least to the political constitution, the debates were interrupted by the entrance of the Sheriff, with an order from the governor, styling them an illegal assembly, and directing their immediate dispersion.

This authoritative mandate was treated with great contempt, and the Sheriff instantly hissed out of the house. A confused murmur ensued, both within and without the walls; but in a few moments all was again quiet, and the meeting adjourned without delay.

Within an hour after this was known abroad, there appeared a great number of persons, clad like the aborigines of the wilderness, with tomahawks in their hands, and clubs on their shoulders, who, without the least molestation, marched through the streets with silent solemnity, and amidst innumerable spectators, proceeded to the wharves, boarded the ships, demanded the keys, and without much deliberation knocked open the chests, and emptied several thousand weight of the finest teas into the ocean. No opposition was made, though surrounded by the king's ships; all was silence and dismay.

This done, the procession returned through the town in the same order and solemity as observed in the outset of their attempt. No other disorder took place, and it was observed the stillest night ensued that Boston had enjoyed for several months.

The number of persons disguised as Indians is variously stated—none put it lower than 60, none higher than 80. The destruction was effected by the disguised persons, and some young men who volunteered; one of the latter collected the tea which fell into the shoes of himself and companions, and put it into a phial, and sealed it up;—which phial is now in his possession,—containing the same tea. The contrivers of this measure, and those who carried it into effect, will never be known; some few persons have been mentioned as being among the disguised; but there are many and obvious reasons why secresy then, and concealment since, were necessary.—None of those persons who were confidently said to have been of the party, (except some who were then minors or very young men,) have ever admitted that they were so. Mr. Samuel Adams is thought to have been in the counselling of this exploit, and many other men who were leaders in the political affairs of the times; and the hall of council is said to have been in the back room of Edes and Gill's printing office, at the corner of the alley leading to Brattle-street from Court-street. There are very few alive now, who helped to empty the chests of tea, and these few will probably be as prudent as those who have gone before them."

No. II.—Page 23.

FEMALE PATRIOTISM.

The following anecdote, which is too well authenticated to be disputed, furnishes one instance, among thousands, of that heroic spirit and love of liberty which characterized the American females during the struggle for independence.

"A good lady—we knew her when she had grown old—in 1775, lived on the sea-board, about a day's march from Boston, where the British army then was. By some unaccountable accident, a rumor was spread, in town and country, in and about there, that the r*egulars* were on a full march for that place, and would probably arrive in three hours at farthest. This was after the battle of Lexington, and all, as might be well supposed, was in sad confusion—some were boiling with rage and full of fight, some with fear and confusion, some hiding their treasures, and others flying for life. In this wild moment, when most people, in some way or other, were frightened from their property, our heroine, who had two sons, one about nineteen years of age, the other about sixteen, was seen by our informant, preparing them to discharge their duty. The eldest she was able to equip in fine style—she took her husband's fowling-piece, 'made for duck or plover,' (the good man being absent on a coasting voyage to Virginia,) and with it the powder horn and shot-bag; but the lad thinking the duck and goose shot not quite the size to kill regulars, his mother took a chisel, cut up her pewter spoons, and hammered them into slugs, and put them into his bag, and he set off in great earnest but thought he would call one moment and see the parson, who said, 'Well done, my brave boy—God preserve you'—and on he went in the way of his duty. The youngest was importunate for his equipments, but his mother could find nothing to arm him with but an old rusty sword; the boy seemed rather unwilling to risk himself with this alone, but lingered in the street, in a state of hesitation, when his mother thus upbraided him. 'You John H*****, what will your father say, if he hears that a child of his is afraid to meet the British?—go along; beg or borrow a gun, or you will find one, child—some coward, I dare say, will be running away, then take his gun and march forward, and if you come back, and I hear you have not behaved like a man, I shall carry the blush of shame on my face to the grave.' She then shut the door, wiped the tear from her eye, and waited the issue; the boy joined the march. Such a woman could not have cowards for her sons. Instances of refined and delicate pride and affection occurred, at that period, every day, in different places; and in fact this disposition and feeling was then so common, that it now operates as one great cause of our not having more facts of this kind recorded. What few there are remembered should not be lost. Nothing great or glorious was ever achieved which women did not act in, advise, or consent to."

No. III.—Page 23.
BATTLE OF BUNKER HILL.

The heights of Charlestown were so situated as to make the possession of them a matter of great consequence, to either of the contending parties. Orders were therefore issued, June 16th, by the provincial commanders, that a detachment of a thousand men should intrench upon Breed's Hill.* Here the Americans, between mid night and morning, with uncommon expedition and silence, threw up a a small redoubt, which the British did not discover till the morning of the 17th, when they began an incessant firing, and continued it till afternoon. With the intrepidity of veteran soldiers, the Americans bore this fire, and proceeded to finish their redoubt and to throw up a breastwork, extending eastward of it to the bottom of the hill.—About noon, General Gage detached Major-General Howe, and Brigadier-General Pigot, with the flower of his army, in two detachments, amounting in the whole to nearly 3,000 men. They landed at a point about 150 or 200 rods south-east of the redoubt, and deliberately prepared for the attack. While the troops, who first landed, were waiting for a reinforcement, the Americans on the left wing towards Mystic River, for their security, pulled up some adjoining post and rail fence, and set it down in two parallel lines near each other, and filled the space between with hay, which the day before was mowed and remained in the adjacent field. The British troops, in the meantime, formed in two lines, and about 3 o clock advanced slowly towards the Americans. The hills and steeples in Boston, and the circumjacent country, were crowded with anxious spectators of the dubious conflict. While some felt for the honor of the British troops, multitudes, with a keener sensibility, felt for the liberties of a great and growing country.—The attack commenced on the part of the British troops. The Americans had the precaution, in obedience to the orders of their commanding officer, to reserve their fire till their enemies had approached within 10 or 12 rods of their works. They then began a well-directed and furious discharge of small arms, which mowed down their enemies in ranks, and occasioned a disorderly and precipitate retreat. Their officers rallied them with difficulty, and pushed them forward with their swords, to a second attack. They were in the same manner put to flight a second time. With still greater difficulty they were forced by General Howe to a third attack. By this time the powder of the Americans began to fail, and their redoubt was attacked on two sides. Under these circumstances, a retreat was ordered; the left wing of the Americans, north-

---
* Historians, through mistake, have called the hill where the battle was fought, *Bunker Hill*, which is a quarter of a mile north of Breed's. or Russell's Hill, where the battle was fought.

east of the redoubt, still continuing their fire, ignorant of what had taken place on the right, till the British had nearly surrounded them. The retreat was affected, with an inconsiderable loss, considering the greater part of the distance they had to pass was completely exposed to the incessant fire of the Glasgow man-of-war, and two floatting batteries. In this retreat Warren fell.

During the heat of this bloody action, by order of General Gage, Charlestown was set on fire, by a battery on Cops Hill, in Boston, and a party from the Somerset man-of-war, lying in Charles River, and nearly 400 houses, including six public buildings, were consumed, with their furniture, &c., valued by nineteen men, under oath, at £156,900 specie; and 2,000 persons reduced from affluence and mediocrity, to the most aggravated poverty and exile.

The number of Americans engaged in this memorable action was only 1,500. There have been few battles in modern wars in which, all circumstances considered, there was a greater slaughter of men than in this short engagement. The loss of the British, as acknowledged by General Gage, amounted to 1,054 men. Nineteen commissioned officers were killed, and 70 wounded. The loss of the Americans was 77 killed, 278 wounded and missing.

The death of Major-General Warren, who four days before had received his commission, and, who, having no command assigned him, fought this day as a volunteer, was particularly and greatly lamented. "To the purest patriotism, and the most undaunted bravery, he added the eloquence of an accomplished orator, and the wisdom of an able statesman."

No. IV.—Page 28.

DORCHESTER HEIGHTS.

On the 22d of February, 1776, it was evident that some great preparations were on foot, in the American army, for some important event. Orders were received, in the hospital department, to prepare lint and bandages, to the amount of two thousand, for fractured limbs and other gun-shot wounds. On the second of March, a very heavy discharge of cannon and mortars commenced from all the works at Cambridge and Roxbury, which continued at intervals for two days. This, it seems, was merely a finesse to draw the enemy's attention to a wrong quarter. On the fourth, the designs of Washington were made known to the army.

"The object in view," says Dr. Thacher, "is now generally understood to be the occupying and fortifying of the advantageous heights of Dorchester. A detachment of our troops is ordered to march for this purpose this evening; and our regiment, with several others, has received orders to march at 4 o'clock in the morning, to relieve them. We are favored with a full bright moon, and the night is remarkably mild and pleasant; the preparations are immense; more than three hundred loaded carts are in motion. By the great exertions of General Mifflin, our Quartermaster-General, the requisite number of teams has been procured. The covering party of eight hundred men advance in front. Then follow the carts with the intrenching tools; after which, the working party of twelve hundred, commanded by General Thomas, of Kingston. Next in the martial procession are a train of carts, loaded with fascines and hay, screwed into large bundles of seven or eight hundred weight. The whole procession moved on in solemn silence, and with perfect order and regularity; while the continued roar of cannon serves to engage the attention and divert the enemy from the main object.

At about four o'clock our regiment followed to the heights of Dorchester as a relief party. On passing Dorchester Neck I observed a vast number of large bundles of screwed hay, arranged in a line next the enemy, to protect our troops from a raking fire, to which we should have been greatly exposed, while passing and repassing. The carts were still in motion with materials: some of them have made three or four trips. On the heights we found two forts in considerable forwardness, and sufficient for a defence against small arms and grape shot. The amount of labor performed during the night, considering the earth is frozen eighteen inches deep, is almost incredible. The enemy having discovered our works in the morning, commenced a tremendous cannonade from the forts in Boston, and from their shipping in the harbor. Cannon shot are continually rolling and rebounding over the hill; and it is astonishing to observe how little our soldiers are terrified by them.—During the forenoon we were in momentary expectation of witnessing an awful scene; nothing less than the carnage of Breed's Hill battle was expected. The royal troops are perceived to be in motion, as if embarking to pass the harbor, and land on Dorchester shore, to attack our works. The hills and elevations in this vicinity are covered with spectators to witness deeds of horror in the expected conflict. His Excellency General Washington is present, animating and encouraging the soldiers, and they in their turn manifest their joy, and express a warm desire for the approach of the enemy; each man knows his place, and is resolute to execute his duty. Our breast-works are strengthened, and among the means of defence are a great number of barrels, filled with stones and sand, arranged in front of our works; which are to be put in motion and made to roll down the hill, to break the ranks and legs of the assailants as they advance. These are the preparations for blood and slaughter! Gracious God! if it be determined in thy Providence that thousands of our fellow creatures shall this day be slain, let thy wrath be appeased, and in mercy grant, that victory be on the side of our suffering, bleeding country.—The anxious day has closed, and the enemy has failed to molest us. From appearances, however, there are strong reasons to suppose, that they have only postponed their meditated work till another day. It is presumed that the martial fire, which has been enkindled in the breasts of our soldiery, will not be extinguished during the night, and that they will not rest quietly under their disappointment. Early in the morning of the 6th, our regiment was relieved from its tour of duty, and I bade adieu to Dorchester heights, without being called to dress a single wound. Not more than two or three men were killed or wounded during the twenty-four hours.—Some of the British troops were seen to embark, and pass down towards the castle last evening, to be in readiness, it was supposed, in conjunction with others, to attack our works this morning; but a most violent storm came on in the night, and still continuing, obliges General Howe to abandon his enterprise; and thus has a kind Providence seen fit to frustrate a design, which must have been attended with immense slaughter and bloodshed. General Howe must now be sensible of his exposed situation, and be convinced of the immediate necessity of evacuating the town of Boston, if he would prevent the sacrifice of his fleet and army."

No. V.—Page 31.
PATRIOTIC SACRIFICES.

"From whatever cause it proceeded, it is certain, that a disposition to do, to suffer, and to accommodate, spread from breast to breast, and from colony to colony, beyond the reach of human calculation. It seemed as though one mind inspired the whole. The merchants put far behind them the gains of trade, and cheerfully submitted to a total stoppage of business, in obedience to the recommendation of men, invested with no legislative powers. The cultivators of the soil, with great unanimity, assented to the determination, that the hard-earned produce of their farms should remain unshipped, although in case of a free exportation, many would have been eager to have purchased it from them, at advanced prices. The sons and daughters of ease renounced imported conveniences, and voluntarily engaged to eat, drink, and wear, only such articles as their country afforded. These sacrifices were made, not from the pressure of present distress, but on the generous principle of sympathy, with an invaded sister colony, and the prudent policy of guarding against a precedent which might, in a future day, operate against their liberties.

The season of universal distress exhibited a striking proof how practicable it is for mankind to sacrifice ease, pleasure, and interest, when the mind is strongly excited by its passions. In the midst of their sufferings, cheerfulness appeared in the face of all the people. They counted every thing cheap in comparison with liberty, and readily gave up whatever tended to endanger it. A noble strain of generosity and mutual support was generally excited. A great and powerful diffusion of public spirit took place. The animation of the times raised the actors in these scenes above themselves, and excited them to deeds of self denial, which the interested prudence of calmer seasons can scarcely credit."

No. VI.—Page 38.
EXECUTION OF CAPTAIN HALE.

The particulars of this tragical event, sanctioned by General Hull, who was knowing to them at the time, are thus related by Miss H. Adams, in her History of New England.

"The retreat of General Washington left the British in complete possession of Long Island. What would be their future operations, remained uncertain. To obtain information of their situation, their strength, and future movements, was of high importance. For this purpose, General Washington applied to Colonel Knowlton, who commanded a regiment of light infantry, which formed the van of the American army, and desired him to adopt some mode of gaining the necessary information. Colonel Knowlton communicated this request to Captain Hale, of Connecticut, who was then a Captain in his regiment. This young officer, animated by a sense of duty, and considering that an opportunity presented itself by which he might be useful to his country, at once offered himself a volunteer for this hazardous service. He passed in disguise to Long Island. examined every part of the British army, and obtained the best possible information respecting their situation and future operations.

In his attempt to return, he was apprehended, carried before Sir William Howe, and the proof of his object was so clear, that he frankly acknowledged who he was, and what were his views.

Sir William Howe at once gave an order to the provost marshall to execute him the next morning.

This order was accordingly executed in a most unfeeling manner, and by as great a savage as ever disgraced humanity. A clergyman, whose attendance he desired, was refused him; a bible, for a moment's devotion, was not procured, though he requested it. Letters, which on the morning of his execution, he wrote to his mother, and other friends, were destroyed; and this very extraordinary reason given by the provost marshal, 'that the rebels should not know that they had a man in their army, who could die with so much firmness.'

Unknown to all around him, without a single friend to offer him the least consolation, thus fell as amiable and as worthy a young man as America could boast, with this as his dying observation, 'that he only lamented he had but one life to lose for his country.' How superior to the dying words of Andre. Though the manner of his execution will ever be abhorred by every friend to humanity and religion, yet there cannot be a question but that the sentence was conformable to the rules of war, and the practice of nations in similar cases.

It is, however, a justice due to the character of Captain Hale, to observe, that his motives for engaging in this service were entirely different from those which generally influence others in similar circumstances. Neither expectation of promotion nor pecuniary reward, induced him to this attempt. A sense of duty, a hope that he might in this way be useful to his country, and an opinion which he had adopted, that every kind of service necessary to the public good, became honorable by being necessary, were the great motives which induced him to engage in an enterprise, by which his connections lost a most amiable friend and his country one of its most promising supporters.

The fate of this unfortunate young man excites the most interesting reflections.

To see such a character, in the flower of youth, cheerfully treading in the most hazardous paths, influenced by the purest intentions, and only emulous to do good to his country, without the imputation of a crime, fall a victim to policy, must have been wounding to the feelings even of his enemies.

Should a comparison be drawn between Major Andre and Captain Hale, injustice would be done to the latter, should he not be placed on an equal ground with the former. Whilst almost every historian of the American Revolution, has celebrated the virtues and lamented the fate of Andre, *Hale has remained unnoticed, and it is scarcely known that such a character ever existed.*

To the memory of Andre, his country has erected the most magnificent monuments, and bestowed on his family the highest honors and most liberal rewards. To the memory of Hale not a stone has been erected, nor an inscription to preserve his ashes from insult."

No. VII.—Page 74.

BATTLE OF TRENTON.

"Washington having obtained information that the advanced party of the enemy, consisting of about fifteen hundred Hessians and British light horse, under command of Colonel Rahl, was stationed at the village of Trenton, concerted a plan for taking them by surprise. For this purpose, he made choice of Christmas night, under the idea that in consequence of the festivity, they might be less vigilantly guarded. At this time the whole force under his immediate command did not exceed three thousand men. At the head of about two thousand four hundred men, one division being commanded by General Greene, and the other by Gen. Sullivan, he crossed the river Delaware in boats, in the night of the 25th of December, during a severe storm of snow and rain. The passage of the boats was rendered extremely difficult and hazardous by the ice, and part of the troops and cannon actually failed in the attempt. Having landed on the Jersey shore, he had nine miles to march, and he reached the village about 7 o'clock in the morning with such promptitude and secrecy. so as to attack the enemy almost as soon as his approach was discovered. A smart firing ensued, which continued but a few minutes, when the enemy, finding themselves surrounded, threw down their arms, and surrended as prisoners. Colonel Rahl, the commanding officer, was mortally wounded and several other officers were wounded and left at Trenton on their parole. About thirty-five soldiers were killed, sixty wounded, and nine hundred and forty-eight, including thirty officers, were taken prisoners, amounting in all to one thousand and forty-eight. Of the continentals. not more than ten, it is supposed, were killed and wounded. General Washington re-crossed the Delaware the same day in triumph, bringing off six excellent brass cannon, about one thousand two hundred small arms, and three standards, with a quantity of baggage, &c. This very brilliant achievement is highly honorable to the commander-in-chief, and to all that were engaged in the enterprise. We are sanguine in the hope that this most auspicious event will be productive of the happiest effects, by inspiring our dejected army, and dispelling that panic of dispair into which the people have been plunged. General Washington allowed the Hessian prisoners to retain their baggage, and sent them into the interior of Pennsylvania, ordering that they be treated with favor and humanity. This conduct, so contrary to their expectations, excited their gratitude and veneration for their amiable conqueror, whom they styled, 'a very good rebel.'"—*Thacher.*

No. VIII.—Page 74.

BATTLE OF PRINCETON.

"After his success at Trenton, General Washington received considerable reinforcements of troops from Virginia and Maryland, and some regiments of militia, which enabled him again to cross the Delaware into the Jerseys, and face the enemy. While at Trenton, Lord Cornwallis advanced to attack him, and a severe cannonade commenced. In the evening, General Washington ordered a great number of fires to be lighted up, and, leaving a sufficient number of men to keep them burning during the night, to deceive the enemy, stole a march with his main army, taking a circuitous route, and, at 9 o'clock the next morning, attacked three regiments of the British, who were posted at Princeton, routed them, and drove them from their redoubts. By this masterly manœuvre, the enemy lost about five hundred in killed, wounded, and prisoners. The loss on our side is very inconsiderable in point of numbers, but we have to lament the death of Brigadier-General Mercer, a brave officer who commanded the Virginia militia. The fact is published, that after General Mercer surrended himself, the enemy, deaf to the voice of humanity, stabbed him with their bayonets, and with the butt end of a musket battered and disfigured his face in a savage manner. It is to be remarked, that on this memorable occasion, Lord Cornwallis was completely out-generaled; while he was expecting to find the continental army at their lighted fires at Trenton, he was astonished and confounded to hear the firing occasioned by this same army, beating up their quarters twelve miles in his rear. His lordship immediately repaired by a forced march to Princeton, but arrived too late to retaliate on his vigilant antagonist, who had taken up his route to Morristown. Finding that the continentals were out of his reach, his lordship proceeded, without halting, to Brunswick. Stratagems in war, when wisely concerted, and judiciously executed, are considered as characterizing a military genius of superior order, and is a quality of inestimable value in every commander. It is often exultingly remarked in our camp, that Washington was born for the salvation of his country, and that he is endowed with all the talents and abilities necessary to qualify him for the great undertaking. The militia of Jersey, immediately on their being liberated from the control of the British, flew to arms, exasperated and stimulated by a recollection of their sufferings, and have become their most bitter and determined enemies; and are very active and vigilant in harassing them on all occasions, keeping a continual watch, and cutting off small parties whenever opportunities offer. It is gratifying to the army, that Congress have conferred on their Generalissimo more ample powers, and appointed him *Dictator* for the *limited* term of six months; to reform and new model the military arrange-

ments, in such manner as he may judge most advantageous for the public service. Much good is expected to result from this measure."
—*Thacher's Journal.*

No. IX.—Page 79.
CAPTURE OF PRESCOTT.

"In the month of July, 1777, Lieutenant-Colonel Barton, of the Rhode Island militia, planned a bold exploit for the purpose of surprising and taking Major-General Prescott, the commanding officer of the royal army at Newport. Taking with him, in the night, about forty men in two boats with oars muffled, he had the address to elude the vigilance of the ships of war, and guard boats, and having arrived undiscovered at the quarters of General Prescott, they were taken for the sentinels, and the General was not alarmed till his captors were at the door of his lodging chamber, which was fast closed. A negro man, named Prince, instantly thrust his beetle head through the pannel door, and seized his victim while in bed. The General's aid-de-camp leaped from a window undressed, and attempted to escape, but was taken, and with the General brought off in safety. In re-passing the water-guards, General Prescott said to Colonel Barton, "Sir, I did not think it possible you could escape the vigilance of the water-guards."—This is the second time that General Prescott has been a prisoner in our hands within two years. This adventure is extremely honourable to the enterprising spirit of Colonel Barton, and is considered as ample retaliation for the capture of General Lee by Colonel Harcourt. The event occasions great joy and exultation, as it puts in our possession an officer of equal rank with General Lee, by which means an exchange may be obtained. Congress resolved that an elegant sword should be presented to Colonel Barton for his brave exploit. It has been ascertained that General Howe has relaxed in his rigid treatment of General Lee, and conducted towards him in a manner suitable to his rank. The Hessian officers, on whom retaliation had been inflicted, are also restored to their former condition as prisoners of war."—*Thacher's Journal.*

No. X.—Page 79.
SIEGE OF FORT STANWIX.

"On the third of August, 1777, Colonel St. Leger, and Sir John Johnson, with a body of Britons, Canadians, tories, and Indians, invested Fort Stanwix, now Fort Schuyler, one hundred and ten miles from Albany. General Herkimer, with about eight hundred militia, was advancing to disperse this motely collection, and to relieve the garrison; but unfortunately he fell into an ambuscade, and suffered a considerable loss. Being himself wounded in both legs, he was seen sitting on a stump, and courageously encouraging his men, by which they maintained their ground, and did great execution among the enemy. Several of the Indian chiefs were slain by the first fire, which so disheartened the remainder, that they were thrown into the greatest confusion, and turning on the tories, and other white people, a warm contention ensued between them, and many of the whites were killed. Colonel Gansevort, the commander of the fort, sent out Lieutenant Colonel Willet, with two hundred and fifty men, who bravely routed the Indians and tories, destroyed their provisions, and took their kettles, blankets, muskets, tomahawks, deer skins, &c., with five colors, and returned to the fort. The brave General Herkimer soon died of his wounds, and one hundred and sixty of his militia men, having fought like lions, were killed, besides a great number wounded. St. Leger's victory over our militia was purchased at a dear price, more than seventy of his Indians were slain, and among them a large proportion of their most distinguished and favorite warriors, and the survivors were exceedingly dissatisfied. The object of the expedition was far from being accomplished; the commander did not, however, despair of getting possession of the fort; for this purpose he sent in a flag, demanding a surrender. He greatly magnified his own strength, asserted that Burgoyne was at Albany; and threatened that, on're fusal, his Indians would destroy all the inhabitants in the vicinity; and so soon as they could enter the fort, every man would be sacrificed. Colonel Gansevort nobly replied in the negative, being determined to defend the fort at every hazard; aware, however, of his perilous situation, he found means of sending to General Schuyler at Stillwater for assistance. General Arnold was now despatched with a brigade of troops to attack the besiegers; but, finding their force greatly superior to his own, he sent back for a reinforcement of one thousand light troops.

An object which cannot be accomplished by force is often obtained by means of stratagem. Lieutenant-Colonel John Brooks, an intelligent officer from Massachusetts, being in advance with a small detachment, found one Major Butler, a noted officer among the Indians, endeavoring to influence the inhabitants in their favor, and he was immediately secured. A man also by the name of Cuyler, who was a proprietor of a handsome estate in the vicinity, was taken up as a spy. Colonel Brooks proposed that he should be employed as a deceptive messenger to spread the alarm, and induce the enemy to retreat. General Arnold soon after arrived, and approved the scheme of General Brooks; it was accordingly agreed that Cuyler should be liberated, and his estate secured to him on the condition that he would return to the enemy, and make such exaggerated report of General Arnold's force, to alarm and put them to flight. Several friendly Indians being present, one of their head men advised that Cuyler's coat should be shot through in two or three places, to add credibility to his story. Matters being thus adjusted, the imposter proceeded directly to the Indian camp, where he was well known, and informed their warriors that Major Butler was taken, and that he himself narrowly escaped, several shot having passed through his coat, and that General Arnold with a vast force was advancing rapidly towards them. In aid of the project, a friendly Indian followed and arrived about an hour after, with a confirmation of Cuyler's report. This stratagem was successful; the Indians instantly determined to quit the ground, and make their escape, nor was it in the power of St. Leger and Sir John with all their art of persuasion, to prevent it. When St. Leger remonstrated with them, the reply of the chief was, "When we marched down, you told us there would be no fighting for us Indians, we might go down and smoke our pipes; but now a number of our warriors have been killed, and you mean to sacrifice us." The consequence was, that St. Leger, finding himself deserted by his Indians, to the number of seven or eight hundred, deemed his situation so hazardous, that he decamped in the greatest hurry and confusion, leaving his tents, with most of his artillery and stores, in the field. General Arnold, with his detachment, was now at liberty to return to the main army at Stillwater; and thus have we clipped the right wing of General Burgoyne. In the evening, while on their retreat, St. Leger and Sir John got into a warm altercation, criminating each other for the ill success of the expedition. Two Sachems observing this, resolved to have a laugh at their expense. In their front was a bog of clay and mud; they directed a young warrior to loiter in the rear, and then, of a sudden, run as if alarmed, calling out *they are coming, they are coming*. On hearing this, the two commanders in a fright took to their heels, rushing into the bog, frequently falling and sticking in the mud, and the men threw away their packs, and hurried off. This and other jokes, were several times repeated during the night for many miles."—*Thacher's Journal*.

No. XI.—Page 79.
BATTLE OF BENNINGTON.

On the 16th of August, 1777, the Americans, under General Stark, defeated the British and Indians, under Lieutenant Colonels Baum and Breyman, at Bennington, Vt. Stark divided his troops into three divisions, and ordered Colonel Nichols, with two hundred and fifty men, to gain the rear of the left wing of the enemy, who were secured by entrenchments. At the same time, Colonel Hendrick made a similar movement on the enemy's right wing, while Stark attacked them in front. The Indians, alarmed at the appearance of being surrounded, endeavored to make their escape in a single file between the two parties, with their horrid yells and the jingling of cow bells. The flanking parties approached each other in their rear, and General Stark making a bold and furious onset in front, a general and close conflict ensued, and continued with more or less severity for about two hours. Though Colonel Baum had nearly twice their numbers, and was defended by breastworks, the force opposed to them proved irresistible, forcing their breastworks at the muzzles of their guns, and obliging them to ground their arms and surrender at discretion, so that the victory on our part was complete. We took two pieces of brass cannon, and a number of prisoners, with baggage, &c. This was no sooner accomplished, than Colonel Breyman, with one thousand German troops, arrived with two field pieces, to reinforce Colonel Baum, who had just been defeated. General Stark's troops were now scattered, some attending the wounded, some guarding the prisoners, and still more in pursuit of plunder; and all exhausted by extreme hunger and fatigue. At this critical moment, Colonel Warner's regiment arrived, and the other troops being rallied, the whole were ordered to advance. A field piece had been taken from Baum in the forenoon, and Stark ordered it to be drawn to the scene of action; but his men, having never seen a cannon, knew not how to load it, the General dismounted, and taught them by loading it himself. An action soon commenced, and proved warm and desperate, in which both sides displayed the most daring bravery, till night approached, when the enemy yielded a second time in one day, to their Yankee conquerors. The German troops being totally routed, availed themselves of the darkness of night to effect their retreat. The whole number of killed, wounded, and prisoners, was nine hundred and thirty-four. including one hundred and fifty-seven tories; of this number, six hundred and fifty-four are prisoners. Colonel Baum received a mortal wound, of which he soon after died. Besides the above, one thousand stand of arms, four brass field pieces, two hundred and fifty dragoon swords, eight loads of baggage, and twenty horses, fell into our hands. The loss on our side, is not more than one hundred in the whole. The officers and men engaged in this splendid enterprise merit all the praise which a grateful country can bestow; they fought disciplined troops, completely accoutred, while they wielded their ordinary firelocks with scarce a bayonet, and at first without cannon. The consequences must be most auspicious as respects our affairs in the northern department. Burgoyne must feel the clipping of another wing, and it must diminish his confidence in his successful career. The event will also be productive of the happiest effects on the spirits of our militia, by increasing their confidence in their own prowess. The following anecdote deserves to be noticed for honor of the person who is the subject of it, though his name has not been ascertained. A venerable old man had five sons in the field of battle near Bennington; and being told that he had been unfortunate in one of his sons, replied, 'What, has he misbehaved, did he desert his post, or shrink from the charge?' 'No, sir,' says the informant, 'worse than that: he is among the slain; he fell contending mightily in the cause.' 'Then I am satisfied,' replied the old man: 'bring him in, and lay him before me, that I may behold and survey the darling of my soul.' On which, the corpse was brought in, and laid before him. He then called for a bowl of water and a napkin, and with his own hands washed the gore and dirt from his son's corpse, and wiped his gaping wounds, with a complacency, as he himself expressed it, which before he had never felt or experienced."—*Thacher's Journal*

No. XII.—Page 79.

BATTLE OF STILLWATER, OR SARATOGA.

The American army, under the command of General Gates, in the vicinity of Stillwater, in the county of Saratoga, in the State of New York, attacked the enemy, under General Burgoyne, on the 19th of September, 1777. At about three o'clock, both armies being formed in a line of battle, the action became general, and the combatants on both sides evinced that ardour and gallantry which shows a determination to conquer or die. The firing for about three hours was incessant, with continued tremendous roar and blaze, filling the field with carnage and death. Few battles have been more obstinate and unyielding—at one point the British are overpowered; but, being reinforced, the Americans are baffled; these, being supported, and renewing their efforts, regain their advantages; the same ground is occupied alternately, the dead and wounded of both parties are mingled together. The British resort repeatedly to their bayonets without effect—the Americans resist and foil their attempts. Captain Jones, of the British artillery, had the command of four pieces of cannon, which he conducted with great skill and valour till he fell, and thirty-six out of forty-eight of his artillery-men were killed or wounded; his cannon were repeatedly taken and re-taken, but finally remained with the enemy for the want of horses to bring them off. During the engagement, a number of our soldiers placed themselves in the boughs of high trees, in the rear and flanks, and took every opportunity of destroying the British officers by single shot: in one instance, General Burgoyne was the object, but the aid-de-camp of General Phillips received the ball through his arm, while delivering a message to Burgoyne; the mistake, it is said, was occasioned by having his saddle furnished with rich lace, and was supposed, by the marksman to be the British commander. In the dusk of evening the battle terminated, the British in one quarter silently retreating, the Americans in another give way, and quit the long-contested battle field. Lieut. Colonel Brooks, with the eighth Massachusetts regiment, remained in the field till about eleven o'clock, and was the last who retired. Major Hull commanded a detachment of three hundred men, who fought with such signal ardour, that more than half of them were killed or wounded. The whole number of Americans engaged in this action, was about two thousand five hundred; the remainder of the army, from its unfavorable situation, took little or no part in the action. The British have suffered a loss, as is supposed, of more than five hundred in killed, wounded, and prisoners. On the side of the Americans, sixty-four were killed, two hundred and seventeen wounded, and thirty-eight missing. Among the killed, are Colonels Adams and Colburn, two valuable officers much regretted. The victory on this important occasion is claimed by the enemy, but the advantages are most decidedly on the side of the Americans: they were the assailants—they held their ground during the day—and, at the close, retired to their encampment without being pursued. The royal army lay all the ensuing night on their arms at some distance from the field of battle."—*Thacher's Journal.*

No. XIII.—Page 79.

RED BANK AFFAIR.

"The Americans had erected several forts and redoubts on the banks of the Delaware river, and on Mud Island, to guard against the passage of the British fleet up this river to Philadelphia. In one of these forts at Red Bank, Colonel Greene, of Rhode Island, was posted, with about four hundred men. General Howe, perceiving the great importance of reducing these works, detached Count Donop, an officer held in high estimation in the royal army, with twelve or fifteen hundred Hessian troops, well supplied with artillery, to take possession of it. Having arrived near the redoubts, he summoned the commander to surrender, to which he resolutely replied, he would defend the place to the last extremity. This fort being originally constructed on a large scale, it was found necessary to run a line across the middle, and divide it into two, so that the external part was left without defence. The Hessian commander ordered his troops to advance under cover of the smoke of his cannon, and storm the redoubt; they soon gained the unoccupied part with loud huzzas on their supposed victory; but on approaching the new line within, where our troops were stationed, the brave garrison poured on them such hot and well-directed fire for about forty minutes, that they were completely overpowered, and fled in every direction.—Colonel Donop, their commander, was mortally wounded and taken, and more than one hundred were killed on the spot, and a greater number wounded and prisoners. The enemy retreated with great precipitation, leaving many of their wounded on the road, and returned to Philadelphia with the loss of one-half their party. Colonel Greene, and his brave troops, acquired great honor for their gallant defence of the fort, which is a key to other posts on the river. Congress has rewarded the Colonel, with an elegant sword. The British army found it difficult to procure the necessary supplies in Philadelphia, and the continental galleys and strong chevaux de frize in the Delaware, rendered a passage of their ship up to the city almost impossible. Admiral Lord Howe determined to attempt the removal of these formidable obstructions, and he ordered six of his ships to engage in this service. They were so unmercifully handled by our galleys, and from Fort Mifflin, at Mud Island, that two of them, one of sixty-four guns, run aground, and were set on fire by the crews who deserted them, and soon after they blew up." *Thacher's Journal.*

No. XIV.—PAGE 79.

SURRENDER OF BURGOYNE.

"After the battle of Stillwater, the situation of General Burgoyne became very precarious. His Indian auxiliaries deserted daily; and his army, reduced to little more than five thousand men, was limited to half their usual allowance of provisions. —His stock of forage was entirely exhausted, and his horses were perishing in great numbers. The American army had become so augmented, as to render him diffident of making good his retreat. To aggravate his distress, no intelligence had yet been received of the approach of General Clinton, or of any diversion in his favor from New York.

In this exigency, General Burgoyne resolved to examine the possibility of dislodging the Americans from their posts on the left, by which means he would be enabled to retreat to the lakes. For this purpose he drew out fifteen hundred men, which he headed himself, attended by Generals Phillips, Reidesel, and Frazer. This detachment had scarcely formed, within less than half a mile of the American intrenchments, when a furious attack was made on its left; but Major Ackland, at the head of the British grenadiers, sustained it with great firmness. The Americans soon extended their attack along the whole front of the German troops, which were posted on the right of the grenadiers; and marched a body around their flank, to prevent their retreat. On this movement, the British light infantry, with a part of the twenty-fourth regiment, instantly formed, to cover the retreat of the troops into the camp. Their left wing, in the meantime, overpowered with numbers, was obliged to retreat, and would inevitably have been cut to pieces, but for the intervention of the same troops, which had just been covering the retreat on the right. The whole detachment was now under the necessity of retiring; but scarcely had the British troops entered the lines, when the Americans, led by General Arnold, pressed forward, and, under a tremendous fire of grape shot and musketry, assaulted the works throughout their whole extent from right to left. Toward the close of the day, a part of the left of the Americans forced the intrenchments, and Arnold with a few men actually entered the works; but his horse being killed, and he himself badly wounded in the leg, they were forced out of them, and it being now nearly dark, they desisted from the attack. On the left of Arnold's detachment, Jackson's regiment of Massachusetts, then led by Lieutenant Colonel Brooks, was still more successful. It turned the right of the encampment, and carried by storm the works, occupied by the German reserve. Lieutenant Colonel Breyman was killed; and Brooks maintained the ground he had gained. Darkness put an end to the action. The advantage of the Americans was decisive. They killed a great number of the enemy; made upward of two hundred prisoners, among whom were several officers of distinction; took nine pieces of brass artillery, and the encampment of a German brigade, with all their equipage. Among the slain of the enemy was General Frazer, an officer of distinguished merit, whose loss was particularly regretted. The loss of the Americans was inconsiderable.

Gates posted fourteen hundred men on the heights opposite the ford of Saratoga; two thousand in the rear, to prevent a retreat to Fort Edward; and fifteen hundred at a ford higher up. Burgoyne, apprehensive of being hemmed in, retired immediately to Saratoga.

An attempt was made to retreat to Fort George.—Artificers was accordingly despatched, under a strong escort, to repair the bridges, and open the road to Fort Edward; but they were compelled to make a precipitate retreat. The situation of General Burgoyne becoming every hour more hazardous, he resolved to attempt a retreat by night to Fort Edward; but even this retrograde movement was rendered impracticable. While the army was preparing to march, intelligence was received, that the Americans had already possessed themselves of Fort Edward, and that they were well provided with artillery. No avenue to escape now appeared. Incessant toil had worn down the whole British army; which did not now contain more than three thousand five hundred fighting men. Provisions were almost exhausted, and there were no possible means of procuring a supply. The American army, which was daily increasing, was already much greater than the British in point of numbers, and almost encircled them. In this extremity, the British General called a council of war; and it was unanimously resolved to enter into a convention with General Gates. Preliminaries were soon settled, and the royal army surrendered prisoners of war.

The capture of an entire army was justly viewed as an event that must essentially affect the contest between Great Britain and America; and while it excited the highest joy among the people, it could not but have a most auspicious influence in the cabinet and in the field. The thanks of Congress was voted to General Gates and his army; and a medal of gold, in commemoration of this splendid achievement, was ordered to be struck, to be presented to him by the president, in the name of the United States."—*Holmes' American Annals.*

No. XV.—PAGF 79.

BRANDYWINE AND GERMANTOWN.

"General Washington having ascertained that it was the great object of Sir William Howe to possess himself of the city of Philadelphia, put in requisition every effort in his power to counteract his measures for this purpose. His force during the whole campaign was considerably inferior to that of the enemy. Battles and skirmishing of more or less importance were frequent, but not decisive, though attended by no inconsiderable loss of human lives. On the 11th of September, the two armies approached each other in the order of battle, and a general action took place at Brandywine, in which the officers and soldiers of both armies displayed a spirit of intrepidity and heroism, scarcely ever exceeded. The British claim the victory; but it was only a partial one, and besides a prodigious sacrifice of lives, they failed in their main object, that of forcing their way to Philadelphia. It is stated that, from particular circumstances, little more than one-half of General Washington's force was opposed to nearly the whole strength of the enemy. Our loss is mentioned in round numbers at one thousand. The Marquis de la Fayette, and General Woodford were slightly wounded. The loss of the royalists, according to accounts published, greatly exceeds that of the Americans."—*Thacher's Journal.*

No. XIV.—PAGE 79.

BURNING OF DANBURY, CONN.

"On the 26th of April, 1777, the notorious Tryon, at the head of two thousand tories and refugees, marched to Danbury, in the state of Connecticut, where they burnt eighteen houses with their contents, and a very valuable quantity of stores, provisions, and 1,790 tents. This wanton devastation alarmed the country, and the militia collected un der Major-General Wooster, assisted by Arnold and Silliman. A smart action soon ensued, and continued about one hour, in which our militia and a small number of continentals conducted with distinguished bravery, but being overpowered by a superior force, they were obliged to retreat. The amount of stores destroyed by the enemy was very considerable, but the loss of valuable officers and men is infinitely more important. General Wooster was mortally wounded, and died soon after. Lieutenant-

Colonel Gould and four or five other officers were killed, and about sixty men were killed or wounded. Among the slain is Dr. Atwater, a respectable character, whose death is greatly lamented. General Arnold had his horse shot under him when within ten yards of the enemy, and a soldier was advancing with fixed bayonet towards him, when, with great presence of mind, he drew his pistol from his holsters, and instantly shot him through the body. On the side of the royalists, the loss, as stated by General Howe, is one hundred and seventy-two in killed, wounded, and missing, but by other accounts it is much more considerable. Among the wounded is Brigadier-General Agnew, and two other field officers."

Thacher's Journal.

No. XVII.—Page 79.

FORTS MONTGOMERY AND CLINTON.

"On the 6th of October, 1777, the British, under Sir Henry Clinton and General Vaughan, succeeded in an assault on Forts Montgomery and Clinton, on the western bank of the Hudson, a few miles below West Point. These fortresses were defended by Governor George Clinton, and his brother, General James Clinton, of New York, having about six hundred militia men, a force greatly inadequate to the defence of the works. The enemy came up the river, landed, and appeared unexpectedly, and demanded a surrender of the forts, which being resolutely refused, were taken by assault, though not without a firm and brave resistance. General James Clinton received a bayonet wound in his thigh, but he and the Governor, with a part of the garrison, made their escape, leaving about two hundred and fifty men killed, wounded, and prisoners. The enemy suffered a severe loss of three field officers killed, and their dead and wounded is estimated at about three hundred. General Putnam, who commanded at Peekskill in the vicinity, having a small force only to guard the deposit of stores, was obliged to retire, and the barracks, stores, and provisions, to a very considerable amount, fell into the hands of the enemy, and were destroyed. With wanton cruelty they set fire to the houses and buildings of every description, and spread ruin and devastation to the extent of their power. To consummate their destructive scheme, General Vaughan destroyed by conflagration, the beautiful town of Esopus, with the church, and every other building it contained. Thus we experience the horrid effects of malice and revenge; where they cannot conquer, they wantonly exterminate and destroy. They are well apprised of the disastrous and desperate situation of their boastful General Burgoyne, and if they dare not march to his relief, they can cowardly retaliate by conflagration with impunity. It is the prevalent opinion here, that by taking advantage of wind and tide, it is in the power of Sir Henry Clinton to convey his forces to this city within the space of five or six hours, and having arrived here, a march of about twenty miles will carry him without opposition to Stillwater, which must involve General Gates in inexpressible embarrassment and difficulty, by placing him between two armies, and thereby extricating Burgoyne from his perilous situation. We have been tremblingly alive to this menacing prospect, but our fears are in a measure allayed by the following singular incident.—After the capture of Fort Montgomery, Sir Henry Clinton despatched a messenger by the name of Daniel Taylor, to Burgoyne with the intelligence; fortunately he was taken on his way as a spy, and, finding himself in danger, he was seen to turn aside and take something from his pocket and swallow it. General George Clinton, into whose hands he had fallen, ordered a severe dose of emetic tartar to be administered; this produced the happiest effect as respects the prescriber; but it proved fatal to the patient. He discharged a small silver bullet, which being unscrewed, was found to enclose a letter from Sir Henry Clinton to Burgoyne. 'Out of thine own mouth thou shalt be condemned.' The spy was tried, convicted, and executed. The following is an exact copy of the letter enclosed:

FORT MONTGOMERY, *Oct. 8th, 1777.*
Nous voici—and nothing between us but *Gates*. I sincerely hope this *little* success of ours may facilitate your operations. In answer to your letter of the 28th of September, by C. C., I shall only say, I cannot presume to order, or even advise, for reasons obvious. I heartily wish you success.

Faithfully yours,
H. CLINTON.
To General Burgoyne."—Thacher's Journal.

No. XVIII.—PAGE 86.

CAPTURE OF MAJOR ANDRE.

The treason of Arnold, and the consequent capture and execution of Major Andre, are events that have been widely circulated in all parts of the world; but the following extracts from the "Life and Correspondence of General Greene," contain several additional facts, which cannot fail of being read with interest:

"It was when Washington was on his march to Kingsbridge, with a view to the attempt on New York, and when he had mustered every man who could carry a musket, that he placed Arnold in command of a corps of invalids at West Point. The commander-in-chief had offered him a command suitable to his rank and reputation in the army; but he made the unhealed state of his wounds, and some other causes, the pretext for declining it; for his negociations for the surrender of West Point had already commenced, or been consummated; and he made interest to obtain that appointment.

Greene was in command of the American army, at the time Arnold's treachery was detected. Soon after the relinquishment of the enterprise against New York, a meeting was concerted to take place between the American commander-in-chief, and the French military and naval commanders. Hartford, on the Connecticut river, was the place assigned for their meeting, and its object was to consult on their future joint operations.

Upon the departure of Washington, Greene was placed in command of the main army. This was on the 17th of September. On the 18th, Admiral Rodney arrived with such an overwhelming reinforcement to the British navy, as must have set the consultations at Hartford all at nought. From that time, Greene's communications to the president of Congress are full of hurried preparations going on at New York for some important enterprise. Little did he or any other suspect to what point that enterprise was directed. It appears that he had established a regular communication for obtaining intelligence from the city by spies; and his correspondents in that place were at a loss whether the expedition was intended against Rhode Island or Virginia. To one or the other of those places the enemy had been careful to throw out hints, or exhibit appearances that the expedition was directed. Yet Greene was not deceived; for in a letter of the 21st to General Washington, he writes, 'Colonel ——— communicated the last intelligence we have from New York; since that I have not been able to obtain the least information of what is going on there, though we have people in from three different quarters. None of them returning, makes me suspect some secret expedition is in contemplation, the success of which depends altogether on its being kept a secret.'

This letter is dated at Tappan, for to that place he had been directed by General Washington, on his departure for Hartford, to remove a division of the army.

On the 23d, the whole mystery was developed by the capture of Major Andre. He had ascended the river in the Vulture sloop-of-war, to hold a personal conference with General Arnold. The British commander had become sensible that no time was to be lost; as most probably, on the return of Washington from Hartford, he would assume the command in person at West Point, or confide it to Greene. The present, therefore, was the most favorable time that would ever present itself; the recent movement of the army nearer that place excited to despatch; and the arrival of Rodney gave the enemy the command of such abundant means of water transportation, without exposing the city to a *coup de main* from the French and American forces, that the British commander would have been culpably negligent, not to have embraced it. Andre was accordingly despatched to make the final arrangements for consummating the treachery of Arnold.

The well known object of Arnold's negociation was to put Clinton in possession of the post at West Point. This is a beautiful little plain, lying on the west bank of the Hudson, a little below where it breaks through the chain of mountains called the Highlands. Its form is nearly circular; in one half of its circumference defended by a precipice of a great height, rising abruptly from the river; and on the other, by a chain of rugged, impassable mountains. It is accessible by one pass only from the river, and that is narrow and easily defended; while, on the land side, it can be approached only at two points, by roads that wind through the mountains, and enter it at the river bank, on the north and south.

Great importance had always been attached to this post by the Americans, and great labor and expense bestowed upon fortifying it: whether judiciously or to good effect, has never been tested. But the place is naturally, scarcely assailable, very healthy, and commands the river, throughout a long circuit that it stretches round the point, and where it is deep and very narrow.

The North river had long been the great vein that supplied life to the

American army; and had the enemy obtained possession of this post, besides the actual loss in men and stores, the American army would have been cut off from their principal resources in the ensuing winter, or been obliged to fall back above the Highlands, and leave all the country below open to conquest; while the communication between the eastern and western states would have been seriously interrupted, if not wholly excluded.

Arnold well knew the bearing of this post upon all the operations of the American army, and afterwards avowed his confident expectation, that had the enemy got possession of it, the contest must have ceased, and Americans been subdued. Clinton, it appears, also well understood the value of this place; and it is probable, that the purchase of it had been arranged with Arnold some months prior to the detection of the plot.— It was well remembered afterwards, that he had been intrigued for some time to get appointed to the command, not only in person, but through the agency of his friends in Congress and the army; and the activity which he displayed in making his escape, and afterwards, as a commander under Clinton, support the belief that the pain and weakness from his wounded legs, on which he founded his claims to a command suited to an invalid, were in a great degree affected. Indeed, in one of his publications he acknowledges, that he had long retained his commission only to find some opportunity to inflict such a blow.

The development of Arnold's plot was communicated to Greene by a letter from Colonel Hamilton, dated Verplanck's Point. It was received the evening of the 25th. The object of the preparations in New York immediately became palpable; and, without delay, he made every disposition for marching to the defence of West Point; so that when General Washington's order reached him, at a quarter past three, on the morning of the 26th, the whole army had already been put under marching orders. The first Pennsylvania brigade under Wayne had been put in motion; so that it actually fell to the lot of Andre to find the 'warrior-drover Wayne' in command, when he was delivered a prisoner at the village of Tappan.—But Wayne did not sit in the board of officers who tried him; perhaps from consideration of delicacy; there may have remained something of personal irritation; the wounds of the pen last longer than those of the sword.

It is very well known that Major Andre was taken near a place called Tarry Town, on the east side of the Hudson, where it forms Haverstraw Bay. Ten years afterwards, the large sycamore near which he was taken, was shown to the traveller; and the incidents at his capture were familiarly known to, and related by, every inhabitant of the village.— Paulding, Williams, and Van Wart, who captured him, were poor, but reputable men, and exhibited a striking instance of disinterestedness and fidelity. Andre offered them large bribes, but they were not to be corrupted, and conducted him a prisoner to Colonel Jamieson, who commanded a scouting party on that side of the river.

The circumstances attending the capture of Andre are differently related by the different authors who have written on the American war. They are all correct as far as they go; but being deficient in a few particulars, excited surprise at the supposed, want of self-possession in so brave a man as Andre. The British army in New York was, at that time, supplied with beef, principally through the aid of a class of men, who obtained the appellation of cowboys. They were a species of settlers, or dealers in live stock, who being well acquainted with the roads and passes, penetrated into the country, and either stole or purchased cattle, which they secretly drove into the enemy's lines. Besides watching the movements of the enemy, one principal object for detaching Jamieson to that quarter was, to check the prosecution of this trade or practice. For this purpose, small scouting parties were occasionally pushed beyond the American posts, to reconnoitre the interjacent country between their posts and those of the enemy. And as the cattle taken from the cowboys, unless stolen, were held to be prize of war; and it was an object with the well-affected to suppress a practice which exposed their stock to depredations, small volunteer parties occasionally waylaid the roads for that purpose. Of this description were the captors of Andre; who, after the fatigue of prosecuting their enterprise, had seated themselves under this tree, in a situation retired from the view of travellers approaching along the road. It is said that they were engaged in a game at cards, when the tread of Andre's horse attracted their notice.

The station they had taken was in view of a point where several roads unite near the village, and Andre, who was visible to the party before they were visible to him, was engaged in examining a sketch of the route, no doubt to determine which of the roads in his view he ought to follow. At the first rustling of the leaves made by the motion of the party in ambush, he precipitately thrust the paper he was examining into his boot, on the opposite side of his horse from that on which the party appeared. This was noticed by one of the party, and led to the examination which produced the detection. On being stopped, he resumed his composure, and exhibited the pass from Arnold, on which he had thus far succeeded in clearing the American posts and patrols; and the party had already released his bridle, when one of them inquired what he had done with the paper he was reading? An indistinct view of the dangerous dilemma in which the question involved him, produced in Andre a momentary hesitation; his embarrassment was noticed by the party, and made them resolve again to detain him. Knowing that the pass from Arnold would not avail him after the discovery of the contents of his boot, Andre then desired them to tell him truly, whether they were 'from above or below?' and on their answering 'the latter,' which was consistent with the truth in fact, though not in the sense he meant it, which was, whether they were whigs or tories; he acknowledged himself to be a British officer on urgent business, and begged them not to detain him. On their persisting to detain him, the whole extent of danger burst upon him, and he liberally tried the persuasive voice of gold. But though he had just witnessed, that one in a much more elevated rank had lent a propitious ear to similar arguments, he found these honest yeomen not to be corrupted. Until then, he had learned, that it is at last in the integrity of the well-informed yeomanry of a country that the strength and security of every free government is to be found. Wo to that government which ever suffers this class of men to remain in ignorance, or to be exposed to corruption!

Upon searching the boot into which the paper had been thrust, a plan of West Point, the strength and disposition of the garrison, and other suspicious papers were discovered; and Andre was immediately conveyed to the headquarters of Colonel Jamieson. By this time, it appears, that Andre had completely recovered his self possession, if indeed, he had ever lost it: and he had the ingenuity to play off on Jamieson a *ruse de guerre*, to which the partiality of his friends, and the feelings of his admirers, have managed to give a character which it by no means merits.

He prevailed on Jamieson to despatch a note to Arnold, informing him that John Anderson (this was Andre's assumed name) was taken. This has been construed into a magnanimous effort to save Arnold; whereas it was obviously an ingenious artifice to save himself. And it must have succeeded, had not the former, instead of taking the hint as it was intended, verified by his conduct the trite adage, 'there is no faith among the dishonest,' by immediately transferring all his attention to his own escape. Arnold could easily have despatched an order to Jamieson to release Andre, or have adopted some fiction or plan for getting him into his own hands, for the purpose of giving him his liberty, and thus have escaped with him. Jamieson obviously entertained no suspicion of Arnold, by sending him this message: and by the time that elapsed before he forwarded to General Washington the papers found upon Andre, it is clear that he waited for some communication from Arnold with regard to the future fate of John Anderson.

It is curious to contemplate the good fortune of this interesting young man, in the favorable views which writers of both nations, indeed all who have ever noticed him, have taken of his conduct. But such is the effect of excited feeling upon the judgment of mankind, or perhaps, such the proclivity of man to follow a popular leader, and to avoid the perplexity of reflection. The breathing pen of Colonel Hamilton was generously employed in describing the magnanimity with which Andre met death; the direction once given to public opinion has been followed, 'nothing loth,' and every subsequent writer has vied with his predecessor in representing Andre's conduct in the most favorable colors. The stern moralist, who, knowing the first to pity, then to imitate, is too often the course through which vice and error steal on society, presumes, in such a case as this, to exclaim, 'pause and reflect;' will be more apt to incur the frowns, than the plaudits of his contemporaries. But there is a time of life when a writer may no longer feel the undue influence of popular applause.

Andre has also been greatly extolled for his magnanimity in communicating to General Washington his real name and character, by the express which conveyed to the commander-in-chief the papers found upon him. But what else remained for him to do? His life was clearly forfeited; and in the character of John Anderson, he must have suffered, 'unpitied and unwept, the summary and ignominious death of a spy, or been detected as Major Andre, with a falsehood on his lips. His only chance of escape was to declare his real character, and place himself under the protection of the circumstances under which he alleges that he came within the American posts; or perhaps, to interest the feelings or the fears of the American commander in his behalf. His letter contains one passage which serves as a plain development of his motives in writing it.—*It was to save his own life by exciting fear for that of others.* The passage alluded to is the following: 'I take the liberty to mention the condition of some gentlemen at Charleston, who, being either on parole or under protection, *were engaged in a conspiracy against us:* though their situation is not similar, they are objects who may be sent in exchange for me, or persons whom the treatment I receive might effect.'

It is truly astonishing, that the ungenerous character of this paragraph has never been properly animadverted upon. Who these 'gentlemen at Charleston' were, is afterwards more explicitly declared, in Arnold's letter to General Washington, of the 1st of October: 'I have farther to observe, that forty of the principal inhabitants of South Carolina have justly forfeited their lives, which have hitherto been spared by the clemency of his excellency Sir Henry Clinton, who cannot in justice extend his mercy to them any longer, if Major Andre suffers, which, in all probability, will open a scene of blood at which humanity will revolt.'

Thus it appears that Andre's hint was greedily caught at by Arnold; and Sir Henry Clinton himself, in his communications, very plainly hints the same thing.

Yet nothing could have been more base and dishonorable than the attempt to save his forfeited life, by drawing down ruin upon a number of innocent men, who, after bravely resisting the enemy, had surrended on terms that had been most dishonorably evaded. The assertion also contained in Andre's letter, that the prisoners alluded to had engaged in a conspiracy, was absolutely destitute of truth; as it was well known, that every individual of those prisoners had, from the first, courted and defied investigation; and there existed no cause for their confinement at St. Augustine, to which place they had been removed, but the prevalence of an opinion that their influence kept others from accepting of the King's protection, the illiberal suggestions of some of the loyalists who could not bear the reproachful looks of those whom they had deserted, and above all, the convenience of retaining such respectable hostages to cover such men as Arnold and Andre.

The introductory paragraph also to Andre's letter cannot be dismissed without a remark. It is in these words.

'What I have as yet said concerning myself, was in the justifiable attempt to be extricated. I am too little accustomed to duplicity to have succeeded.' [That is to say, I have hitherto been doing what no man who sufficiently values the obligation of truth would do, or at least, expose himself to the danger of being obliged to do, even for 'the justifiable attempt to be extricated,'] I have hitherto dealt out nothing but falsehoods; but for want of practice, my firmness fails me.'

In the first place, this paragraph is uncandid; for if his disguise could any longer have availed him, he would have retained it; in the next place, there is no small cause to believe that this was not the first time in which Major Andre had played off the practical falsehood of assuming a disguise, and acting the spy.

It is believed by many, that in the character of a spy, he had been greatly instrumental in involving in captivity, the very men whom he now wished to involve in the horrors of retaliation.

Let political expediency disguise it as it may, still the character of a soldier cannot be blended with that of a spy, without soiling the pure ermine of the former. And, however, his sovereign may applaud and reward the officer who tempts his enemy to treachery, there is something so foul in the constitution of the crime, that we cannot look upon him who seduces another to the commission of it, but as the instigator or propagator of crime. The breath of treachery gives a taint to the reputation of the man who but holds converse with it.

Indeed, there appears to have been a combined attack upon morals made by all the *particepes criminis* in this black transaction. One can hardly read with patience the letters of Clinton, Robertson, and Arnold, boldly insisting that Andre was not punishable as a spy, because he came within the garrison under the sanction of a flag, or under the protection of the commander; although in fact, with that commander he was concerting measures to get possession of the post where that officer commanded; that he was himself innocent, because he prostituted the usual protection of innocent and honorable purposes to the perpetration of the basest treachery. And to complete the ridicule of the scene, the chief justice of the state is brought upon the carpet to support this holy doctrine.

This was at a conference which was held by appointment at King's Ferry, between General Robertson and General Greene, on the subject of Andre's treatment. Robertson brought with him from New York, Chief Justice Smith, and the Lieutenant Governor to support him in the argument; but whether it was that the man of the sword was afraid to encounter the man of the gown in argument, Greene would not suffer Smith to land, and the conference resulted in nothing but mutual confirmation in pre-existing opinions. On the 2d of October, Andre was executed as a spy on a gibbet, at the village of Tappan, where the principal part of the army was then encamped.

As his case was one of many novel features, and threats of retaliation had loudly resounded, General Washington did not order his execution summarily, as by the laws of war he would have been justified to do, but commanded a board of general officers to be convened, and submitted the case to their consideration.

Greene was appointed to preside, and Colonel John Laurens was present in the capacity of judge advocate general, which station he held in the army. LaFayette and Steuben were members of the court; and, if dignity, worth, and service can give weight to the decision of the court, never was one constituted more worthy to be respected. There was in it six Major Generals and eight Brigadiers. They were unanimously of opinion, that Andre must suffer as a spy."

ADDITIONAL APPENDIX.

The Old Senate House, at Kingston, N. Y.

[From the Fishkill Times, July 15, 1885.]

The cut at the head of this article is a fair representation of the old stone house, at Kingston, known as the old Senate House. This is one of the oldest buildings in this State, having been erected by Col. Wessel Ten Broeck, in the year 1676, and is consequently considerable over 200 years old. It is 70 feet long, and built of stone with walls about two feet in thickness. The heavy oak timbers put in when it was first erected are sound, and apparently good for several centuries to come. The Fourth Provisional Congress assembled at White Plains July 9th, 1776, and immediately adopted the Declaration of Independence. The next day the body changed its appellation to the "Convention of the Representatives of the State of New York." On the 29th of August following, it adjourned to Fishkill, and from here it moved to Kingston. A committee, of which John Jay was chairman, was appointed to draft a constitution for the State. Their work was completed and the new constitution was adopted on the 20th of April, 1777. The committee met in this house, and under its venerable roof this important document was drafted. The first election under this constitution was held July 30th, 1777. George Clinton was elected Governor and installed in presence of the military and citizens assembled at Kingston. After the organization of the State Government the Senate held its sessions in this house until the British forces, under command of General Vaughan, sacked and burned the village of Kingston in October following. Part of the roof of this house was burned at that time and restored soon after. Gen. Armstrong, the boy hero of the Revolution, afterwards Secretary of War, lived in this house in 1804, previous to his departure as Minister to the French Court. A marble fireplace, erected by him, still adorns one of the rooms. This house has for many years been the property of Frederick E. Westbrook, Esq., son of Rev. Cornelius D. Westbrook, D. D., who was for many years pastor of the Reformed Dutch church in this village. Dr. Westbrook's last years were spent in this house, where he died in March, 1858. Dr. Westbrook's father, Gen. Frederick Westbrook, was an officer of the Revolution, and a Brigadier-General in the war of 1812. He died in this village in 1823, and was buried in the old burying ground near the entrance to the chapel.

[From the Fishkill Times, July 1, 1885.]

A Revolutionary Heroine.

In the year 1776 there resided at White Plains, Westchester county, N. Y., a family consisting of the Rev. Samuel Mills, his second wife, who was a sister of General Humphrey, and several children by his first wife, the oldest being a daughter, then some ten or twelve years of age The father was an ardent patriot, or as the British and their Tory allies would have termed him, a bitter rebel. When after the battle of Long Island, the British landed at Throgg's Neck, and commenced their advance into the country, Mr. Mills considered it prudent for him to leave his home and seek safer quarters farther in the interior. Being left alone with the children, Mrs. Mills busied herself during the few hours allowed her before the arrival of the enemy, in providing for the safety of the children and the property left in her charge. First she took the little ones into the woods and lodged them in the cabin of some friendly Indians. She then returned to her home, and after throwing her spoons into the well, carried off and hid all the portable property she could before the invaders came and fired the house. Powerless to prevent, she witnessed the destruction of her home and all its contents which she had not been able alone to remove. Remaining near the spot all night, in the gray dawn of the morning she discovered a soldier who had straggled from his command asleep by the side of a fence Stealthily approaching, she secured his musket, and compelling him to surrender, marched him at the point of the bayonet to the American camp and delivered him up as a prisoner of war. The little twelve-year-old girl, who on that eventful day was taken by her step-mother to that Indian wigwam, in after years was the mother of the late Samuel M. Stevens. Mr. Stevens, for many years resided near this village, and his widow and two sons, William and George, and daughter Sarah, now reside in this place. Mrs. Stevens still has in good preservation, the curtains which Mrs. Mills that day stripped down from her spare-room bed before the red coats applied their torch to her dwelling. The spoons, which were afterwards recovered from the well, were some years ago sold for old silver.

THE OLD COLONEL BRINCKERHOFF MANSION.

[From the Fishkill Times, July 8, 1885.]
The Old Col. Brinckerhoff Mansion.

The old Col. Brinckerhoff house, a fine illustration of which appears in this number of the TIMES, remains substantially the same as when first erected nearly a hundred and fifty years ago. It is constructed of stone, except the gables, which are of brick imported from Holland. In the western gable appears the date of its erection, 1738, in colored brick, as can be plainly seen in the cut. This house stands a short distance south of the road which runs from the village of Fishkill to Hopewell, near the little hamlet called Swartwoutville. During the Revolutionary war it was frequently occupied by General Washington. His letter to Gen. Lincoln announcing the appointment of the latter by Congress to the command of troops for the defence of Charleston, dated "Headquarters, Fishkill, Oct. 3d, 1778," and numerous other letters and orders were written at this house. He occupied the bedroom back of the parlor, which remains the same as it then was, except that a door has since been cut through communicating with the hall.

The Colonel was a devout member of the old Dutch church, at Fishkill. When Washington first became a member of his family he is said to have stated "I am commander-in-chief in my own house, and wish everybody under my roof to attend family prayers." Of course Washington complied. Col. Brinckerhoff died in 1785, at the age of 82 years, and was buried near the entrance of the old burying ground at Fishkill. His grave stone is still standing, and as sound and legible as when first erected a hundred years ago.

Col. Brinckerhoff, by his will dated Dec. 29th, 1784, gave the farm on which he lived, including this house, to his grandson, John Brinckerhoff Van Wyck, from whom it descended to his son, Alfred Van Wyck, who held it for many years. Mr. Van Wyck sold it about 30 years ago and moved to Illinois, where he still resides. It is at present owned and occupied by Mr. Myers Brownell.

Washington's Headquarters.
BY E. M. RUTTENBER.

The building now so generally known as Washington's Head-quarters at Newburgh, is situated in the south-east part of the city. It is constructed of rough stone; is one story high, fifty-six feet front by forty-six feet in depth, and is located on what was originally Lot No. 2, of the German Patent. The title of the lot was vested, by the Patent referred to, in Herman Schoneman, a native of the Palatinate of Germany, who sold, in 1721, to James Alexander, who subsequently sold to Alexander Colden and Burger Meynders, by whom it was conveyed to Jonathan Hasbrouck. The north-east corner of the building, more particularly shown by the walls and the timbers of the roof remaining in the attic, is the oldest portion; it was erected by Hasbrouck in 1750. The south-east corner was added by him for a kitchen, and in 1770 he erected the west half and embraced the whole under one roof.

Jonathan Hasbrouck, from whom the building takes the name of "The Hasbrouck House," was the grandson of Abraham Hasbrouck, one of the Huguenot founders of New Paltz. He was a man of marked character; of fine physique, being six feet and four inches in height; was colonel of the militia of the district, and was in frequent service in guarding the passes of the Highlands. His occupation was that of a farmer, a miller, and a merchant. He died in 1780.

In the spring of 1782, Washington made this building his Head-quarters, and remained here until August 18th. 1783, on the morning of which day he took his departure from Newburgh. At this place he passed through the most trying period of the Revolution: the year of inactivity on the part of Congress, of distress throughout the country, and of complaint and discontent in the army, the latter at one time bordering on revolt among the officers and soldiers.

It was at this place, on the 22d day of May, 1782, that Col. Nicola proposed, by letter to Washington, that he should become King, for the "national advantage," a proposal that was received by Washington with "surprise and astonishment," "viewed with abhorrence," and "reprehended with severity." The proposition it-

self was of little significance, and of no general importance whatever. It has, however, been so colored up by the fervent imagination of some writers, that a passing reference to it seems proper.*

The inattention of Congress to the payment of the army, during the succeeding winter, gave rise to a more important episode in the history of the war. On the 10th of March, 1783, the first of the famous "Newburgh Letters" was issued, in which, by implication at least, the army was advised to revolt. The letter was followed by an anonymous manuscript notice for a public meeting of officers on the succeeding Tuesday. Washington was equal to the emergency. He expressed his disapprobation of the whole proceeding, and with great wisdom, requested the field officers, with one commissioned officer from each company, to meet on the Saturday preceding the time appointed by the anonymous note. He attended this meeting and delivered before it one of the most touching and effective addresses on record. When he closed his remarks, the officers unanimously resolved "to reject with disdain" the infamous proposition contained in the anonymous address.

The meeting of officers referred to was held at the New Building, or "Temple" as it was called in the New Windsor encampment, but Washington's address was written at his Headquarters, in Newburgh. The "Newburgh Letters," to which it was a reply, were written by Major John Armstrong, Aid-de-camp to General Gates, who, as senior officer of the army, had command of the encampment, with his quarters at the Ellison house, now more generally known as "Knox's Head-quarters." The anonymously called meeting was not held. The motives of its projectors we will not discuss; but its probable effect, had it been successful, must be considered in connection with Washington's encomium of the result of the meeting which he had addressed: "Had this day been wanting, the world had never known the height to which human greatness is capable of attaining."

Notice of the cessation of hostilities was proclaimed to the army April 19th, 1783. It was received with great rejoicings by the troops encamped at New Windsor, and, under Washington's order, was the occasion of an appropriate celebration there. In the evening, signal Beacon lights proclaimed the joyous news to the surrounding country. Thirteen cannon came pealing up from Fort Putnam, and were followed by a *feu-de-joic* rolling along the lines. "The mountain sides resounded and echoed like tremendous peals of thunder, and the flashing from thousands of fire arms, in the darkness of the evening, was like unto vivid flashes of lightning from the clouds." From this time furloughs were freely granted to soldiers and entire regiments who wished to return to their homes, and when the army was finally disbanded by Congress, in November, those absent were discharged from service without being required to return. Practically, however, the army was disbanded by furlough prior to June 20, when

---

*The slander should never be repeated that Nicola represented the army. He was not its representative in any sense, but spoke for himself alone. There is no evidence that he even consulted with any one, nor was it ever claimed that he did. He held no important rank in the army, but was simply Colonel of the Invalid Continental Regiment at Philadelphia. He had no service in the field.

the remnant of short term men were marched from New Windsor to West Point. As the furloughed regiments moved off the encampment grounds at New Windsor, there were many sad parting scenes.

"Painful," says Thacher, "was the parting; no description can be adequate to the tragic exhibition. Both officers and soldiers, long unaccustomed to the affairs of private life, were turned loose upon the world. Never can the day be forgotten when friends, companions for seven years in joy and sorrow, were torn asunder, without the hope of ever meeting again, and with the prospect of a miserable subsistence in the future."

Major North adds: "The inmates of the same tent, for seven long years, grasped each others' hands in silent agony. To go, they knew not whither; all recollection of the art to thrive by civil occupation lost, or to the youthful never known.. Their hard-earned military knowledge worse than useless; and with their badge of brotherhood, a mark at which to point the finger of suspicion—ignoble, vile suspicion!—to be cast out on the world long since by them forgotten. Severed from friends and all the joys and griefs which soldiers feel! Griefs, while hope remained—when shared by numbers, almost joys! To go in silence and alone, and poor and hopeless; it was too hard! On that sad day how many hearts were wrung! I saw it all, nor will the scene be ever blurred or blotted from my view!"

Perhaps both of these pictures are overdrawn, but it is true that the men were literally hurried away—were literally poor and without where to lay their heads.

"Why was the army brought hither?" and "What portion of the building was particularly occupied by Washington?" are questions so frequently asked that a few words of explanation appear to be necessary. The presence of the army of the Revolution north of the Highlands, and in the vicinity of the river, was for the purpose of counteracting the plans of the British Ministry, who hoped, by obtaining control of the navigation of the river, to cut off the Eastern Provinces from the Southern, with a view to confine the rebellion to the former and render its reduction certain. The Hudson thus became the strategic line of the contending forces, to which the possession of the Highlands was the key. While English cannon thundered at New York and Quebec, the extremes of the line, the forces of the patriots guarded the Highland passes; on both sides of the river the campfires of the army were lighted, while from the centre of the field—first at his Head-quarters in New Windsor, and subsequently at the Hasbrouck House—Washington, through the secret service, watched the movements of his powerful antagonist. Once, twice, the centre of the line had been lost, and recovered almost by a miracle. Sir Henry Clinton's victorious banners were given to the breeze from the Highland battlements October 7, 1777, and his messenger sped away to bid Burgoyne hold on. It seemed but the question of a day; but accident led the messenger into the hands of a rallying militia—the silver bullet which he conveyed revealed his purpose. Burgoyne, after waiting his arrival until he could wait no longer, surrendered at Saratoga, and forts Clinton and Montgomery, blackened by fire and strewn with the dead, returned to the patriot forces. The treason of Arnold was not less accidentally prevented from accomplishing its purpose. And in this connection how singular is the fact, that while accident or miracle twice saved the cause of liberty, the immediate agents through whom so great a boon was gained—Taylor and Andre—suffered death at the hands of hangmen!

To the second question we answer: Washington's family consisted of himself, his wife, and his Aid-de-camp, Major Tench Tighlman. The large room, which is entered from the piazza on the east, known as "the room with seven doors and one window," was used as the dining and sitting room. The north-east room was Washington's bed-room, and the one adjoining it on the left was occupied by him as a private office. The family room was that in the south-east; the kitchen was the south-west room; the parlor the north-west room. Between the latter and the former was the hall and stair-case, and the store-room, so called from having been used by Col. Hasbrouck and subsequently by his widow as a store. The parlor was mainly reserved for Mrs. Washington and her guests. A Mrs. Hamilton, whose name frequently appears in Washington's account book, was his housekeeper, and in the early part of the war made a reputation for her zeal in his service which Thacher makes note of and Washington acknowledges in his reference to an exchange of salt. There was little room for the accommodation of guests, but it is presumed that the chambers were reserved for that purpose. Washington's guests, however, were mainly connected with the army and had quarters elsewhere.*

The building is now substantially in the condition it was during Washington's occupation of it. The same massive timbers span the ceiling; the old fire-place with its wide-open chimney is ready for the huge back-logs of yore; the seven doors are in their places; the rays of the morning sun still stream through the one window; no alteration in form has been made even in the old piazza—the adornments on the walls, if such the ancient hostess had, have alone been changed for souvenirs of the heroes of the nation's independence. In presence of these surroundings, it requires but little effort of the imagination to restore the departed guests. Forgetting not that this was Washington's private residence, rather than a place for the transaction of public business, we may, in the old sitting-room, respread the long oaken table, listen to the blessing invoked on the morning meal, hear the cracking of joints, and the mingled hum of conversation. The meal dispensed, Mrs. Washington retires to appear at her flower beds or in her parlor to receive her morning calls. Colfax, the captain of the Life-Guard, enters to receive the orders of the day—perhaps a horse and guard for Washington to visit New Windsor, or a barge for Fishkill, or West Point, is required; or it may be Washington remains at home, and at his writing-desk conducts his correspondence, or dictates orders for army movements. The old arm-chair, sitting in the corner yon-

---

*Chastellux relates that when he visited the Head-quarters in December, '82, the room which served as a sitting-room in the day-time was his bed-room at night.

der, is still ready for its former occupant.

The dinner hour of five o'clock approaches; the guests of the day have already arrived. Steuben, the iron drill-master and German soldier of fortune, converses with Mrs. Washington. He has reduced the simple marksmen of Bunker Hill to the discipline of the armies of Europe, and tested their efficiency in the din of battle. He has leisure now, and scarcely knows how to find employment for his active mind. He is telling his hostess, in broken German-English, of the whale (it proved to be an eel) he had caught in the river. Hear his hostess laugh? And that is the voice of Lafayette, relating perhaps his ventures in escaping from France, or his mishap in attempting to attend Mrs. Knox's last party. Wayne, of Stony Point; Gates, of Saratoga; Clinton, the Irish-blooded Governor of New York, and their compatriots—we may place them all at times beside our *Pater Patriæ* in this old room, and hear amid the mingled hum his voice declare: "Happy, thrice happy, shall they be pronounced hereafter, who have contributed anything, who have performed the meanest office in erecting this stupendous fabric of Freedom and Empire on the broad basis of independency; who have assisted in protecting the rights of human nature, and in establishing an asylum for the poor and oppressed of all nations and religions."

In France, fifty years after Washington lived here, Marbois reproduced, as an entertainment for Lafayette, then an old man, this old sitting-room and its table scene. From his elegant saloon he conducted his guests, among whom were several Americans, to the room which he had prepared. There was a large open fire-place, and plain oaken floors; the ceiling was supported with large beams and whitewashed; there were several small-sized doors and only one window with heavy sash and small panes of glass. The furniture was plain and unlike any then in use. Down the centre of the room was an oaken table covered with dishes of meat and vegetables, decanters and bottles of wine, and silver mugs and small wine glasses. The whole had something the appearance of a Dutch kitchen. While the guests were looking around in surprise at this strange procedure, the host, addressing himself to them, said: "Do you know where we now are?" Lafayette looked around, and as if awakening from a dream, exclaimed, "Ah! the seven doors and one window, and the silver camp goblets such as the Marshals of France used in my youth. We are at Washington's Head-quarters on the Hudson fifty years ago."*

Fortunate will it be for America if, in the coming time, her children, drawing inspiration from those old walls and from the lessons of patriotism, of honor, of official integrity, of political action, which were here inculcated, shall sincerely and reverentially respond: "The seven doors and one window—*we are at Washington's Head-quarters on the Hudson!*"

After the retirement by Washington the Hasbrouck family resumed possession of the house, and remained there until a short time anterior to 1849, when the title of the property

---

* While quoting this story as current literature, it is but just to history to say that Lafayette was never in the Hasbrouck house during its occupation by Washington. He was in France.

became vested in the people of the State of New York, under the foreclosure of a mortgage given to the commissioners to loan certain moneys of the United States. For many years it was called "the old Hasbrouck house," but the memory of Washington and of the events which clustered around it during his residence here, ever brightening as time advanced, caused this name gradually to fade away before the undying one by which it is now known.

By an act of the Legislature, passed April 10, 1850, the property was placed in the care of the Board of Trustees of the then Village of Newburgh, to be preserved as nearly as possible as it was at the time of its occupation by Washington, and to erect a flag-staff from which should be unfolded the United States flag, upon which should be inscribed : "*Liberty and Union, now and forever, one and inseparable.*"

The interior of the building had been modernized in some respects, but the Trustees of Newburgh, true to their trust, appointed a committee, and by them every part of the building was carefully restored to the condition it was in at the time of its occupation by Washington. This being done and the flag-staff erected, on the 4th of July, 1850, the place was formally dedicated, with appropriate ceremonies, on the green in front of the building.

The property thus set apart and dedicated to be forever kept to awaken patriotic memories, passed to the care of the city authorities of Newburgh, on the passage of the city charter in 1866, where it remained until 1874, when the Legislature, by act of May 11th, appointed a Board of Trustees to hold and maintain it. This Board, composed of Wm. C. H. Sherman, David Carson, David Moore, James G. Graham, Jos. H. H. Chapman, Cyrus B. Martin, Peter Ward, Joel T. Headley, Edward C. Boynton, and James W. Taylor, is now (through its successors) in the discharge of the duty assigned to it.

Washington's Headquarters.

BY MARY E. MONELL.

Sung at the Dedication of the Old Building, July 4, 1850.

Free men, pause! this ground is holy;
  Noble spirits suffered here;
Tardy justice, marching slowly,
  Tried their faith from year to year—
    Yet their patience
Conquered every doubt and fear.

Sacred is this mansion hoary;
  'Neath its roof-tree, years ago,
Dwelt the father of our glory.
  He whose name appalled the foe·
    Greater honor
Home nor hearth can never know.

Unto him and them are owing
  Peace as stable as our hills;
Plenty, like yon river flowing
  To the sea from thousand rills·
    Love of country,
Love that every bosom thrills.

Brothers! to your care is given,
  Safe to keep this hallowed spot;
Though our warriors rest in heaven,
  And these places know them not,
    See ye to it
That their deeds be ne'er forgot.

With a prayer your faith expressing,
  Raise your country's flag on high;
Here, where rests a nation's blessing,
  Stars and stripes shall float for aye!
    Mutely telling
Stirring tales of days gone by.

ADDITIONAL APPENDIX.

The Crosby Memoirs.

Enoch Crosby finished his life where Capt. Barnum's narrative left him, at his quiet home near Brewsters, in Putnam county, N. Y. He died on the 26th of June, 1835, and was buried with his family in the old Gilead burying-ground. A plain marble slab 21 inches wide and 2 inches thick, bearing the following inscription, marks his last resting place:

```
         In
      memory of
   ENOCH CROSBY,
       who died
    June 26, 1835,
    aged 85 years,
   5 mo's and 21 d's.
```

His first wife, one son and two daughters are buried by his side, and have headstones similar to his. His Family Bible, containing the family record, is said to be still in existence, though our reporter was unable to find it. His family consisted of two sons, Enoch and Lewis, and four daughters, Betsey, Rebecca, Sally and Hannah. Enoch married a daughter of Hackaliah Bailey, of Somers, Westchester county, and moved to Sing Sing, where for many years he kept a prominent hotel. He owned and ran a line of stages between Sing Sing and Somers, which was extended to Patterson, Putnam county, a part of the time. He also owned an interest in the Red Bird stage line which ran to Albany.

Lewis lived at the old homestead, and died in 1836, at the age of 46 years. Betsy died in 1806, aged 21 years. Rebecca died in 1841, also aged 21 years. We were not able to learn when Sally died, but were informed that neither she, Betsey nor Rebecca was ever married. Hannah married Philip Rundell, and lived near her old home. She died April 16, 1871, aged 71 years. As far as we could learn, Hannah and Enoch left no children. Lewis had six sons, Edward, Joseph, Ira, Benjamin, Henry and Charles, and one daughter, Zilla. Edward is a physician, and resides near Salem, Westchester county. Joseph died in 1869, aged 54. Ira is living in Steuben county, N. Y. Benjamin keeps a hotel in New Canaan, Conn. Charles is dead. Henry is living at Jefferson Valley, Westchester county. Zilla never married; she died in 1863, at the age of 46.

Enoch Crosby was married twice. After the death of his first wife, who was the mother of all his children, about the year 1824 he married the widow of Col. Benjamin Green, of Somers, Westchester county. His second wife died about 1828, and was buried by the side of her first husband in Mount Zion Methodist church yard, in the town of Somers.

The Fishkill Centennial.

The one hundredth anniversary of the disbanding of the Continental Army, by an order from Washington dated June 2d, 1783, furloughing his non-commissioned officers and men, who then struck their tents in Fishkill and made preparations to return to their homes, was celebrated at Fishkill Village on Saturday, June 2, 1883. Not only did the inhabitants of the village turn out *en masse*, but vehicles of all sorts brought people from the out-lying districts, while the cars brought many more from the towns and villages along the lines of the Newburgh, Dutchess and Connecticut, and the New York and New England Railroads. The village was in gala attire, almost every house being decorated with the National colors, portraits of Washington, etc. Crowds of people thronged the streets, especially in the vicinity of the Mansion House, where the procession formed. Mr. A. R. Wiltsie acted as Grand Marshal, and Messrs. W. H. Wood, H. W. Smith, W. E. Dean, H. R. Scofield, Absalom Niver and Frank Wakeman as Aids.

THE PROCESSION.

Piano's Brass Band of 19 pieces.

A choir of 18 male singers, led by Dr. C. M. Kittredge.

The Centennial Committee—J. J. Monell, C. M. Kittredge, J. H. Cook, G. W. Owen, F. B. Goodrich, J. E. Dean, R. B. Van Kleeck, C. M. Wolcott.

Committee of Arrangements—H. H. Hustis, J. T. Smith, J. W. Spaight, Lyman Robinson, I. E. Cotheal, E. Luyster, Augustus Hughson, H. F. Walcott, Isaac Cary, H. B. Rosa, A. W. Armstrong, I. O. Norris, E. M. Goring, F. I. Jackson, L. C. Rapalje, Garrett DuBois, Storm Emans, L. V. Pierce, C. W. Horton.

The Clergy—including the pastors of all the churches in the town.

The Speakers of the occasion.

Members of the Press.

The thirteen Vice-Presidents, representing the 13 original States: Walter Brett, J. B. Burnett, J. L. Scofield, John Place, Lewis Tompkins, W. H. Mase, F. K. Scofield, Major E. C. Boynton, E. M. Ruttenber, T. V. W. Brinkerhoff, J. G. Van Wyck, M. V. B. Brinckerhoff, Dr. L. H. White.

Thirty-eight young ladies dressed in white, with sashes of red, white and blue, each bearing a small silk flag, represented the present number of States.

Veterans, citizens and invited guests.

After the procession had formed, it marched through Broad, Jackson and Main streets, and arrived at "The Battery," where the exercises were to take place, at 3 o'clock. A large platform had been erected for the speakers, officers, band, singers, etc., and the entire field was surrounded with suitable decorations. A cannon had been planted near by, and a salute of 13 guns was fired during the moving of the procession. About 3000 persons had gathered in and about the Battery to take part in the occasion. When the procession arrived the platform was soon filled, and the exercises began.

Hon. J. J. Monell, of Fishkill Landing, arose and spoke as follows:

Fellow-citizens—From the opening to the close of the Revolutionary war a strong military force was stationed at this village, extending through the passes of the Highlands toward West Point. Its object was to keep up communication with the Eastern States, to supply the troops at West Point and the lower Hudson, and to harass and prevent the British troops from joining Burgoyne at Albany. Fishkill became an armed encampment, and one of the most important places in Dutchess county. After eight long years of watching and suffering, on the 2d of June, 1783, an order from the Commander-in-Chief reached the camp, directing that "arrangements be made for marching the troops of their respective States to their homes." Peace had been proclaimed, the war was over, the battles had been

ADDITIONAL APPENDIX. 131

fought, the victories won, and America was free! A shout of joy went up throughout all the camp. To commemorate the Centennial of this event we have this day assembled.

We also meet preparatory to the erection of an appropriate monument to honor and perpetuate the memory of all those who died in the encampment and were buried in the Revolutionary grave-yard at the foot of yonder mountain.

"They fell devoted but undying.
The very gale their praise seems sighing.
The waters murmur with their name.
The woods are peopled with their fame.
Their memory wraps the dusky mountain,
Their spirits sparkle in the fountain."

On all important occasions, before and after battle, in times of trial, in the hour of victory, at the proclamation of the Proposals of Peace, and at the dissolution of the army, Gen. Washington always ordered that the chaplains should recognize the Supreme Ruler of the universe. Following his example, and from the impulses of our own hearts, Dr. John H. Hobart, rector of the old Revolutionary church in this place, has been selected to open this celebration with prayer, to be followed by a psalm of praise, in which it is hoped all the people will join. As Dr. Hobart has recently been severely afflicted by the loss of a beloved sister, Rev. Robert B. Van Kleeck, a descendant of Henry Schenck, who was Quarter-Master at Fishkill during the Revolution, will perform the services.

Rev. Mr. Van Kleeck then offered prayer, which was followed by the choir singing "Praise God from whom all blessings flow."

Hon. J. J. Monell then introduced Mr. Benson J. Lossing, the historian, who was selected to act as chairman, as follows:

We are favored to-day by the presence of a citizen of Dutchess county who is a brilliant example of what our institutions can do for man. From being a printer's boy, he has risen by his own exertions to be one of the first historians of the age, and has done more than any other person to delineate and perpetuate the events of the Revolution. He has been honored by the colleges of our own country and by the universities of Europe, and he honors us this day by consenting to act as chairman of this meeting. I introduce to you the Hon. Benson J. Lossing."

Upon taking the chair, Mr. Lossing said

Ladies and gentlemen—Citizens of Fishkill: I thank you for the great honor you have conferred upon me by inviting me to preside on this most interesting occasion. I am officially supported by thirteen distinguished citizens, and sustained by the presence of charming representatives of *all* our States; what more could I desire?

This summer you are privileged to celebrate not only the disbandment of the Continental army, but the bicentennial of three important events in the history of the ancient and undivided town of Fishkill, namely:

1. The advent within its domain of the first white child born in Dutchess county.

2. The purchase of the land of this region from its barbarian inhabitants, and so planting the seeds of settlement and civilization and empire in this county; and

3. The marriage of the chief purchaser, an ex-Mayor of New York city, with the attractive young widow, Helena Van Ball, whose daughter, seventeen or eighteen years afterward, became Madame Brett, a personage distinguished in your local annals and honored by her worthy descendants among you.

On the 19th of last April the citizens of Newburgh celebrated the centennial of Washington's announcement of peace, in accordance with a proclamation by the Continental Congress on the 11th; to-day the citizens of Fishkill celebrate the centennial of Washington's order for the virtual disbandment of the Continental army, the logical sequence of the proclamation of the 11th and the announcement of peace on the 19th of April.

One hundred years ago to-day, Washington wrote to Gen. Putnam that the Secretary of War and the Paymaster-General were at headquarters at Newburgh, the latter "empowered to settle all accounts" with the soldiers—the final act of the war.

The definitive treaty of peace had already been negotiated by the agents of the high contracting powers, and only needed the proper signatures. These were appended in September following.

You are assembled to-day to celebrate the last of the two final events in the history of the old war for independence, namely: the disbanding of the army which had been instrumental in securing peace and independence for our beloved country.

I congratulate you, citizens of Fishkill, because of the privilege you enjoy of being residents of a precinct so hallowed and consecrated by great deeds, the memory of which more eloquent tongues than mine will this day awaken.

The choir sang the grand old hymn, "The Star Spangled Banner." Hon. J. J. Monell then addressed the chair and said:

Mr. Chairman, the following Vice Presidents have been selected by the Centennial Committee:

Mr. Walter Brett, a descendant of Madame Brett. She was the first white woman who settled in this town—an heiress who inherited over 28,000 acres of land extending from the Hudson river along Fishkill creek, four hours journey, sixteen miles. She was greatly beloved in her day, and her memory is still held in great honor by her numerous descendants. She died in 1764, and was buried in the graveyard attached to the Reformed Church of this village. When the steeple was erected it was over her grave; an appropriate monument to her memory.

Mr. Joseph B. Burnet, of New Windsor, grandson of Major Robert Burnet, who was a delegate to the Temple, when, under the inspiration of Washington, the officers of the army, neglected by Congress, resolved to stand by their country Major Robert Burnet heard Washington say, when he could not see clearly to read his address, "You see, gentlemen, I am growing blind, as well as gray, in the service of my country."

Gen. Jacob L. Scofield, born in the lifetime of Washington, and an officer in the war of 1812, has lived under every Administration of this Government.

Messrs. John Place, Lewis Tompkins, and Willard H. Mase, representatives of the mercantile and manufacturing interests of the town. Men who have risen to places of influence by their own efforts, examples of what our institutions can do to improve the condition of man.

Major Edward C. Boynton, of Newburgh, late of the United States army, who wrote the history of West Point, and has recently compiled the general orders of Washington, issued at Newburgh.

Mr. E. M. Ruttenber, the historian of Newburgh, of Orange county, and of the Indian tribes of the Hudson, who for years has devoted his leisure hours to collect the historical events of this region.

The remaining five—Messrs. Frederick K. Scofield, Jacob G. Van Wyck, T. Van Wyck Brinkerhoff, Matthew V. B. Brinckerhoff, and Dr. Lewis H. White—represent old Revolutionary families, who gave up their homes to the occupation of Revolutionary officers, and did all they could for their comfort. Many of these persons occupy the same houses that their ancestors did, rich in historic associations.

These thirteen Vice-Presidents are chosen to represent the thirteen original States.

Each of the thirty-eight young ladies personates one of the 38 States; they represent the stars on the blue ground of our flag, the 38 stars in the dome of our National Capitol, the 38 States that are woven and interwoven into the very texture of our Constitution, so as to be "one and inseparable, now and forever." They, with the ladies in charge of them, represent "Heaven's first, best gift to man—woman." And now, let the toast be, "Dear woman!" and let the Band respond.

Amid much applause, the Band played and the choir sang "Let the toast be, Dear Woman!" repeated three or four times.

Mr. Lossing then introduced Hon. Theodoric R. Westbrook, of Kingston, a Justice of the Supreme Court, and a native of Fishkill Village, who made the opening address. He spoke as follows:

Ladies and Gentlemen—Upon the elevation of a century of years which our country has now attained, of the greatness of which we are forcibly reminded by the presence of these young ladies representing the thirty-eight States of the Union, we are assembled to look backward to their beginning; to rescue so far as we can from oblivion the events which then transpired in this locality; and, while we contemplate the past and the present, to remember the Hand which has led us, and shaped and directed the occurrences making the history of the intervening period.

In the immediate locality of this assembly there were no battles, but the scenes of carnage were not far away. Quite near us are Stony Point, Forts Clinton, Montgomery, and Putnam, and West Point—historic and classic ground made memorable, not only by the deeds of patriotic valor, but by treason, almost successful, of a trusted general. Many of the actors in those great events were familiar with the landscape upon which we now look. They saw the same old hills, and beheld the same old buildings. The ground around and about us is hallowed by recollections of those who here, from time to time, took counsel together concerning the important events in which they were participants.

On the 28th day of August, 1776, the Provincial Convention of this State—as its Legislature was then called—then in session at White Plains, selected Fishkill as the place to which should be removed the treasury and archives of the State, and in which the subsequent sessions of that body were to be held. They were accordingly resumed at this point on the 3d day of September, 1776. The Episcopal church, still standing and subsequently occupied as a hospital, was selected, because then unoccupied, but on assembling there it was found to be "foul with the dung of doves, and without seats, benches, or other conveniences," and thereupon the convention adjourned to the old Reformed Dutch church, which still rears its spire heaven-ward, and whose walls still stand, the silent witnesses of the wisdom and patriotism of its then occupants. That historic building continued to be the place of meeting of the convention until its removal to Kingston, where it continued its labors from February, 1777, to May of the same year. Here also, in the same old church, the Committee of Safety met. There, too, as tradition informs us, the prisoners captured by our soldiers were confined. Ah, could those walls but speak, what tales they could tell! What words of wisdom they heard, what secrets they bear of dangers averted by action determined upon within their enclosure! What hopes and aspirations there uttered, and what forebodings of evil, almost inaudibly whispered, they in silence listened to! The details of what there transpired shall never be disclosed to us, but from the character of the bodies which there assembled we are sure that much of the history marked by the stirring events of the Revolution was there formulated and resolved upon. The old church-yard, too, what a sacred and hallowed enclosure it is! There repose the bodies of Col. John Brinckerhoff, General Jacobus Swartwout, General Frederick Westbrook, Capt. Gridley, and of many other patriots and soldiers of the Revolution. Sleep on, and sleep sweetly, dear kindred dust, until the archangel's trump shall wake you upon the glorious resurrection morn!

Let me resume the history of the convention which assembled here: The draft of the Constitution was submitted to the convention in Kingston on the 12th day of March, 1777, and was adopted on the 20th of April. Concerning it, the late Mr. Gulian C. Verplanck said: "The Constitution of the State of New York was printed in 1777, and was the first as well as the most important book ever printed in the State. The people could find but one press in their domain with which to print the work of their representatives. It was done at Fishkill by Samuel Loudon, who had been a Whig editor and printer in the city of New York, and who had retired with his press to Fishkill, where was the chief deposit of stores, hospitals, etc., for the northern army of the United States."

The same Samuel Loudon also published here till the close of the war a newspaper called "The Fishkill Packet." This paper was the official organ of the Whigs of the Revolution, and contained four pages of eight by ten inches in size. Upon the press of Loudon was also printed the official orders of the American army.

It would be interesting to pause at this point to consider how great a work in the establishment of our liberties that humble paper wrought. Beside the printing of the State Constitution and the orders of Washington, how many hearts were cheered and hands strengthened by its stirring words during the long years of the bloody struggle for freedom!

With Loudon and other patriot refugees who fled hither from New York upon its occupation by the British, was a Mr. Van Steenberg, who was the schoolmaster of the Collegiate Reformed Dutch Church of that city, and here established a school. At it many of the inhabitants of this locality were educated. Who can calculate the influence for good of that seminary of learning, thus early established, upon this neighborhood? We know it bore fruit in the virtue and intelligence of the occupants of the homes all around us.

On the 14th of October, 1776, Fishkill, in addition to being the depository of the treasure and archives of the State, was turned into an armed encampment. Chastellux gives this general description of the place in 1780: "This town, in which there are not over fifty houses in the space of two miles, has long been the principal depot of the American army. It is there they have placed their magazines, their hospitals, their workshops, etc., but all these form a town by themselves, composed of handsome large barracks, built of wood at the foot of the mountains." The barracks referred to by the writer extended from the place recently occupied by the late Sidney E. Van Wyck to the foot of the mountain, and near by was the soldiers' burial place, where many now unknown patriot dead repose. From what cause it was largely filled let the following extract from the same author describing the invalid camp, tell: "The houses were made of logs and were erected by the soldiers. To this place the troops, however healthy and fit for service, were sent when they became destitute of clothing. They remained at the barracks as long as they had rags which could be patched into a covering, but when they became, naked they were sent into this hiding-place." What a tale this is in simple words! We shudder as we fill in all the details of horrors here portrayed in general terms. In hunger, and in cold, with no food or clothing, our heroes died. No stone marks their resting places, their names are not preserved to us, but He who called them into being knows where they sleep. In the volume of His book their deeds are all recorded. and by and by, in His own good time, shall their virtues and their works be proclaimed so loudly that the universe shall hear, and applaud.

The Van Wyck mansion was the officers' headquarters, and must often have been honored by the presence of Washington, Lafayette, Steuben, Putnam and others. Lafayette was sick in this village for six weeks of a fever, and while ill remained at the house more recently owned by Matthew V. B. Brinckerhoff. The Baron Steuben and his military family occupied the residence of Mr. Samuel Verplanck, near the Landing, in which the constitution of the now historic society of the Cincinnati was formally signed on May 13th, 1783.

A word should here be spoken concerning Washington's headquarters* when in this locality, and of their owner, Col. John Brinckerhoff, who died full of years and honors March 26th, 1785. The house is thus described by one who is present with us to-day, and who may be justly styled the Historian of the Revolution, Mr. Benson J. Lossing: "It is an old-fashioned house built of stone, with the date 1738 on one of its gables, formed of brick imported from Holland." According to the same authority, "a letter written by Gen. Washington to Gen. Lincoln, announcing the appointment by the Continental Congress of the latter gentleman to the command of troops for the defence of Charleston," was here penned, and "is dated at Col. Brinckerhoff's, October 3d, 1778." Mr. Lossing also states: "In the Brinckerhoff mansion Washington remained a few days at this time, dating his letters written there, after the one just mentioned: "Headquarters, Fishkill." Whenever Washington was at Fishkill he made Col. Brinckerhoff's his headquarters. He occupied the bedroom back of the parlor, "which remains the same (at date of 1874) excepting a door that opens into the hall, which has been cut through."

In Fishkill lived John Bailey, who had also fled from the City of New York. He was a mechanic, and in his shop were forged many of the weapons of the patriot soldiers, and among them was a sword worn by the Father of his Country, now deposited with other national relics at the city of Washington, and bearing the inscription "J. Bailey, Fishkill." To

---

* See illustration on page 121.

this same individual Gen. Washington alludes in a curious letter dated October 7th, 1779, as the person who could supply him with a two-bladed pocket knife, of which he was then in need, having lost "an old and favorite one," by which loss he was "much distressed."

Party spirit ran high during those days in this locality, but at least two-thirds of the inhabitants were loyal to home and country, and the ladies were ever active in their contributions for our needy and suffering soldiers. As proof of their loyalty, it may be mentioned that on the 14th day of August, 1776, they possessed themselves by force of a quantity of tea stored here by Alderman Lefferts, of New York, disposed of it at six shillings per pound, and distributed the proceeds of the sale for the benefit of the patriot cause.

During the week now closing stirring recollections of another great and successful struggle—one fought to preserve the Union which our fathers formed—have been awakened. All over this broad land have our people gathered to decorate with flowers the graves where departed heroes sleep. As I recalled the stirring reminiscences of the war to achieve, and of the war to preserve, "*Liberty and Union*," and remembered the issue of each, I could not but think that the Union of the States will be perpetual, ever blessing the world with the vision of a government by the people for a people prosperous as never before witnessed on earth, and of a nation great in all that makes true greatness beyond all present human conception!

The choir then sang "Columbia, the Land of the Brave," rendering the chorus amid the waving of their flags by the 38 young ladies. Mr. J. Hervey Cook, of Fishkill-on-Hudson, was then introduced as the next speaker, and said:

Mr. President, Ladies and Gentlemen—Go back with me one hundred years. June 2, 1783, has been alike charming, and in all nature there is the most attractive loveliness, but is there not a fuller joy in Newburgh, New Windsor, Cornwall, West Point, and Fishkill, than can be felt upon this gladsome day? United in heart as now, those who have been long in camps, and in action upon many a field, hear from yonder old headquarters the orders of their beloved Washington, summoning them once more to the Cantonment, and they strike their tents and hasten, while prayers go up from devout lips, and loud shouts and huzzas cause the welkin to ring, to be echoed and re-echoed among these hills and mountains.

From that holy Temple where their leader had refused the crown that the people might be sovereigns, the non-commissioned officers and soldiers day after day are furloughed in obedience to the voice of Congress, never in the providence of God to return, and are taking that reluctant leave of each other which springs from an affection that has been born of being fellow sharers in perils, sufferings, enjoyments and triumphs, and they hurry away to the heart-touching welcomes awaiting them in their homes, where the loved shared with them the blessings which freedom brings. It is not the proclamation of uncertain war, nor the declaration of independence, but the divine assurance of peace. It is the taking off the harness more gloriously than it was put on.

The story of Fishkill in the Revolution has never yet been fully told I know this is saying much in the presence of this multitude, who have been listening to the most eloquent utterances, and seeing around me these historical writers, with the author of "The Field Book of the Revolution" in the chair, who has given therein with pen and pencil so much to endear him to Americans, but even he—and I say it with deference—could tell but little of what could not be crowded into a volume, having to range through the thirteen States. But some of you may know much more than I can narrate to you, and you ought to, for they were your own ancestors who were living here then, and acting with them.

When the news came to the Provincial Congress in New York of the battle of Lexington, where
"the embattled farmers stood,
And fired the shot heard round the world,"
we see Nathaniel Sackett hastening back to Fishkill, like another Paul Revere, to spread the general alarm, and organize the Committee of Observation. At that first meeting there was a Spartan woman present who declared, with patriotic zeal, that if the exigencies required it, her own sex would take up arms. Who of you can claim her in your lineage, need boast no more.

Many went out to battle, and many never to return. Fathers and sons and brothers were frequently arrayed against each other, as tories were in all ranks of society still loyal to their king, who had cut off by his mis-rule the natural allegiance. The names of those patriots are familiar to you, and many of them you bear. In this brief space I could not name them all, and to speak of a few would be making an inglorious distinction. How they looked, you have often heard, and there are those of you who remember seeing in your childhood some of those heroes in their age.

But those spirits are around us now. Along this old Post Road leading down through the Highlands, which was formerly an Indian path, and was laid out by Lord Loudon in the French and Indian war, we see them moving one way and the other.

Near the close of August, 1776, the Provincial Legislature is meeting in yonder old Trinity Church, no longer ornamented with a spire, and soon moves into the old Dutch Church near by for reasons which the historian gives, which is so changed that the fathers scarcely know it. seeing but here and there a trace of the Dutch left in it. The president, Abraham Yates, is seen riding backward and forward to the old Teller house, in Matteawan, where he makes his stay. Many remarkable men are gathered in this Convention. That elderly, courtly gentleman is Philip Livingston, to become afterward a signer of the Declaration of Independence, and Lewis Morris is to be alike honored. Among them are Pierre Van Cortlandt, Leonard Gansevoort, General John Morin Scott, Robert Van Rensselaer, with James Duane, the eminent lawyer. Another to have higher distinction is Robert R. Livingston, who is to be associated with Adams, Jefferson, Franklin and Sherman in drafting the Declaration of Independence, and to be named as the first Chancellor, and to administer the oath to Washington as President of the United States. But there is one more already famous for having written the Petition to the People of Great Britain in the first Continental Congress, which Jefferson pronounced "the production of the finest pen in America," and he is to have greater glory here. This young man can be none other than John Jay, who will have brighter honors—to be with Adams, Franklin and Laurens in negotiating the Treaty of Peace, and the first Chief Justice.

I must tell my eloquent friend why this Convention went from here to Kingston. Scott, in writing Washington at the time, says it was on account of "inconvenience of lodging," and he opposed it with much vigor, declaring it was highly important that they should remain to further the obstructions in the river, to be nearer New York, and to strengthen the patriots who were in the midst of so many tories.

A number of those members were to be in that brilliant Convention in Poughkeepsie, to act upon the adoption of the Federal Constitution, and you remember how conspicuously they shone along side of Hamilton, George Clinton, and Melancthon Smith, in those long and able discussions. Gen. Swartwout was a member from here of that body, and gave his vote against it, not wishing to favor it without further amendments. It was not what Hamilton wished, who had proposed a much stronger government, but who gave to its passage a mighty strength,

hoping that time would mould it as he would like to see it. How this village then appeared, you have learned through your fathers around the old hearth-stones. Scattered two miles around were only about fifty houses, quaint in their looks, and some of them going back to the first settlement two hundred years ago. The hospitals, magazines, workshops, barracks and military stores, stretching along on either side down to the mountains, were like a military town, and you must not forget that there were thousands of soldiers. There were major-generals, brigadiers and many other officers. Many patriots took refuge here after the disasters on Long Island. Putnam came from Peekskill on the capture of Fort Montgomery, and in this retreat was the most trying time to him of the war. You may think it strange that he should be questioned, upon whose tombstone is inscribed, "He dared to lead where any dared to follow," but so it was. It was not enough that he endured sufferings and hardships, and was so cruelly scarred in the old French and Indian war, nor that he should have been among "the bravest of the brave" with Warren at Bunker Hill, although overpowered by the superior numbers of Sir Henry Clinton. The youthful Hamilton must criticise him, and Washington must yield to the prejudices aroused, to relieve him for a while from command. But the Commander-in-Chief one hundred years ago this very day sat down in the old Headquarters and wrote with warmth this Roman general that he would "never be forgotten." Among those generals were Poor, Learned, Parsons, McDougal and the Clintons. The Baron Steuben had his headquarters in the Scofield house, in Glenham, and at the last at the Verplanck house near the river, where the other day the centennial of the Society of Cincinnati was duly celebrated. The valiant soldier of Frederick the Great gave us his best services, like DeKalb and Kosciusko. We see the Mad Wayne at Fishkill Landing rapidly dashing off a note to Sackett in mysterious language, meditating upon another attack like that which at Stony Point gave a brilliancy to his name. Across those ferries to and from Newburgh and New Windsor, and up and down along the old roads leading to this old village, those men are seen coming and going.

In the old Brinckerhoff house Lafayette lay very sick with a fever. He was so young, so unselfish, so Godlike in those qualities which adorn human nature. I need not speak his praise.

There is another soldier I must be permitted to speak of, who went out from this county, the gallant Richard Montgomery, who fell at Quebec.

Washington was familiarly known. In camp, on horseback, or in his headquarters at Col. John Brinckerhoff's, he was grave and thoughtful, and there are many anecdotes remembered. The Commander-in-Chief on his way to Connecticut spent the night here with Benedict Arnold just a week before he went over to the enemy to betray us, and he was on this road going toward West Point, riding down through those Highlands, when he learned that he who had been rash in his courage, but had done much in the service to merit distinction, had become a traitor. Well might he ask in sorrow, "Whom can we trust now?" Here Joshua Hett Smith, supposed to be in complicity with Arnold, was captured, as was also Claudius Smith, who was hanged in Orange county as a tory.

In your old church-yard lies the dust of many of your fathers, who won for themselves the patriot's immortal name, but how many there were who died from wounds and disease in yonder church hospitals, who have long since mouldered and mingled with mother earth in the neglected burial plot down near those mountains, who, though nameless to us, are in the guardianship of those spirits that keep holy watch over their country and ours, whom we can never call by name until the books are opened in which the recording angel has written the beauty of their heroic lives. They are no longer distinguished by the States from which they came, but lie together as fellow patriots.

The fathers have long since entered upon their high reward. The children, too, have nearly passed away, and here are their children's children rising up to call them blessed.

Descendants of the men of the Revolution, God Almighty has given you His own peculiar blessing, in giving you such a lofty line, which is more than to claim a kinship with kings. There is no battle-field that has more hallowed ground, for it was consecrated through all those years. The buildings are becoming fewer and fewer in which they were, and while they need no monuments, we should set up memorial stones everywhere for other ages to look upon, to be the common heritage of freemen. Those beacons shall forever remain, from whose proud heights our fathers saw the sun of Liberty rising through the golden gateways, whose divine rays are radiating in the fullness of their effulgence, never to depart while God sits upon His throne and rules in His majesty among the children of men.

The choir then sang "Our Braves," to the tune of Kellar's "American Hymn."

Hon. James G. Graham, of Newburgh, was then introduced and spoke as follows:

What more beautiful than a day in June? And surely it is fitting that a day like this, when nature is in the "bloom of her beauty," and the landscape is blossoming with the ensign of the Republic, should be chosen for these patriotic ceremonials. It is fitting, too, that ministers of religion, and ministers of justice, and men of business—that age, with whitened locks, and youth, with growing aspirations; the strength of manhood and matronly worth and culture—and the grace and beauty of maidenhood—

"On their hearts the dew of youth,
On their lips the smile of truth;"

that all these should gather on this

centennial day, and lay some offering on the altar of patriotic memories—and more than all, should strive to learn the lessons which our Revolutionary history is teaching.

It is indeed a day for solemn thought. In the march of time, another one of the centuries has passed. You have gathered here with reverent steps, from the valley of the Central Hudson, in honor of the great events which have made this region famous forever. May you not recall, with pride, the fact that nowhere in all the land are riverside, and mountain, and valley so pervaded with deep historic significance, as in this Highland region. Curtis has well said that "the Hudson is rich in Revolutionary reminiscences, and the beauty of its scenery is touched with the glamour of romantic and historic associations."

Do we realize as we should our rare privilege in having our homes, not only where the surroundings of Nature are so grandly beautiful, but where there also ever rests over all, like the glory of sunset, the golden radiance of Revolutionary traditions?

The claims of this village, and of this town, to an honored place in Revolutionary history, have been justly and eloquently presented by Judge Westbrook and Mr. Cook. They have told you of the sword made here for Washington and still preserved; and as the song of the "Sword of Bunker Hill" has been heard at thousands of assemblages all over the land, why should not the story of the "Sword of Washington" be woven into a national song, and be heard in days to come, by many a camp fire, and on many a day of patriotic rejoicing?

The fact that the first constitution of the State, adopted at Kingston in 1777, had to be brought to Fishkill to be printed, speaks emphatically of her patriotic public spirit at that early day in the struggle, and I regard as one of my most treasured Revolutionary relics a copy of that old New York "Packet," printed by Samuel Loudon, at Fishkill, in March, 1777, which I now hold in my hand. It contains proceedings of the "Committee of Safety," then in session in Kingston, and also many other items of interest in reference to the pending struggle.

This press had been driven from New York by the British forces, and the printer states he "has fixed the printing office at the house of Mr. Isaac Van Wyck, in Fishkill." It also states that the "post office for the State of New York is kept by Samuel Loudon, at Fishkill," and that "a post office is opened at headquarters in Morristown, New Jersey, through which we receive the Philadelphia mail once a week. The Boston upper post riders, by way of Hartford, arrive at Fishkill Wednesday evening; the lower post, by way of New London, arriving on Saturday evening."

The hearts that thrilled as its contents were read, more than a hundred years ago, have long since ceased to beat, and the eyes that pored over it with eager interest have long been closed in dreamless sleep. When these centennial days are past I shall lay it again away, fondly dreaming, perhaps, that it may still be cared for, and that some descendant who may treasure the memory of Revolutionary days, may meet with your descendants here one hundred years from to-day, and bring with him, then, this old relic of 1777. For surely these memorable events will be worthy to be celebrated anew as each century rolls round. Even in our wildest dreams we cannot hope to picture the Republic as it will be when another century shall have passed; with our flag floating over the whole continent, and our population reaching a hundred millions. These grand mountains, only, may not change. They will still stand like sentinels, stationed by the Eternal in the early morning of time, still keeping watch and ward over the valley below; and then, perhaps, even as to-day, the flowery spring-time will be passing onward to the golden summer through gates of pearl, and beneath a sky of cloudless blue.

It is fitting, too, that your neighbors from beyond the Hudson should join with you in these ceremonies to-day, for their history was most intimately connected with that of Fishkill in those eventful days. The ferry between Fishkill and New Windsor was crossed over by Col. Morgan and his brave troopers, in 1775, on their way to join the American army near Boston. He led them through this same valley and through youder pass in the mountain. During the whole period of the Revolution the same ferry was constantly used in connection with military movements and the transportation of military supplies.

May I ask you to follow me across the river, and look on some of the famous grounds that lie beyond it. New Windsor was in truth one of the birth places of that spirit of resistance and revolution which culminated at last in Independence. Her sons of Liberty were early in their resistance to the Stamp Act, and their leader, George Clinton, in the Colonial Legislature, was among the foremost in urging appeal to arms. His brother, Gen. James Clinton, fought bravely in the French War, as well as in the Revolution. They seemed, in truth, born soldiers, and lovers of Liberty. The home of George Clinton, during the war, was on the river bank, where the Ludlow, or Chrystie House, now stands. And what a proud record his public life presents—for seven terms Governor of New York, and twice Vice President of the United States; and during much of his early service as Governor, holding important military commands. He died with his armor on, while in the public service, as Vice President.

The Ulster "Plebeian" of April 12, 1812, which I have before me, contains the proceedings in Congress in honor of the memory of George Clinton, the patriot, statesman and hero.

Washington had his headquarters at the Thomas Ellison house, on the river bank, in 1778, and also in 1780, and in 1781, while preparing for Yorktown. At the last of March, 1782, he established his headquarters at the old Hasbrouck house at Newburgh There, he remained almost continuously until August 17, 1783. It was sometimes the scene of social enjoyment, but oftener of the gravest anxieties. The army in October, 1782, went into "quarters" beyond Snake Hill, and there remained until June, 1783, with detachments also in neighboring localities. A district of but a few miles square thus embraced not only the headquarters of the great commander, but those of Steuben, and Knox, and Heath, and all his other generals—the cantonment of the army at New Windsor, and what is worthy of deepest veneration of all, the burial grounds of the soldiers who died there.

What other region in all our borders is thus crowded full of historic grounds and historic traditions? This alone should secure for it the visits and veneration of lovers of liberty from all climes. But it has stronger title to remembrances by reason of the momentous events of which it was the theatre. Impartial history has awarded Washington the praise of consummate generalship. Frederick the Great, one of the most famous of European generals, after the Revolution was over presented him a sword inscribed, "From the *oldest* to the *greatest* General of the age." Washington had won renown at Trenton and Monmouth, and was fresh from his crowning triumph at Yorktown; but towering above them all in importance and moral grandeur, were his triumphs won at the old Headquarters at Newburgh and at the "Temple" in New Windsor. Washington's Headquarters at Newburgh are forever associated with the essential grandeur of Washington and the sure foundation of the Republic. It was there that the Commander in-Chief, alone, prevented the great victory, after the long and terrible conflict, from ending in an incalculable catastrophe, and alone secured the well-ordered and lawful peace for which the war had been waged.

After the addresses you have already heard, it would be needless to detain you by farther and fuller reference to the wonderful scenes of which the "Temple" was the witness. Had Washington accepted the offer of kingly authority, made by Col. Nicola on behalf of many of the officers, you cannot doubt that the army, then in a mood of angry discontent, would have followed and recognized his sole authority. A monarchy, instead of a Republic, would have been established in this young colonial empire, which had at last secured independence.

Do you realize, then, how momentous was the decision of Washington when he refused the crown? How it shaped the course of American history, and secured the establishment of an American Republic? Surely the "Headquarters" and "Temple Hill" should be the shrine to which every lover of republican liberty should journey, with something of that spirit of veneration which impels the follower of Mahomet on a pilgrimage to Mecca, or the Christian traveler, as he treads the streets of Jerusalem, or the "sacred mountains" round about her.

The places of special historic interest in your vicinity should be marked by some lasting memorial, and above all, the burial place of continental soldiers, here and at Temple Hill, should be guarded from further desecration, and made beautiful with shrubs and flowers. Then the song birds will gather there and chant their morning hymns, and the sunshine will linger lovingly above them.

As the wonderful story of these closing Revolutionary days is recalled and brought often before you, you are transported back, in fancy, through the years of the century and look upon the camps of the soldiers on the hillside. You hear the words of prayer and praise on Lord's day, at the Temple; you see Washington sitting at sunset at the door of the Headquarters, forgetting his cares as he gazes on the river and the mountain suffused with the "rose flush of departing day," and as the night comes on you hear the tread of the sentinel marching on his lonely round, and near the grounds where we are gathered see again many a battle-worn soldier, and at times some honored general meets you. You are startled as some form rushes past you in the darkness, but in a moment you recognize it as Harvey Birch, fleeing from his prison toward the mountain. What is the clattering tumult on the distant highway where the cloud of dust is rising? It is Morgan and his band of troopers dashing on toward Boston.

As this day is the centennial of the beginning of the virtual disbandment of the continental army, I may, in conclusion, refer briefly to the closing scene.

We can never too highly honor the veterans who, in the war of the Rebellion, preserved that Republic which the men of the Revolution had established. But yet, how marked, in some respects, were the contrasts in history, at the close of the respective struggles. In the last war, the Government faithfully kept all its engagements as to pay and clothing and supplies for the soldiers in its service; although in cost, and numbers engaged, that war exceeded, many hundred fold, the Revolutionary struggle —and who can forget the grand array of all these Union veterans, who when the war had ceased, passed in review at Washington, before the President and other chief officers of the Government, with martial bearing and banners floating, and music lending its enchantment to the pageant; and as they reached their various homes they were welcomed with shouts of rejoicing and words of grateful speech and song; and they were well worthy of all these honors—they can never be fully repaid.

But now go back to 1783, and see how these "Continentals" are leaving, after seven long years of sacrifice and suffering. Think for a moment what their triumph had secured. They had won Independence for the colonies, and laid the foundations of an American Republic, stretching now from ocean to ocean and embracing 50,000,000 of people. Surely, in view of such sacrifices and such results secured, they were worthy, if ever soldiers were, to have their dues paid in full measure and "running over." They were worthy, if ever successful warriors were when parting from their officers and brother soldiers, to be clothed in "purple and fine linen," and even to wear, as did the victors of old, robes "richly inlaid with silver and gold."

How different the picture presented there in those June days one hundred years ago! With long arrearages of pay, for which the prime of their manhood had been sacrificed, and with clothing scanty and threadbare, these Continental soldiers broke camp and turned their faces homeward. With no grand review, no floating banners, no ranks keeping step to martial music, and passing proudly before their great commander and all his generals. Day after day in succession, the troops of the several States struck their tents, and said their sad words of parting. Faithful soldiers whose sense of duty and love of country was proof against all temptations. The flag which had floated over the encampment for nearly a year, torn and battle stained, but which to them was more beautiful than if woven of summer sunset hues—this old flag was taken down and folded away forever.

Yes! there, as the "Army of the Continentals," you "passed out of mortal sight, but into immortal history." And your grateful countrymen of this imperial republic, on this centennial of your disbandment, with eye of faith and loving reverence, behold you now not in "ragged regimentals" and with faces saddened and careworn, but they behold you radiant with joy, and wearing the glittering robes of crowned Champions of Freedom, where

> "On Fame's eternal camping ground
> Your silent tents are spread,
> Where glory guards with solemn round
> The bivouac of the dead."

But now the lengthening shadows admonish me to close. It is an hour of mingled sadness and pleasure. Sadness, that those who are gathered on this festal "centennial" day will never again all meet for this pious duty. The old will soon be gathered to their fathers, and even the young cannot expect that their life, long though it may be, can span the coming century. This will be your last centennial commemoration of the closing Revolutionary days. And yet, it is an hour of rejoicing—that the season to which so many have looked forward with patriotic longing has come, and we have all been permitted to offer some tribute, however humble, to the memory of these veterans of the Revolution. We have been allowed, as it were, to sit at the feet of these patriarchs of the Republic, and to hear again from their lips the great lessons of "trust in Providence" and of "unconquerable patriotism," and "love of country," which their lives so splendidly illustrated. And we have an abiding faith that long after the ceremonials of to-day shall be past the lessons of these heroic lives will be seen and felt in the lives of all our citizens, and that thus we may rise to a nobler individual manhood, and a higher national life may gladden the future of the Republic.

The name and fame of these illustrious men of the Revolution are now left, in some measure, to *your* keeping. But, matchless and towering above them all, stands the majestic character of Washington. "Like the magnolia in Spring, one cloud of snowy bloom—like the tree of the tropics, under the blossoms, the rarest fruits, profuse and perennial." The loving reverence of his countrymen has long since crowned him with that noblest of titles, "the Father of his Country." Here we leave him, and we go forward refreshed, strengthened, inspired, by the light of the life which, like a star, serene and inextinguishable,

"Flames in the forehead of our morning sky."

The choir then sang "America."

The Chairman made a few closing remarks, when the choir sang the "Doxology," and the Benediction was pronounced by Rev. M. Bross Thomas, of the Reformed Church, Fishkill, which closed the exercises, and the vast crowd dispersed, having appropriately honored the great centennial anniversary of the disbanding of the Revolutionary army.

OLD TRINITY CHURCH, FISHKILL, N. Y., AS IT FORMERLY APPEARED.

[From the Fishkill Weekly Times, of Feb. 17, 1886.]

Trinity Church, Fishkill, is one of the oldest church edifices in the State of New York. It was the third church organized in the town of Fishkill, and the first of its denomination in Dutchess county, or anywhere above the Highlands on the east side of the Hudson. As originally built, it had a tall, tapering spire, surmounted by a ball and vane, as was usual a century ago. The early records are lost, but from the best evidence obtainable it is believed that the church was built about 1760.

At that time the people in this section were few in number and poor in worldly goods, and it was no light matter to procure funds for erecting what was then considered a large and expensive structure. A gentleman who now resides in this village informs us that his grandfather was one of the original contributors to the building fund for this church, and in order to pay his subscription he was compelled to mortgage his farm to an amount which he was never able to pay during his lifetime. The land was not sacrificed, however, and still remains in the family, and last year a great-grandson of this contributor, who now tills the same acres that his liberal ancestor first broke up, sold over twenty tons of grapes from his vineyard, beside abundance of other products of the farm.

The first service was held by the Rev. Samuel Seabury, in 1756. The first rector was Rev. John Beardsley, who was appointed by the society for the propagation of the gospel, and accepted the charge Oct. 26, 1766. This church was connected with Christ Church in Poughkeepsie for nearly fifty years. Rev. Mr. Beardsley was removed to New York Dec. 16, 1777, by order of the Council of Safety. It appears the church was then without a pastor over nine years, during part of which time it was used both by the military and civil authorities as a hospital for the sick and wounded, and a meeting place for the Constitutional Convention of this State.

The next rector was Rev. Henry Van Dyck, who accepted the rectorship Jan. 22, 1787. He remained until the spring of 1791, and was succeeded by Rev. George H. Spierea, Nov. 12, 1792. He in turn was succeeded by Rev. John J. Sayers, Jan. 5, 1795. Mr. Sayers continued in the rectorship two years, and was succeeded by Rev. Philander Chase, afterward Bishop of Ohio and also of Illinois. Bishop Chase was the founder of Kenyon College, at Gambier, Ohio, and Jubilee College, at Robin's Nest, Illinois. Mr. Chase left here in 1805, and was succeeded by Rev. Barzillai Bulkley, Aug. 6, 1806.

Mr. Bulkley was succeeded in 1812 by Rev. John Brown, who was followed in 1816 by Rev. Mr. Ten Broeck. He remained a short time, and left, when the church had no settled minister for a number of years, being supplied through missionary sources until 1833, when Rev. R. B. Van Kleeck, D. D., was duly installed as rector. He was succeeded in 1837 by Rev. Colly A. Foster, who was followed in 1838 by Rev. Richard F. Burnham. Rev. Robert Shaw succeeded Mr. Burnham in 1841, and was succeeded in 1844 by Rev. Wm. H. Hart. Mr. Hart remained about three years, and was followed by Rev. Christian F. Cruse, D. D., in 1847. Rev. F. W. Shelton succeeded Dr. Cruse in 1853, and was followed by Rev. John R. Livingston in 1855. Mr. Livingston served the church long and faithfully, and, dying in the harness, was succeeded in the ministry, in 1879, by Rev. J. H. Hobart, D. D., the present incumbent.

The church book comprises minutes of each vestry from 1785, and, like all old records, contains many curious entries:

"At a meeting of the Trustees of Trinity Church at Fishkill, on the 11th day of August, 1788, present, John Cook, Peter Mesier, Jeremiah Cooper, James Cooper, and Elbert Willett, Jr., the following resolution was entered into, to wit: That said Trustees should meet Quarterly on the first Monday in May, first Monday in August, first Monday in November and first Monday in February, hereafter. In case of absence of any of the Trustees at any time of meeting, the person or persons so neglecting shall forfeit and pay respectively for every such neglect the sum of four shillings, two pence, for the benefit of the church. Resolved by the vestry, all voting, that the damages this church received by the publick was duly appraised by James Weekes, Isaac Van Wyck, and Capt. Cor's Adriance.

From the year 1776 to 1783:
The use of the church.... £140 0 0
"   "   "   "   " yard   20 0 0
Damages to the same by
    the publick   .. 189 4 11
                                  £349 4 11

This statement given to John Cook, to be Liquidated by the Publick.

Resolved—The compensation so obtained shall be applyed in finishing and repairing the church so far as it will go, and for no other purpose whatever."

By a resolution passed in 1789 it was ordered that the church should receive two shillings from the parents for every child baptized.

In 1803 money was raised to repair the steeple, but if the work was done it does not appear to have been effectual, for in a few years after complaints were made that the spire was unsafe, and in 1817 it was removed.

The apprehensions about the spire were probably not unreasonable, as the carpenter who removed it said that as he worked at the top, in the early morning, he could see his shadow swaying backward and forward on the ground a long way to the westward. The base was left standing, and from that time to about 1860 the church had a short tower with an ornamental balustrade, as shown in the accompanying illustration. Then the building was repaired and this tower removed, since which it has appeared as shown in the larger engraving.* Some years later the interior was considerably changed also. The high pews were removed, and more comfortable ones substituted, and the tall pulpit, with its antiquated sounding board, which stood near the centre of the church, was dispensed with.

In the burying-ground which surrounds the church on all sides except the front, a great many of the early residents lie buried. Forty or fifty years ago, when interments were frequent in this ground, it was no unusual thing to dig up pieces of blankets, which had probably been wrapped around the remains of those who died in this edifice when it was used as a hospital.

In September, 1865, the church celebrated its Centennial, when interesting services were held and an address was delivered by Rev. Dr. Brown, who more than fifty years before had been its rector.

---

* See page 92.

The Reformed Dutch Church, Fishkill.

The Reformed Dutch Church of Fishkill was organized in 1716 by the Rev. Petrus Vas, pastor of the church at Kingston. At that time there was but a sparse population in this section. The census taken two years before gave 445 as the total population of Dutchess county, which was then much larger than at present. That the people were not only few but poor, is evidenced by the tax-list of 1717, which gives a total valuation for the county of £1,300. Six years later, in 1723, there were only 195 taxable inhabitants in this county. The first church building was erected in 1731, and was of stone, and part of these walls still remain in the present edifice. [See cut on page 47.]

The first pastor was the Rev. Cornelius Van Schie, who was installed Oct. 4, 1731. He remained but a few years, and accepted a call to the church in Albany. Calls were then sent to the Classis of Amsterdam, and afterward to Germany, but no pastor was obtained until 1745, when the Rev. Benj. Meynema was installed, and held the position for ten years, when he resigned. The third to occupy the position was the Rev. Jacob Vannist. He died in the ministry after serving two years and a half, and was buried beneath the pulpit. His headstone, still standing at the end of the church, states that he died April 10, 1761, in his 27th year. In December, 1763, the Rev. Henricus Schoonmaker assumed the charge, and officiated nearly two years, and was then succeeded by the Rev. Isaac Rysdyck, who was installed in September, 1765. In the spring of that year the church lost one of its members, who had attained a very remarkable age. The silver tankard used in celebrating the Lord's Supper was presented to the church in January, 1820, and bears the following inscription: "Presented by Samuel Verplanck, Esq., to the First Reformed Dutch Church in the town of Fishkill, to commemorate Mr. Englebert Huff, by birth a Norwegian, in his lifetime attached to the Life Guard of the Prince of Orange, afterwards King William III. of England. He resided for a number of years in this county, and died with umblemished reputation at Fishkill, 21st of March, 1765, aged 128 years."

During the pastorates of Messrs. Schoonmaker and Rysdyck the R. D. churches in this country were divided into two parties, called the Coetus and Conferentie, between which the contention was very sharp and bitter, insomuch that they shut the churches against each other, and sometimes broke them open by force. Until then all clergymen had been educated and licensed in Holland, which was very inconvenient, and caused great delay in obtaining pastors. The Coetus partisans advocated their education and ordination here, while the Conferentie looked on such a proposal as revolutionary and impious. Mr. Schoonmaker belonged to the former party, and Mr. Rysdyck to the latter. When the former was ordained in Poughkeepsie the church doors were closed against him, and the services were held under an apple-tree near by. It is related that on one occasion the Coetus party broke open the church door here with an ax, and that the heads of families sat during the service with clubs in their hands. Truly it was then a "church militant" in the fullest sense. These differences were finally adjusted at a meeting held in New York in June, 1772, although contention in the churches did not cease until 1778. On the 12th of May of that year a meeting was held in this church, when the two consistories were combined, one-half of each retiring, and the others remaining as the official board of the united church.

Dominie Rysdyck, in addition to his pastoral duties, was principal of a grammar school which had previously been established here, and was the first academy in this county. He was considered the most learned theologian in the Dutch Church at that time, and was as familiar with Latin, Greek and Hebrew as with his native tongue. During the latter part of his ministration he preached alternately in Dutch and English, the services having previously been always conducted in Dutch. He died Nov. 20, 1790, and was buried at New Hackensack. His successor, Rev. Isaac Blauvelt, who was born and educated in this country, was installed Oct. 26, 1783. He gave one-third of his time to the Middle Presbyterian Church, dividing the remainder between this and the Hopewell church. In 1790 he removed to Paramus, N. J. The next pastor was Rev. Nicholas Van Vranken, who was installed Nov. 23, 1791. He preached two Sabbaths each month here, and divided the other two between Hopewell and New Hackensack. He died May 20, 1804, after a brief illness, in the 42d year of his age. He was buried in the churchyard of this church, near the entrance, where his grave-stone is still standing. During his ministration preaching in Dutch was discontinued.

After his death the union of the three churches was dissolved, Fishkill becoming a separate charge, over which Rev. Cornelius D. Westbrook, D. D., was installed, March 9, 1806. His pastorate was a long one, lasting until July, 1830. During his ministry the church at the Landing was organized, Dr. Westbrook preaching in this church morning and evening, and there in the afternoon. In October, 1830, Rev. George H. Fisher became pastor of this church, and remained here five years. He was followed by Rev. F. M. Kip, D. D., in August, 1836. Dr. Kip's pastorate was long and successful, extending over a third of a century. In September, 1866, the 150th anniversary of the organization of the church was celebrated with appropriate services, in the presence of a large concourse of the children and friends of the church, on which occasion Dr. Kip preached a historical discourse, from which we gather many of the facts in this sketch. Dr. Kip resigned the charge in May, 1870, and was followed by Rev. Peter E. Kipp, who was installed in August of the same year. On account of impaired health, he resigned in January, 1875, and was succeeded by Rev. Asher Anderson, who was installed in August following. After laboring here with great zeal and success about five years Mr. Anderson accepted a call to a church in Passaic, N. J., and Rev. M. B. Thomas was called to the charge, being installed in March, 1881. Mr. Thomas still holds the position, being the thirteenth pastor in regular succession since the organization of the church, 170 years ago. If we count the two who jointly held the position during the controversy between the Coetus and Confer entie parties as one, there have been but twelve pastors since the church was founded, which would make them average over fourteen years each.

[From the Fishkill Times, March 24, 1886.]

The Wharton House, Fishkill, N. Y.

The accompanying illustration* was engraved expressly for the TIMES from a photograph recently taken for us by Mr. C. A. Palmer, of Matteawan, and is an exact representation of the renowned "Wharton House" as it appears at the present day. This ancient edifice stands on the easterly side of the old Post Road, about one mile south of the centre of this village, not far from the foot of the mountain which it faces. Like most of the houses in this region built a century or more ago, it was fronted toward the south, without regard to position or direction of the road which runs by it. It is not known when it was built. but from deeds in the possession of Mr. J. J. Van Wyck of this village, we learn that the land on which it stands, which then included a tract of 959 acres, was purchased by Cornelius Van Wyck, of Hempstead, Long Island, from Catharine Brett, familiarly known in local history as "Madam Brett," on the 10th of April, 1733. In 1757 Mr. Van Wyck by will divided his land between his sons, Cornelius and Richard. The portion where this old homestead stands fell to the share of Cornelius, while the portion nearer the village went to Richard. Cornelius, the second, in turn divided the property between his two sons, Cornelius C. and Isaac, the latter retaining the southerly part,

---

* See page 60.

containing the old mansion. His brother on his tract, soon after the close of the Revolutionary War, built the house now owned and occupied by Mr. George R. Shaw. The old house which is the subject of our sketch was undoubtedly erected by Cornelius, the original settler, as in his will he provides that his widow shall occupy the west room and the small room back of it, with the furniture contained in both, during her life. That it was occupied as an official headquarters during the greater part of the Revolution, is a matter of history on which there is no dispute. The name of "Wharton" is, however, entirely fictitious, and is derived from Cooper's story of "The Spy." No family of that name ever owned or occupied the premises.

As stated above, Cornelius Van Wyck, the original settler, bequeathed it to his son Cornelius. From him it descended to his son Isaac, who was born, spent his life and died there, and bequeathed it to his son Isaac I., and he in turn to his son Sidney E. He died childless in 1883, and the old homestead passed into the hands of Mr. David Hustis, who owns it at the present time. Isaac I. Van Wyck bequeathed the southerly part of his farm to his son Joseph J., and on his death, in February of last year, it passed to his son Joseph J., who now holds it. Another and larger portion of the original purchase a little further down the valley, but adjoining the above, belongs to Mr. Jacob G. Van Wyck, another descendant of the fifth generation from the original settler, being a grandson of Mr. Cornelius C. Van Wyck.

Across the road from the old headquarters was the camp of the troops, their barracks extending for a quarter of a mile to the foot of the mountain. On a knoll in the camp grounds stands the black walnut tree which, during the time the troops were quartered here, was used as a whipping-post where deserters and tories were punished with the lash. This tree is fully six feet in diameter at the base, and the iron rings to which the culprits' hands were tied have long been overgrown and hidden from sight. Directly in front of the old mansion across the little brook whose crystal waters come purling down from the mountain, is the old burying-ground where hundreds of brave men who, in the midst of privation and suffering which we shudder to think of, gave their lives for their country, lie in unmarked and unhonored graves.

THE Cold Spring *Recorder* says: A traveler, just at the close of the Revolution, was crossing the Fishkill mountains at the time when it took a hatful of Continental money to buy a breakfast. He had no money, but he had a copy of a famous little book, one of the earliest printed books in America, called "The New England Primer," which contained the shorter catechism of the Scotch Church. It was a little book, but it had pictures with rhymes, such as "In Adam's fall we sinned all." He counted out a number of these pages after eating his breakfast, and handed them to the old lady who served him. She didn't know much about reading, but she took them, looked at them closely, spelled out a few pious words, and said: "That's right; I am so glad that Congress has at last got some money with a little religion on it."

From the Fishkill Weekly Times of Oct. 21, 1885.

Fishkill in the Olden Time.

Our friend Mr. John B. Jones, of New Hackensack, contributes to our columns some interesting anecdotes of "ye olden time," which we print below:

Having heard from my grandmother a few incidents of the olden time, I thought perhaps they might be interesting to your readers.

About the year 1760 Benjamin Roe bought of Samuel Verplanck a tract of land near Myers' Corner, now divided into five farms. The country then was almost a wilderness, a few families of Indians living still in the neighborhood. Mr. Roe built a residence, which is still standing, and is now owned and occupied by James H. Kent. One acre of land was paid for by Mrs. Roe knitting a pair of stockings for Mrs. Verplanck.

On one occasion a squaw, who had a wigwam near by, came to the house, having some young Indians with her. As there was a number of cats and kittens around, Mrs. Roe asked the children if they would like one. They said "Yes," and she gave one to them. They immediately took it to the woodpile and cut off its head with an ax, and when their mother came out one of them held the kitten up by its hind legs and said, "Have some good braw to-morrow."

During the Revolutionary War the Roe family were loyal to the country, and one night a company of tories took possession of the house for the purpose of plunder. They tied the old man to the bed, and made his daughter Ruth pilot them around the house. Mr. Roe had at that time a considerable amount of silver money in the house, which he intended to pay on his farm, and it is supposed that some of the men were aware of that fact. While they were searching the house they examined the chest which contained it, but did not find it, as the chest had a double bottom. The daughter, who was afterwards my grandmother, had a gold ring on her finger, which she slipped into her mouth. One of the men, taking hold of her hand, wanted to know what had become of the ring? She had silver buckles on her shoes, which they appropriated. One of the men said, "There used to be two watches hanging over that mantel-piece; what has become of them?" The watches belonged to the two sons, who were away at that time and had the watches with them.

The men found a small amount of Continental money, which they took, saying it would be of no use to them, but they could give it to some of their friends. Grandmother thought she knew one of the men, although they wore masks, and she called him by name; but he said she was mistaken. However, some time after the war one of my grandmother's cousins was at a party on the other side of the river, and this man's sister was one of the company, having silver buckles on her shoes. This cousin said to her, "You have my cousin Ruth's buckles on your shoes." The girl commenced crying, and said she "couldn't help what her brother had done."

Grandmother said she kept the men as long as she could, hoping that some of the colored people would manage to get word to the soldiers who were quartered at that time near by, at the house then owned by a Mr. Schenck, now occupied by Mrs. P. Flagler. A short distance from Mr. Roe's house was a log-cabin occupied by their slaves, the man named Ish and his wife Nan. When Nan was asked why she did not put her husband out of the back window and send word to the soldiers, she said she was afraid they would kill Ish.

In the year 1782 my grandfather Abraham Sleight married Ruth Roe in this house, the ceremony being performed by the Rev. Isaac Rysdyck, who came from Holland, and was at that time pastor of the Reformed Dutch churches of Poughkeepsie, Fishkill, Hopewell, and New Hackensack, preaching in the Dutch language. He served as such pastor for twenty-five years until his death, and was buried under the pulpit of the church at New Hackensack.

J. B. JONES.

From the Fishkill Weekly Times of Feb. 4, 1885.

Revolutionary Reminiscences.

MR. EDITOR: You ask for incidents of Revolutionary times. I will give you some that I remember hearing when a boy, from the actors in those scenes. My grandfather, Abraham Sleight, was a soldier of the Revolution. This is the only story of his that I now remember, perhaps because it was the most striking one. He was once struck by a spent cannon ball. It hit him below the knee, but did not break his leg. He could show that he received the wound when facing the British, as the skin in front, below the knee, was calloused to the bone. He secured the ball and kept it as a relic of the times. I remember seeing it; it was about the size of a large orange.

An old colored woman, living near the New Hackensack church, used to tell about seeing, when she was a girl, Gen. Burgoyne's army, after his surrender, pass along the road as prisoners of war on their way south. She said they passed over the hill where Dr. Underhill now lives, and down by Fishkill village.

An old man worked on the farm for my father who went by the name of Hush (pronounced Hoosh) Haines. He said his true name was Godfrey, but when he was a small boy his father one day sent him to a neighbor's to get some bush beans to plant. When he got there he had forgotten the name, but asked for "hush" beans. After that he was always called Hush Haines. At the time Burgoyne's army passed he was a young man, living with his father in the old stone house now occupied by Mrs. Charlock, on the Hopewell road. Uncle Hush, as we all called him, said that on that day he was away from home with his father's horses, and did not get home until in the night, and it was very dark. The wagon-house was opposite the house, close to the road. Going into the wagon-house to hang up his harness, he stumbled and fell over something, and reaching down to find out what it was, he passed his hand over the cold face of a dead man. Hush said he never was so frightened in his life. The harness did not get hung up, but he got out as rapidly as possible. He did not know that Burgoyne's army had passed along the road that day. The next morning he heard that one of the soldiers had been accidentally killed and laid in the wagon-house as the army was passing.

That winter the other stone house

ADDITIONAL APPENDIX.

down at the end of the lane was the headquarters of Gen. Lafayette and staff. Hush said he had seen the French officers go out on the swamp near the road, cut holes in the ice, run spears down in the mud, and pull out frogs on the spears. They preferred frogs to quail or rabbits, which were plenty in the swamps at that time. Hush said the officers had great sport hunting for the frogs. It seems that eating frogs is not a new thing for Frenchmen.

Uncle Hush used to tell one story with great gusto, in which he was the hero. He said the tories and cowboys used to steal the farmers' cattle and horses, and run them into the British lines, down near White Plains, in Westchester county. Col. Brinckerhoff then lived in the house now occupied by Mr. Matthew V. B. Brinckerhoff. The Colonel had a valuable team of horses, and to prevent them from being stolen he kept them in the house cellar, at the north end of the house. In the day time the door was not fastened, but at night it was bolted and barred on the inside. The Colonel slept in a room directly over the horses, and kept his musket loaded and primed standing by his bed near the window, so that he could point the gun out and fire at a moment's warning. Hush had heard him say that he would give any man a hundred dollars that could steal the horses out of the cellar in the night.

One hundred dollars was more money than Hush had ever seen in his life. He thought he would take the chances for that hundred. One day he managed to get into the cellar and hide himself without being seen by any one. He laid low and kept still. It was a common thing at that time for old men to take their toddy for a "night-cap," in order to sleep well. Hush did not move until he was sure all in the house were sound asleep. He could tell by the snore over his head that the "night-cap" was working like a charm. He then knew just how to go to work to get the door open and not make any noise. Then he untied the horses and led them very carefully out through the yard and into the road. He then stopped and listened, but heard no sound. He was on good terms with the old dog, who would not bark at him. He then mounted one of the horses, and, leading the other, soon had them in his father's stable. The next morning his father was out early, and going as usual to the stable to see if his own horses were safe, saw the other horses and knew them. He came back to the house and went to the stairs and sang out:

"Hush! do you know how Colonel Brinckerhoff's horses got in our stable?"

"I put 'em in."

"You did?"

"Yes, sir."

"Come right down, then, and take them home in a hurry!"

Hush said he got up, started down, but did not take the horses. When he got to the Colonel's house the Colonel was out on the front stoop tearing around in a great rage, and giving orders to have the neighbors all notified to start out in pursuit of the thief and horses. Hush modestly asked the Colonel what was the matter? The answer was:

"My horses have been stolen!"

"Colonel, didn't you say if any one could get your horses out of that cellar you would give him a hundred dollars?"

"Yes—what if I did?"

"If you will give me that hundred dollars I will return the horses."

"How can you do it?"

"The horses are up in our stable."

"Did you get them horses out last night?"

"Yes, sir."

"Well, now, Hush, you go home and bring the horses back."

Hush said he took them home and tied them in the cellar. He never received the hundred dollars, but got a new suit of clothes.

EDGAR SLEIGHT.

Our Nation's Progress.

About one hundred and ten years have elapsed since the thirteen American colonies commenced their struggle for national independence. During this short period, compared with the usual life of nations, our country has grown and increased at a rate never witnessed on this planet before. An energetic and enterprising people, possessing a land abounding in resources, enjoying the blessing of peace at home and abroad, might well be expected to grow in greatness; yet our advancement has vastly exceeded the most sanguine expectations of the founders of our government, and astonished the other nations of the world. Our system of government, which wise men considered weak and lacking the elements of perpetuity, has stood the test of time and carried us safely and triumphantly through one of the greatest civil wars to which a nation was ever subjected.

What the future of this land will be, the wildest dreamer cannot now predict; but if the growth of the nation in intelligence and virtue keeps pace with the advances of science and wealth, our favored land will soon occupy a proud position at the head of all the nations of the earth. Let every boy and girl who reads this little book, and learns something of the privations our fathers endured to give them the grand heritage they possess, resolve to do their part to preserve and promote our glorious institutions to

THE END.

BARTHOLDI'S STATUE OF LIBERTY ENLIGHTENING THE WORLD, erected on Bedloe's Island, New York Harbor.

CPSIA information can be obtained
at www.ICGtesting.com
Printed in the USA
LVOW01s0459010216
473132LV00023B/605/P